# WOMEN IN MISSION

*American Society of Missiology Series, No. 40*

# WOMEN IN MISSION

*From the New Testament to Today*

**Susan E. Smith**

ORBIS BOOKS

**Maryknoll, New York 10545**

Founded in 1970, Orbis Books endeavors to publish works that enlighten the mind, nourish the spirit, and challenge the conscience. The publishing arm of the Maryknoll Fathers and Brothers, Orbis seeks to explore the global dimensions of the Christian faith and mission, to invite dialogue with diverse cultures and religious traditions, and to serve the cause of reconciliation and peace. The books published reflect the opinions of their authors and are not meant to represent the official position of the Maryknoll Society. To obtain more information about Maryknoll and Orbis Books, please visit our website at www.maryknoll.org.

**Library of Congress Cataloging in Publication Data**

Smith, Susan, 1940-
    Women in mission : from the New Testament to today / Susan Smith.
        p. cm. — (American Society of Missiology series ; no. 40)
    Includes bibliographical references and index.
    ISBN 978-1-57075-737-2
1. Women in missionary work. 2. Women missionaries. I. Title.
    BV2610.S65 2007
    266.0082—dc22
                                    2007008572

To the Sisters of the Congregation of Our Lady of the Missions

# Contents

# Preface to the American Society of Missiology Series

The purpose of the American Society of Missiology Series is to publish—without regard for disciplinary, national, or denominational boundaries—scholarly works of high quality and wide interest on missiological themes from the entire spectrum of scholarly pursuits relevant to Christian mission, which is always the focus of books in the Series.

By *mission* is meant the effort to effect passage over the boundary between faith in Jesus Christ and its absence. In this understanding of mission, the basic functions of Christian proclamation, dialogue, witness, service, worship, liberation, and nurture are of special concern. And in that context questions arise, including, How does the transition from one cultural context to another influence the shape and interaction between these dynamic functions, especially in regard to the cultural and religious plurality that comprises the global context of Christian life and mission.

The promotion of scholarly dialogue among missiologists, and among missiologists and scholars in other fields of inquiry, may involve the publication of views that some missiologists cannot accept, and with which members of the Editorial Committee themselves do not agree. Manuscripts published in the Series, accordingly, reflect the opinions of their authors and are not understood to represent the position of the American Society of Missiology or of the Editorial Committee. Selection is guided by such criteria as intrinsic worth, readability, coherence, and accessibility to a range of interested persons and not merely to experts or specialists.

The ASM Series, in collaboration with Orbis Books, seeks to publish scholarly works of high merit and wide interest on numerous aspects of missiology—the scholarly study of mission. Able presentations on new and creative approaches to the practice and understanding of mission will receive close attention.

The ASM Series Committee
Jonathan J. Bonk
Angelyn Dries, O.S.F.
Scott W. Sunquist

# Preface

There is little doubt that the theology and practice of Catholic mission have changed significantly over the last half century. It has been my good fortune to have been involved in mission during those years. Like so many Catholic sisters, I initially taught in the Catholic school system, but Vatican II's call to religious women and men to reassess their apostolic involvement allowed me to move from school to overseas ministry, first in Bangladesh, then in Papua New Guinea, and finally to work briefly with the Jesuit Refugee Service in Ethiopia. Furthermore, I also spent several years working with the New Zealand Catholic Commission for Evangelization, Justice, and Development,[1] which alerted me to the integral role that work for justice had to play in the mission of the church. In the 1980s I was privileged to live and work with Ngati Porou, one of New Zealand's Maori tribes, an experience that contributed much to my understanding of mission, particularly the historic and present role of Europeans in their involvement with indigenous peoples.

It was in the latter part of my life that I turned to the world of academia, a time that has allowed me to reflect critically on mission and on the importance of missiology not only for academics but also for those actively engaged in mission. In my doctoral thesis, I researched the missionary history of my religious congregation, the Sisters of Our Lady of the Missions, and in particular sought to explain how the different developments had their genesis in, and contributed to, the changing theological landscape of the post–Vatican II church.

As I pursued my research, the important but often neglected role of women in mission emerged as something that needed further examination. In narrating, analyzing, and interpreting the contribution of women to Christian mission, one initial question was deciding how to periodize their story. A quick review of some contemporary studies of Christian mission presented possible solutions. David Bosch's *Transforming Mission* offered six historical paradigms that provided a convenient way of understanding the Christian history of mission. In this magisterial work, Bosch, following Hans

---

1. By 1998, the New Zealand Catholic Commission for Evangelization, Justice, and Development had evolved into a new organization, Caritas Aotearoa New Zealand, a member of Caritas Internationalis.

Küng, identifies six major paradigms: the apocalyptic paradigm of primitive Christianity, the Hellenistic paradigm of the patristic era, the medieval Roman Catholic paradigm, the Reformation paradigm, the Enlightenment paradigm and the emerging ecumenical paradigm[2]—paradigms with which we have become familiar in the years since the publication of *Transforming Mission* in 1989.

More recently, in their 2001 work *History of the World Christian Movement*,[3] Dale T. Irvin and Scott W. Sunquist offered a different periodization. Their first volume is divided into six historical periods ending in 1453, the eve of the Protestant Reformation. Parts II and III are concerned with the life of the Christian community in the first three centuries of its life, while part IV examines the growth of the Constantinian church from 300 to 600. Part V looks at the challenges the church faced in both the East and West in the period 600-1000 C.E. Part VI, which concludes volume 1, tells the story of the Christian church as it faces a multiplicity of political, religious, and theological challenges that mark the end of the Middle Ages.

Stephen B. Bevans and Roger P. Schroeder present yet another way of periodizing the history of Christian mission.[4] Part I is primarily concerned with the emergence of the church as missionary, that is, when the first Christians recognized their mission to proclaim the good news to "Samaria and the ends of the earth" (Acts 1:8). In part II, the authors identify six important eras in the story of Christian mission: first, the story of the postapostolic church in the second and third centuries; the second period tells the story of the church from 313, the year of Constantine's "Edict of Milan" through to 907, when events in China brought to a close the growth of the East Syrian Church in Asia and in China; in the third period, the authors describe the growth of the church in the East and the West, and the capture of Constantinople and the fall of the Byzantine Empire in 1453 as Islam consolidated its control of that part of the world we now refer to as the Middle East, North Africa, and parts of southern Europe. In the next section, Bevans and Schroeder take up the story of Christian mission after 1492, the discovery of the Americas, the impact of the Reformation on Christian missionary activity, and the decline of such activity in the eighteenth century, a decline that was startlingly reversed in the nineteenth century. Their story of Christian mission concludes with developments in the twentieth century, highlighting

2. See David J. Bosch, *Transforming Mission: Paradigm Shifts in Theology of Mission* (Maryknoll, N.Y.: Orbis Books, 1991). Bosch indicates his reliance on Hans Küng's "Paradigm Change in Theology: A Proposal for Discussion," in *Paradigm Change in Theology*, ed. Hans Küng and David Tracy (Edinburgh: T & T Clark, 1989), 3-33.

3. See Dale T. Irvin and Scott W. Sunquist, *History of World Christian Movement*, vol. 1 (Maryknoll, N.Y.: Orbis Books, 2001).

4. See Stephen B. Bevans and Roger P. Schroeder, *Constants in Context: A Theology of Mission for Today* (Maryknoll, N.Y.: Orbis Books, 2004).

the challenges that faced a Eurocentric Christianity that sometimes struggled with, and sometimes embraced, the emergence of local churches in the Two-Thirds World.[5]

While these three works offer important narrative structures whereby the reader can appreciate better the story of Christian mission, they are less helpful in providing a way forward whereby the women's part in that story is better understood. Bosch virtually ignores the role of women. Irwin and Sunquist, writing twelve years later than Bosch, attempt to alert the reader to the important role women played from New Testament times until the present, but their references to women can best be described as verging on the minimalist. Bevans and Schroeder attempt a more comprehensive study of women's role in the story.

One difficulty confronting the writer who is attempting a feminist interpretation of the story of women as missionaries is that in these three works, the criteria used to periodize history derive from an androcentric reading of history revolving around events or movements that had their genesis in the lives and actions of eminent missionaries and theologians such as Paul, Augustine, Aquinas, Luther, or George Carey, and powerful political figures like Constantine, Charlemagne, or Henry VIII. For example, while the significant changes associated with Constantine's Edict of Milan most certainly led to changes in the exercise of Christian mission, it is more difficult to identify if it brought about changes in women's missionary roles.

As Barbara MacHaffie points out, histories of Christianity and, by extension, histories of Christian mission "have been traditionally 'his stories'" rather than "her stories."[6] In other research associated with understanding better the story of women as missionaries, I have become aware that there is little written in this area. The situation is changing, as Dana Robert's *American Women in Mission: A Social History of Their Thought and Practice*[7] indicates. Leslie Flemming, Mary Huber, and Nancy C. Lutkehaus have published important works on the nineteenth- and twentieth-century involve-

---

5. I am using the terms "One-Third World" and "Two-Thirds World" rather than "Western" and "non-Western," "North," and "South," or "developed" and "less-developed." While they are not entirely satisfactory, they are more appropriate than "Western," "North" or "South." These suggest a geographic categorization that is far from accurate, as it is difficult to fit countries like South Africa, Australia, and New Zealand into such categories. Similarly "developed" and "less-developed" are more difficult to use today given the rapid economic development of the Asian nations, of China, India, and Brazil. By "One-Third World" I am referring to those countries in which Europeans or peoples of European descent predominate. By "Two-Thirds World" I mean those countries that are predominantly populated by African, Asian, and Latin American peoples.

6. Barbara J. MacHaffie, *Her Story: Women in Christian Tradition* (Minneapolis: Fortress Press, 1986), 1.

7. See Dana L. Robert, *American Women in Mission: A Social History of Their Thought and Practice* (Macon, Ga.: Mercer University Press, 1996).

ment of women in mission.[8] Attention is devoted to the stories of particular Protestant and Catholic women's missionary groups.[9] There is also a lot of "in-house" writing, particularly by members of Catholic religious orders of women about their founders. It should be noted that much of this work is essentially hagiographic in nature and lacks a critique of the theologies and ecclesiologies that motivated such women to found religious communities dedicated to mission.

The following pages constitute an attempt to redress some of those lacunae by offering a history of that mission and of the theological developments that were influential in determining how women exercised their mission. This work does not presume to be a detailed history of women in the mission of the Christian church. Furthermore, there will be an emphasis, though not an exclusive focus, on Catholic women in the modern era, that is, from the discovery of the Americas onward. This is not intended to denigrate in any way the extraordinary work of many women from other churches, but it is intended to address a specific lack in contemporary missiological studies. This work means that another voice can participate in the burgeoning conversation that seeks to understand from a feminist perspective women's position in the story of Christian mission.

In part I, the New Testament evidence will be examined by referring first to those letters that can unequivocally be identified as genuinely Pauline: 1 Thessalonians, Galatians, 1 and 2 Corinthians, Philippians, Philemon, and Romans. Certain texts in these letters suggest that women had an important role in the mission of primitive Christianity, and incidentally, this allows for an interpretation of Paul as other than unredeemably misogynist. As the Deutero-Pauline letters indicate, however, by the end of the first century, the situation was changing and a patriarchal culture was ensuring that women's primary role was to be domestic rather than public. The canonical Gospels and the Acts of the Apostles offer conflicting messages regarding the role of women. Women disciples of Jesus are above all faithful disciples, as their presence at the cross and the tomb of Jesus indicates. In particular, their role as first witnesses of the resurrection is pregnant with missionary overtones. As some texts, particularly Luke-Acts, indicate, the good news can and is sometimes interpreted as bad news for women. Any consideration of the New Testament must also include a study of the roles of women in the apocryphal Gospels, particularly the gnostic Gospels, given the efforts of feminist scholarship to locate in such texts evidence of women being accorded a proactive and public role. The early-first-century story suggests a movement

---

8. See Leslie A. Flemming, ed., *Women's Work for Mission: Missionaries and Social Change in Asia* (Boulder, Colo.: Westview Press, 1989); Mary Taylor Huber and Nancy C. Lutkehaus, eds., *Gendered Missions: Women and Men in Missionary Discourse and Practice* (Ann Arbor: University of Michigan Press, 1999).

9. See Penny Lernoux, *Hearts on Fire: The Story of the Maryknoll Sisters* (Maryknoll, N.Y.: Orbis Books, 1993).

from women and men working together in a manner that hints at a certain egalitarianism to a situation that is determined by patriarchal mores governing social and ecclesial structures.

Part II is concerned with a much longer period. It bypasses the periodization located in Bosch, Irvin and Sunquist, and Bevans and Schroeder, because their schemata reflect the story of men in mission rather than that of women in mission. Part II stretches from the second century through the middle of the twentieth century because throughout these centuries any expression of, or movement toward, the egalitarianism that is characteristic of the earliest New Testament texts is systematically and often ruthlessly expunged from the Christian communities. There are attempts on the part of some women to recapture something of the pro-active roles of Prisca or Eudoia and Syntyche as the lives of Hilda, abbess at Whitby in the seventh century, Leoba, Walburga, the Beguines, Carmelite nun Teresa of Avila (b. 1515), the sixteenth-century founder of the Ursuline sisters, Italian Angela Merici, and Englishwoman Mary Ward, who founded the Institute of the Blessed Virgin Mary in 1609, indicate. Generally speaking, however, the history of these centuries is uniformly depressing because women's efforts to move beyond the domestic realm were greeted not only with scorn but on occasion with imprisonment or exile. In the aftermath of the French Revolution, the numbers of women, Catholic and Protestant, involved in mission exploded so that as the nineteenth century drew to a close, women began to outnumber men; nevertheless, their role was still ancillary to that of men.

Part III explores the changes occurring in missionary practice in the latter half of the twentieth century. After World War II, the situation of women began to change, particularly in the Catholic world, where the influence of Vatican II (1961-65) and, slightly later, liberation theology radically subverted traditional ways of understanding the mission of women. This is not to argue that women's attempts to move beyond their traditional and biologically determined roles of nurturing and caring were greeted with approval and acclaim by key figures in church and society. However, women missionaries, influenced by liberationist theologies, particularly feminist theologies, began to envisage their task as other than domesticating women and girls for their roles as wives and mothers in a patriarchal culture and a patriarchal church. Rather, mission was about liberation so that women could become the subjects of their own development. This work occurred in different ways. It can be seen in the efforts of women missionaries to work with women who are oppressed and with them to identify strategies that allowed them to move beyond those situations that prevented them from confronting the reality of patriarchal culture's oppressive elements. It is also apparent at a scholarly level where authors such as Elisabeth Schüssler Fiorenza, Rosemary Radford Ruether, and Elizabeth A. Johnson are identifying the parameters of theologies that legitimate such developments and show them to be consistent with Christian tradition. The movement from mission as domestication to mission as liberation was for both the practitioners of mission and those among whom they lived and worked radically subversive of more traditional understandings of mission, encapsulating as it were a movement toward egalitarian and inclusive structures.

It remains for me to attempt a definition of mission. This is not easy, and indeed defining mission today is a highly controverted task. First, mission can be understood as the work of conversion, so that souls are saved. Linked to this understanding is an eschatological model of mission that may direct people's attention toward life after death in such a way that this life has little intrinsic value other than as a place of preparation for a better life.

Second, mission can also be driven by the need to plant the church in those places where it is not yet established. In this perspective, mission is understood as *plantatio ecclesiae*, and is particularly important for institutional Catholicism, although I venture to suggest that it is assuming less importance for many Catholic missionaries working at grassroots level among the poor and dispossessed.

Third, mission is increasingly understood not simply in geographical or ecclesial categories but in socioeconomic categories as Christians recognize their responsibility toward those who may live in One-Third World and Two-Thirds World situations and who experience economic, cultural, ethnic, and gender discrimination and oppression. In this perspective, the reign of God has both a present and an eschatological quality. Christians who actively work to ensure a more just society see this work as a continuation of the mission of Jesus (see Luke 4:18-20) and part of a wider movement that will bring about the reign of God in its fullness.

Fourth, and assuming more importance in our contemporary world where religion is often identified as a cause of disquiet, tension, and even armed struggle, interreligious dialogue is assuming more importance as Christians seek to understand the beliefs and traditions of other religious groups.

Finally, inculturation has emerged as yet another important missionary priority as members of a particular local church strive to understand and express more effectively the relationship of the good news to their cultural context.

All these different ways of understanding mission are important, and I hesitate to establish a priority among them. However, it is possible to comment on the significance of these different approaches for women. If mission is understood as the work of conversion and as directing peoples' attention toward life after death, it suggests a model predicated on a spiritual/material dualistic model that may cause discomfort for many contemporary Christian women concerned at the impact of dualistic attitudes toward women and toward women's bodies. If mission understood as *plantatio ecclesiae* is emphasized, then it has as its unacknowledged goal the establishment of hierarchical and patriarchal structures, and, for this reason, contemporary women missionaries may experience unease at being closely involved in such work. On the other hand, if we understand mission as liberation, as interreligious dialogue at both the formal and informal level, or as inculturation, this points to an understanding of mission that is grounded in an incarnational theology. It also permits women missionaries to move beyond a role that is subordinate to that of the ordained minister. It is an understanding of mission that is perhaps best described as reignocentric insofar as its primary focus is not on saving souls nor on the establishment of the institutional church. Rather, it focuses on the coming of the reign of God by striving to be part of those movements and struggles that want to ensure that people can live with dignity and respect.

Many people have journeyed with me as I wrote this book. First, members of my own religious congregation who have challenged and supported me over the years; second, the many lay women and men, priests and religious of other congregations, with whom I have worked and from whom I have learned so much; and, finally, the faculty and staff of the School of Theology at the University of Auckland, whose insights have helped me to critique and refine my own thinking about mission. In particular, I am indebted to the careful reading of the various chapters by Jenny Harrison, Diana Atkinson, Diane Strevens, Dr. Marie Foale, RSJ, Dr. Ann Giloy, RSJ, Dr. Tom Ryan, SM, to Joan Parker, RNDM, for her careful proofreading, and last but not least Dr. Bill Burrows, managing editor of Orbis Books, who has provided constant and invaluable help not only with this book but also with my earlier thesis writing. Without their support, none of this would have happened.

# Part 1

# THE NEW TESTAMENT STORY
# OF MISSIONARY WOMEN

# 1

# *Women as Co-workers with Paul*

In Christian tradition, Paul has the dubious distinction of being both acclaimed and maligned; acclaimed because he was a key figure in ensuring the spread of Christianity beyond Palestine, and maligned because he is often judged to be both antiwomen and anti-Semitic. Before making a decision as to how Paul ought to be judged, it is important to appreciate that the first-century Greco-Roman world was a patriarchal society that clearly distinguished between the public and male domain and the private and female domain. This distinction, indeed opposition, between male and female meant the emergence of a series of "culturally charged binary oppositions"[1] as follows:

| Male | Female |
|------|--------|
| spirit | flesh |
| soul | body |
| active | passive |
| rational | emotional |
| city | home |
| culture | nature |
| authority | obedience |

Such binary oppositions had their origins in Greek philosophy and in certain texts from the Hebrew scriptures, particularly Genesis 2-3, later interpreted in other biblical books in decidedly nonwoman-friendly ways (see Sir 25:24; 1 Tim 2:13). These two streams flowed into each other, allowing for a veritable torrent of discrimination against women in church and society. The cultural context in which early Christianity developed was patriarchal,

---

1. Daniel Boyarin, *A Radical Jew: Paul and the Politics of Identity* (Berkeley: University of California Press, 1994), 18.

androcentric, and dualistic. It was a world in which men were history makers and women were homemakers.

A major task in assessing the role of Paul is discerning to what extent his letters reflect continuity or discontinuity with that cultural world. According to some commentators, Paul shared the dominant male patriarchal mindset of the time. "In contrast to Jesus, the writings of Peter, Paul, Timothy, and of the Church Fathers like Jerome, Tertullian, Augustine and John Chrysostom emphasized women's inferiority and declared that women should be subordinate to men,"[2] or again, while acknowledging that Paul greets women in his letters, Italian anthropologist Ida Magli states that "Paul expressly imposes silence on women in his writings to the different communities [and] this is a clear sign that such behavior, inasmuch as it was subversive to orderly masculine life, not only occurred, but had also become customary."[3] Such bad press from scholars certainly permits, at both the popular and academic levels, identifying Paul as a misogynist. But it is possible to arrive at another understanding because those letters considered genuinely Pauline—1 Thessalonians (ca. 50-51, or 41-43), Galatians (54-55), Philemon (ca. 55), 1 and 2 Corinthians (56-57), Philippians (56), and Romans (57-58)[4]—allow for a different perspective. Paul is revealed as one who, despite the inherently patriarchal character of his society, sought to actively involve women in the mission of early Christianity. Making such a claim is not intended to suggest that Paul was a prototype feminist, but it does not permit judging Paul as a misogynist. In order to show that Paul involved women as missionaries with him, I propose to refer to those letters identified as genuinely Pauline in chronological sequence in order to assess their positive or negative impact on women as missionary in primitive Christianity.

## 1 THESSALONIANS

First Thessalonians is the first canonical book of the New Testament and was written perhaps as early as 41 C.E. Thessalonica was a predominantly Gentile community in Macedonia. Paul commends the Thessalonians because the new Christians had "turned to God from idols, to serve a living and true God" (1 Thess 1:9). The fact that women are not mentioned in this letter has led feminist biblical scholar Lone Fatum to comment that involv-

---

2. Bonnie S. Anderson and Judith P. Zinsser, *A History of Their Own: Women in Europe from Prehistory to the Present*, 2 vols. (New York: Harper & Row, 1989), 1:74.

3. Ida Magli, *Women and Self-Sacrifice in the Christian Church: A Cultural History from the First to the Nineteenth Century*, trans. Janet Sethre (Jefferson, N.C.: McFarland, 2003), 19.

4. See Raymond E. Brown, *An Introduction to the New Testament* (New York/London: Doubleday, 1997).

ing oneself "in the interpretation of 1 Thessalonians is like forcing one's way into male company, uninvited and perhaps unwanted."[5] First Thessalonians nowhere explicitly refers to women, although in Acts 17:4, where Luke describes Paul's visit to Thessalonica, he refers to Greek women and men coming to listen to Paul's preaching.

First Thessalonians does not indicate that Paul involved women with him in his ministry, but identifies his co-workers as Silvanus and Timothy (1 Thess 1:1). It is difficult, however, to locate antiwomen tendencies in this letter. There are two characteristics of Paul's first letter that are important in understanding Paul's approach to mission. On the one hand, he appears to favor egalitarian rather than hierarchical structures, as his use of fraternal imagery for both his co-workers and the community at Thessalonica makes clear (see 1:4; 2:9, 14, 17; 3:7; 4:1, 9, 10, 13; 5:1, 12, 26). On the other hand, his use of maternal imagery in 1 Thess 2:4-8, in which he likens his role to that of a mother nursing her child, suggests a sensitivity to and awareness of women in the community. Therefore, it is difficult to extrapolate from 1 Thessalonians the antiwoman tendencies that Magli, for example, finds in Paul's letters.[6]

## GALATIANS

Paul's main purpose in writing the decidedly polemic letter to the Galatians was to register his opposition to those who insisted that Gentile converts were obliged to follow the prescriptions of the Law, particularly the law of circumcision, prior to their full initiation into the Christian family. Not that Paul regarded being Jewish as a barrier to becoming Christian. "The problem for Paul was not *remaining* a Jew, but *becoming* a Jew, so he wrote, 'if you let yourselves be circumcised, Christ will be of no benefit to you'" (Galatians 5:2).[7] Paul argued that baptism in Christ allows for the birth of a law-free community. His letter offers important insights for women and their mission in the world.

Galatians 3:28 ("There is no longer Jew or Greek, there is no longer slave or free, there is no longer male and female; for all of you are one in Christ Jesus") is a text with important missiological implications, particularly for those committed to a liberation model of mission. The text originated as part of a baptismal formula in the early church and was incorporated by Paul into

---

5. Lone Fatum, "1 Thessalonians," in *Searching the Scriptures: A Feminist Commentary*, ed. Elisabeth Schüssler Fiorenza, 2 vols. (New York: Crossroad, 1993, 1994), 2:250.

6. See Magli, *Women and Self-Sacrifice in the Christian Church*, 15-19.

7. Sheila Briggs, "Galatians," in *Searching the Scriptures: A Feminist Commentary*, ed. Elisabeth Schüssler Fiorenza, 2 vols. (New York: Crossroad, 1993, 1994), 2:222.

his letter to help explain what new creation in baptism meant. Paul assures the Galatians that through faith, they are "in Christ," thereby becoming members in the new eschatological community. Paul probably believed that equality belongs to the age to come, not to the present age. In other words, Paul did not intend Galatians 3:28 to provide a blueprint for a revolution in the Roman Empire! The text suggests, however, that baptism should mean that ethnic, gender, and economic distinctions within the community should not be the reason for identifying women, slaves, and Gentiles as inferior. For the Christian community, the collapse of socioeconomic distinctions that followed baptism should allow women (and slaves) to "negotiate new social roles and claim leadership roles which formerly had been held inappropriate for women, even of high class and ethnic religious status."[8]

"There is no longer male and female" recalls Genesis 1:27, "So God created humankind in his image, in the image of God he created them; *male and female he created them*" (italics added). "Male and female" in Genesis 1:27 is sometimes thought to refer to an androgynous being, and it is not until Genesis 2:21-22 that we learn of the fateful division of that androgynous being into man and woman. In the early church, this text could be interpreted in two ways: first, some Christians thought of themselves as a new genus of humankind; and, second, as the restored original humankind. In Galatians 3:28, Paul seems to have opted for the first interpretation and is desirous of moving beyond the original creation story found in Genesis 1, because through Christ, there is a new creation. Through baptism in Christ, the creation order of Genesis is transcended.[9]

German New Testament scholar Norbert Baumert asserts that Galatians 3:28 should not be seen as the Magna Carta for equal rights between women and men. He argues that just as the text "does not constitute a cry to slaves to rise up in liberation, nor an appeal against nationalism, so its intention is also not to establish equal rights for men and women."[10] Baumert is correct insofar as Paul's letter to Philemon suggests that Paul is not advocating the abolition of slavery. Rather, Paul is asking that the relationship between slave and master be one of love and mutual respect rather than one of servility and domination. In fact, he uses the metaphor of slavery to teach about discipleship in his letters (see Rom 7:25; 1 Cor 7:22; 9:19; Phil 2:7). Baumert's approach to the text offers little support for the contemporary missionary seeking a scriptural mandate for her mission of solidarity with the marginalized. However, both literary-critical and rhetorical-critical methodologies allow her to identify the links between Paul's text and her context. A literary-

---

8. Ibid., 2:219.

9. Wayne Meeks, "The Image of the Androgyne: Some Uses of a Symbol in Earliest Christianity," *History of Religions* 13 (1974): 165-208.

10. Norbert Baumert, *Woman and Man in Paul: Overcoming a Misunderstanding*, trans. Patrick Madigan and Linda M. Maloney (Collegeville, Minn.: Liturgical Press, 1996), 296-97.

critical approach means that the reader can approach the text as literature rather than as history, and thus find contemporary meaning in the text. A rhetorical-critical approach invites the reader to take as her entry point into the hermeneutical task her own social location and to ask questions of the text in the light of that location.

We need to ask if Paul's polemic against the Law meant that he favored a significant discontinuity with Jewish law with respect to women's role in the life of the faith community. Did Paul's belief "that bondage to law had been replaced for Christians by a freedom, given with the Spirit (4:21-5:1)"[11] have emancipatory effects for women? In Galatians, Paul holds that both Jewish and Gentile Christians were freed from observance of the ritual and purity requirements of the Law, which implies that women could renegotiate their roles in the Christian community.

In assessing the impact of Paul's teaching on the law in Galatians and its effect on women, it is important to recognize that first-century Judaism was more pluralistic than we have been accustomed to believe, and not all Jews, particularly those in the Diaspora, subscribed to a the strict interpretation by the Pharisees of the Mosaic Law. For example, women were not always physically separated from men in synagogue prayer, and, according to Bernadette Brooten, they served as leaders in the synagogue, as donors and patrons, which suggests that they had control over some resources.[12] Jewish women could inherit property and were able to seek divorce from their husbands.[13] Even though there were groups in Judaism who insisted on a strict observance of the Torah, "there were other communities that allowed women a much wider participation, including leadership roles which in the Mishnah's idealized world were denied them."[14] Although the dominant rabbinic interpretation favored the exclusion of women from the public realm, Paul seems to have held that his experience of the Spirit constituted a moral guide that persuaded him to accept women in leadership roles in the community.

## 1 AND 2 CORINTHIANS

An important city in ancient Greece, Corinth developed into a thriving metropolis after it was re-established as a Roman city in 44 B.C.E. by Julius Caesar, and it was this bustling port city that Paul first visited about the year 50 C.E. It is uncertain whether Paul's visit led to the establishment of the first Christian community in Corinth, or whether there was already a Christian

---

11. See Briggs, "Galatians," 228.
12. See Bernadette J. Brooten, *Women Leaders in the Ancient Synagogue: Inscriptional Evidence and Background Issues* (Chico, Calif.: Scholars Press, 1982).
13. Ibid., 106-27.
14. Briggs, "Galatians," 231.

community associated with the household of Prisca and Aquila (Acts 18:1-11). Religiously, the population of Corinth was diverse. Greco-Roman religions were well established; the cult of Isis, the Egyptian goddess, had many adherents, and there were temples honoring Greek deities such as Apollo and Hermes. There is also evidence of a significant Jewish community, as Paul's use of the Septuagint makes clear.

Paul frequently refers to the Christians at Corinth as *adelphoi*, rightly translated in the New Revised Standard Version (NRSV)[15] as "brothers and sisters" (see 1 Cor 1:10, 11, 26; 2:1). Earlier modern translations such as the RSV or *The Jerusalem Bible*, opting for a literal translation, use "brothers" only, although classical Greek understood *adelphoi* as generic rather than gender specific. The word *adelphoi* occurs in all Paul's letters and points to his warm and affectionate relationship with a community that was dear to him. In particular, it indicates that in Paul's communities, women and men were both addressed by the apostle.

Paul is concerned about discord within the community generated by Christians allying themselves with important missionary figures in the early church: Christ, Apollos, Cephas, or Paul himself. He learns from members of Chloe's household while he is in prison in Ephesus of the subsequent friction ("For it has been reported to me by Chloe's people that there are quarrels among you, my brothers and sisters," 1 Cor 1:11). Chloe was most probably leader of a household church. In early Christianity, the household was "the basic structural unit of the early Christian church,"[16] and leadership in the household church often belonged to women. Christians gathered in households to celebrate the Lord's Supper, to hear the gospel proclaimed and explained, and to provide hospitality for traveling missionaries such as Paul and his companions. The fact that Paul mentions Chloe indicates her important leadership and missionary role in the early church; this verifies Antoinette Wire's claim that Paul would have regarded people such as Chloe as "social equals."[17]

The reference to "Chloe's people" may be a reference to her immediate or biological family, but it more likely refers to members of an extended household, which would have included freedmen and women and slaves. We are introduced "immediately to the reality of social stratification in the Corinthian community: membership included people of higher and lower social status. Chloe most likely owned slaves,"[18] something that can cause

---

15. Bruce M. Metzger and Roland E. Murphy, eds., *The New Oxford Annotated Bible with the Apocryphal/Deuterocanonical Books* (New York: Oxford University Press, 1993). Unless otherwise stated, all scriptural references will be from this edition.

16. Raymond F. Collins, *First Corinthians*, ed. Daniel J. Harrington (Collegeville, Minn.: Liturgical Press, 1999), 74.

17. Antoinette Wire, *The Corinthian Women Prophets* (Philadelphia: Fortress Press, 1990), 42.

18. Margaret Y. MacDonald, "Reading Real Women through the Undisputed Letters of

unease for the contemporary reader. However, "the evaluation of the social status of people in the ancient world is a complicated issue. Social position was determined by a variety of factors: the status of one's family, one's finances, one's sex, and birth into freedom or slavery all played a part in determining one's social location."[19] Obviously, Chloe was a woman of means, and even though slaves would have been members of her household, Paul does not criticize her as he later criticizes Philemon, suggesting that the early Christian community was more concerned about the attitude of slave owners toward slaves than about the institution of slavery as such. The story of Chloe alerts us to the possibility of the reversal of status that primitive Christianity offered women, whose societal roles were restricted by patriarchal culture.

Paul is often accused of dualism in his teachings on sexuality. One of the more controversial texts that offers support for that position is 1 Corinthians 7, in which Paul responds to questions addressed to him by the Corinthians concerning those married or preparing to marry, and the widowed. While we are not required to engage in a detailed study of these passages, they are interesting insofar as they throw light on Paul's attitude toward women. In 1 Corinthians 7:5 ("Do not deprive one another [of conjugal rights] except perhaps by agreement for a set time, to devote yourselves to prayer"), Paul is responding to questions that probably had their genesis in practices associated with the cult of Isis. The cult of Isis prescribed sexual abstinence before cultic prayer, something which the Jewish tradition required; and Jewish law also prescribed sexual abstinence at the time of menstruation. According to Raymond Collins, Paul could agree to abstinence for a married couple when: "1) the abstinence is mutually agreed upon by husband and wife; 2) it is limited to a relatively short period of time; and 3) its purpose be prayer."[20] Therefore, it seems inappropriate to ascribe dualistic tendencies to Paul in his teaching on sexuality. It is perhaps more important to note his emphasis that with respect to sexual abstinence mutual agreement is required of husband and wife.

A more explicitly significant text regarding the roles of women in the early church is found in 1 Corinthians 11:3-7:

> But I want you to understand that Christ is the head of every man, and the husband is the head of his wife, and God is the head of Christ. Any man who prays or prophesies with something on his head disgraces his head, but any woman who prays or prophesies with her head unveiled disgraces her head—it is one and the same thing as having her head

---

Paul," in *Women and Christian Origins*, ed. Ross Shepard Kraemer and Mary Rose D'Angelo (New York/Oxford: Oxford University Press, 1999), 201.

19. Ibid.

20. Collins, *First Corinthians*, 259.

shaved. For if a woman will not veil herself, then she should cut off her hair; but if it is disgraceful for a woman to have her hair cut off or to be shaved, she should wear a veil. For a man ought not to have his head veiled, since he is the image and reflection of God; but woman is the reflection of man.

Paul is concerned about what head covering women who pray and prophesy in public should wear. This is a text that has generated an immense amount of scholarly and not so scholarly debate, because it implies that women should be subordinate to men. Certainly Paul appears to be more influenced by the Yahwist creation account in Genesis 2-3 than by the Priestly tradition found in Genesis 1:27 with its emphasis on male and female being created in the image and likeness of God. What is important for our purposes is that the text demonstrates that Corinthian women prayed and prophesied in public, and therefore were actively involved in witnessing to the good news in the public domain.

Another controversial text is 1 Corinthians 14:33b-35 ("women should be silent in the churches. For they are not permitted to speak, but should be subordinate, as the law also says. If there is anything they desire to know, let them ask their husbands at home. For it is shameful for a woman to speak in church"). There is ongoing scholarly debate about these verses on two counts. First, some contemporary Pauline scholars hold that these "unfriendly" verses are an interpolation or later editorial insertion,[21] citing as their main reason the fact that women do pray and prophesy (see 1 Cor 11:3-7). Antoinette Wire, who does not acknowledge the interpolatory character of the two verses,[22] believes they indicate that Paul is concerned about women praying and prophesying in public, which suggests that the household churches were becoming the public face of the various Christian communities in Corinth.[23]

In addition to conflicting opinions concerning the authorship of 14:33b-36, there is some dispute regarding the context that gave birth to the text. This contention assumes particular importance for those who believe that these verses are Pauline in origin, given that they seem to be in opposition to other, more positive references to women in the genuine Pauline letters. Elisabeth Schüssler Fiorenza argues that Paul's prohibition against women

21. Metzger and Murphy, eds., *The New Oxford Annotated Bible*, 244; Winsome Munro, "Women, Text and the Canon: The Strange Case of 1 Corinthians 14:33-35," *Biblical Theology Bulletin* 18 (1988): 270; Donald Senior, ed., *The Catholic Study Bible: New American Bible* (New York: Oxford University Press, 1990), 27.
22. See Antoinette Wire, "1 Corinthians," in *Searching the Scriptures: A Feminist Commentary*, ed. Elisabeth Schüssler Fiorenza, 2 vols. (New York: Crossroad, 1993, 1994), 2:185-89.
23. Robert W. Allison, "Let Women Be Silent in the Churches (1 Cor 14:33b-36): What Did Paul Really Say and What Did It Mean?" *Journal for the Study of the New Testament* 32 (1988): 27-60; Curt Niccum, "The Voice of the Manuscripts on the Silence of the Women: The External Evidence for 1 Cor 14:334-5," *New Testament Studies* 43 (1997): 242-55.

preaching most probably derived from those Jewish-Hellenistic traditions which taught that women were subordinate to men, and from a concern that the community at Corinth might have been mistaken "for one of the orgiastic, secret, oriental cults that undermined public order and decency."[24] In other words, the contextualized nature of such prescriptions needs to be acknowledged, and once that has happened, they should not be considered as normative for all ages and communities. The particular challenge facing Pauline exegetes is to show that "the passage is consistent with Paul's pervasive egalitarianism and his treatment of his female co-laborers."[25] Such scholarly debate and textual evidence make it clear that women were part of the public face of church leadership in Corinth.

In the concluding verses of 1 Corinthians, Paul, Prisca, and Aquila, "together with the church in their house" (1 Cor 16:19), send greetings to the Corinthians. The reference to Prisca confirms her importance in the life of the early church. We first read about Prisca and Aquila in Acts 18:2-3, 18, 26-27. Apparently Prisca and Aquila have been living in Corinth after being exiled along with other Jews from Rome in 49 C.E., and they provide hospitality for Paul while he visits Corinth. It then appears that they journeyed with Paul to Ephesus and ministered with Apollo before he returned to Corinth. They remain in Ephesus, and from there send greetings back to Corinth. Prisca is referred to as a co-worker of Paul in Romans 16:3, and there is a further reference to her in 2 Tim 4:19. Given that this missionary couple traveled extensively, they may have been reasonably well off. On the other hand, Luke reports that they are leather workers (Acts 18:3), and so members of the artisan class, which would not qualify them as affluent. The fact that Prisca's name appears before that of her husband in four of the six New Testament references (Acts 18:18, 26; Rom 16:3; 2 Tim 4:19) suggests that her role in the early church was more important than that of her husband.

Second Corinthians does not refer explicitly to women as 1 Corinthians does. At one level, the second letter reads negatively for women. As we saw in 1 Thessalonians, Paul interprets his relationship to the community at Corinth in familial categories, but in this instance, Paul emphasizes the authority that he enjoys as father, an authority analogous to that of the *pater-familias* in Greco-Roman society. Paul threatens to punish them (10:6), a threat he again makes in 13:1-2. Throughout 2 Corinthians, Paul asserts his authority against his opponents who claim that a special relationship with Moses affirms their place as teachers and preachers (see 2 Cor 3:1-18). Paul argues that their written letters of recommendation are inferior to his own qualification as a minister of a new covenant through the Spirit who gives

24. Elisabeth Schüssler Fiorenza, *In Memory of Her: A Feminist Reconstruction of Christian Origins* (New York: Crossroad, 1983), 230-31.

25. Allison, "Let Women Be Silent," 31.

life. Paul is prepared to move beyond a reliance on law and tradition to validate his mission to the Corinthians. Perhaps women can find in Paul's willingness to break with the established tradition through the transforming power of the Spirit hope in their own struggles against those committed to maintaining traditional positions on the place and status of the women in mission. Although 2 Corinthians does not explicitly concern itself with women's roles in the community, Paul's refusal to be restricted in his mission by faithfulness to those aspects of the Mosaic Law that could hinder the full participation of women in the community is important as women seek to revision their missionary roles.

## PHILIPPIANS

Paul's letter to the Philippians is suffused with joy, warmth, and love, despite Paul's writing it from prison. The Christian community at Philippi was the first Gentile church to be founded by Paul in Europe, and points to the Christian movement's growth beyond Asia Minor, with its significant Diaspora Jewish communities, to the Gentile world. Philippi was a city in which "the citizenship, language, culture and religion of Rome had been the city's dominant public frame of reference for over a century."[26] In a 1994 paper, Wendy Cotter argues that the more romanized a city was, the more the dignity and rights of women, particularly higher-class women, were asserted. According to Cotter, this improved social status of women is discernible in at least six ways. First, women householders not only had responsibility for overseeing the goods of the household, but also for guarding the lives and virtue of those within the household. Second, Roman houses, as distinct from Greek and Hellenistic homes, were not built so as to separate women from men, and this meant that Roman women could dine with men without appearing indecent. Third, Roman custom regarding marriage appears to have made the wife less subordinate to her husband than was the custom in the nonromanized parts of the empire. Fourth, Roman women were able to go out to the theater or visit friends unaccompanied by a male. Fifth, Roman law permitted women to retain their own inheritance and to possess land. This could lead to women owning and running their own businesses (see Acts 16:13-15, which recounts the story of Lydia, who owns a purple-dye trade business in Philippi).[27] Sixth, because they could be women of independent means, they were better placed than their Greek counterparts to act

---

26. Marcus Bockmuehl, *The Epistle to the Philippians*, ed. Henry Chadwick (London: A & C Black, 1998), 6.

27. The story of Paul's visit to Philippi is told in told in Acts 16:9-40, and Luke has high praise for Lydia's leadership. There is no reference to Lydia in Philippians, but her presence in Acts confirms that leadership in Philippi was not restricted to men.

as benefactors of clubs and organizations.[28] Cotter believes that Paul's positive attitude toward women in the more romanized part of the empire was conventional rather than countercultural, and this explains why he allows women to join him in the mission of the early church. Philippian women "enjoyed more personal freedom and participation in social and economic life than women in most of the eastern Mediterranean lands, [i]t is therefore not surprising that women played a significant role in the early years of the Philippian church."[29]

In Philippians 4:2-3 ("I urge Euodia and I urge Syntyche to be of the same mind in the Lord. Yes, and I ask you also, my loyal companion, help these women, for they have struggled beside me in the work of the gospel, together with Clement and the rest of my co-workers, whose names are in the book of life"), Paul is referring to two Gentile women, Euodia, whose Greek name meant "good journey," and Syntyche, another Greek name, which can be roughly translated as "good luck," urging them to be united as they struggle in the work of the gospel, together with Clement, identified by Eusebius as bishop of Rome, although contemporary commentators are not so positive about this. Marcus Bockmuehl points out that in the King James Version, the feminine "Euodia" is incorrectly translated as the masculine "Euodias,"[30] evidence indeed that translation is always an interpretative process!

Given the affirmation of these two women, it would be helpful if the possible causes of their disunity could be identified. Perhaps it was their competition and quest for power and authority in the community, or conflict over the material support offered by their respective house churches to Paul, or the challenges posed by Jewish Christianity to the young Gentile Christian community. Paul does not say but he is opposed to all such disputes because they harm the unity of the Philippian church. In the famous christological hymn (Phil 2:5-11), the Philippians are instructed to imitate Christ, who emptied himself and took the form of a slave. Paul too has willingly lost everything in order to know Christ Jesus his Lord, and he invites others to imitate him in his self-stripping (Phil 3:17). He urges Euodia and Syntyche "to be of the same mind in the Lord" (Phil 4:2). The fact that Paul asks "his loyal [unnamed] companion,"[31] to mediate between the two women to ensure that they are of the same mind suggests that their conflict was quite divisive for the community. "Settlement of the dispute that involves these two women is vital because they have struggled beside Paul in the work of

---

28. See Wendy Cotter, "Women's Authority Roles in Paul's Churches: Countercultural or Conventional?," *Novum Testamentum* 36 (1994): 350-72.
29. Carolyn Osiek, "Philippians," in *Searching the Scriptures: A Feminist Commentary*, ed. Elisabeth Schüssler Fiorenza, 2 vols. (New York: Crossroad, 1993, 1994), 2:238.
30. See Bockmuehl, *The Epistle to the Philippians*, 238.
31. "Loyal companion" may also be translated as a proper male name, "Syzygus," although neither the NRSV nor the NAB translates it as such.

the gospel, together with Clement and his co-workers."[32] Throughout Philippians, Paul challenges the community to seek unity (1:7; 2:2, 5; 3:15, 19; 4:10), citing the example of Jesus and of Paul himself.

It is difficult to extrapolate from Philippians what form of leadership was exercised by Euodia and Syntyche. The text suggests that the two women were more than leaders and benefactors of two house churches. After all, Paul has identified them as "loyal companions" and "co-workers" who have struggled with him. The Greek for "have struggled with" can be translated more literally as "fighting alongside," and, according to Bockmuehl, is "a gladiatorial term continuing the athletic imagery of 1:27; 3:12-14."[33] In other words, Paul's language suggests that the two women were actively involved with him in the public work of the proclamation of the good news. Margaret MacDonald believes that these two women, Gentile converts to Christianity, were actively engaged as co-workers with Paul in his mission to gain both Jewish and Gentile followers as the Christian movement expanded into Western Europe. She attributes particular significance to the fact that in the ministry of both women, the public and private realms meshed in a way that did not diminish the value of either. Euodia and Syntyche were missionary co-workers with Paul, and at the same time, they were leaders, *diakonoi*, of household churches. Despite Paul's concern at their behavior, there is no suggestion that they are enemies of Paul, nor should they be linked with "the dogs" or "evil workers" (see Phil 3:2), that is, those who attempt on the basis of Christianity's Jewish origins to impose complete Jewish observance on Gentile converts (see Galatians; 2 Cor 10-13). Generally, Paul's enemies remain nameless, while more often than not he names his friends and co-workers. These two women emerge as good friends of Paul and as important leaders in the Philippian church; they deserve to have their names written in the book of life. The expression "the book of life" first occurs in Exodus 32:32 and Psalm 69:28, and in Jewish and Christian apocalyptic material (e.g., Rev 3:5; 13:8). Euodia and Syntyche deserve to be numbered among the saved.

## PHILEMON

Paul wrote this short letter to three important Christians in Colossae: Philemon, owner of the slave Onesimus, whom Paul had baptized in prison (see Phlm 10b); "Apphia our sister," "sister" indicating that she was a fellow Christian; and to Archippus, who is identified as "our fellow soldier," possibly a reference to one who gave material or financial support. While Paul accepts the institution of slavery, he believes that in Christ there ought to be equality within the community. As already indicated, the primitive Christian communities were not in a position to challenge the institution of slavery,

---

32. MacDonald, "Reading Real Women," 204-5.
33. Bockmuehl, *The Epistle to the Philippians*, 239.

and, furthermore, the expectation that the parousia was imminent militated against a strident advocacy of social reform.

There is ongoing discussion concerning Apphia. Traditionally it was assumed that Apphia was Philemon's wife, although the text does not say as much. Philemon was a leading member of a house church community in Colossae, but the fact that Paul addresses three people—Philemon, Apphia, and Archippus—separately "suggests that each was prominent in the community. Paul also honors each with a different title. Apphia is called 'sister' (*adelphē*) . . . this is a term that could be applied to a female member of a missionary partnership (cf. 1 Cor 9:5; Rom 16:15)."[34] Philemon, Apphia, and Archippus emerge as leading members of a household church in Colossae.

Given the decisive role of household churches in the early missionary expansion of the Christian community, I propose to digress here in order to expand on the nature of such communities. Paul's missionary proclamation was addressed primarily to the middle stratum of Greco-Roman society, and to the lower urban classes. Rural populations were untouched by Paul's preaching because he concentrated on the cities that straddled the important trade routes of the empire. There were three different models that would have influenced Paul's communities when they gathered to worship in the homes of better-off Christians.

First, in Palestinian and Diaspora Judaism, the home was more than a living space for the Jewish family. The social and religious functions of the house *bêt-'āb*, ("father's house") meant that "the household for the Israelite, was the place of inclusion, authority, and spiritual continuity (by its role in teaching and preserving the faith and traditions)."[35] It was where the family gathered to remember and celebrate its religious identity and traditions. The centrality of the household in Jewish religious life should not be underestimated. It was only after the destruction of the Temple in 70 C.E. that synagogues as special buildings set apart for religious activities became common.

Second, in the Roman Empire, the patriarchal home with the father as the head was the cornerstone of the city and empire. As a rule, the home was basic for the household's economic well-being, because the things on which the family lived were produced there. The Greco-Roman household included not only members of the biological family. It also included unmarried female members of the family, slaves, freed persons, and tenants. The word "family," which most appropriately translates as "*oikos* (plural, *oikia*), signifies family as household, in much the same way as *bayit* in the OT which this word frequently translates as. In the Greco-Roman world, the *oikos* (Latin, *familia*) was a comparable social unit to the Israelite *bêt-'āb*. It included not

---

34. MacDonald, "Reading Real Women," 206.

35. C. J. H. Wright, "Family," in *The Anchor Bible Dictionary*, ed. David Noel Freedman (New York: Doubleday, 1992), 768.

only blood relatives of the head of the house, but also other dependents—slaves, employees, and that peculiarly Roman phenomenon known as 'clients' (i.e., freedmen, friends, and others who looked to the head of the house for patronage, protection, or advancement)."[36]

Third, voluntary associations of like-minded people or gatherings of people engaged in similar work also provided another model for the primitive Christian community in its search for an appropriate structure. For example, in the Greco-Roman world there were at least three major categories of voluntary associations: funerary, religious, and professional. In voluntary associations, as distinct from the Jewish and Greco-Roman patriarchal households, egalitarian rather than hierarchical structures seemed to predominate, and interest rather than biology or economics determined membership. Members usually came from the lower classes, though a minority came from more affluent classes. People gathered for both social and religious reasons. Schüssler Fiorenza offers another variation of the voluntary association because she argues that in the first century, wealthy women opened "their premises and houses to oriental cults and their ecstatic worship celebrations."[37] Therefore, Christians were not alone in gathering in homes for religious purposes, and indeed the fact that Christianity spread from home to home must be considered an especially fortunate decision for the church's mission because it adapted already present structures that offered sufficient room for religious minorities to develop. A house that belonged to a well-to-do person would hold between thirty to sixty people.

There are several reasons that explain the success of the household model of church for the early Pauline communities. A household church would be less likely to attract unwelcome attention from pagan officials (see 1 Thess 4:12). While adapting the societal family structure, in the home itself Christians could live as members of the eschatological church. Thus, the home as the place used for worship was also the locus of daily life, and it became the place where faith, love, and hope were practiced, thereby precluding the possibility of a dichotomy between worship and daily life. Early Christianity's eschatological character would have had an immense appeal among those who considered themselves to be the victims or at least the nonbeneficiaries of imperial institutions. Baptism in Christ demanded that the new Christians distance themselves from their old lives, social connections, and pagan religions, and household churches became the place where the newly formed community could gather. Through baptism, all were made brothers and sisters of equal status (Gal 3:28), and while this meant social structures as such

---

36. Ibid., 768.
37. See Schüssler Fiorenza, *In Memory of Her*, 176.

did not change, attitudes did: spouses were obliged to mutual consideration and yielding love, and the relationship of slave to master was to be grounded in love and respect. Paul's central concern was always the unity of the church. Competing groups were foreign to what the church should be (1 Thess 4:17; 5:10; Phil 2:5-11; 4:2-3).

As far as worship was concerned, household churches seem to have lacked cultic accessories, vestments, symbols, and ritual preparations, and it does not appear as if a separate priestly class had emerged. The two most important acts of worship would have been baptism, which led to full membership in the church as members were received into the body of Christ and required to live in a manner befitting their status (1 Thess 4:1ff.), and the gathering of the community for the Lord's Supper. First Corinthians 11:20 suggests that the Lord's Supper was preceded by a regular meal. At the center of the Supper meal were the words of institution, which recalled the death and looked forward to the parousia of the Lord. There is little to indicate that there was an obligatory order to be followed, and the disturbances to which Paul alludes in 1 Corinthians 11:17-22 could have happened only in a condition of relative flexibility, although as Paul indicates, fidelity to tradition was also important.

## ROMANS

Romans, the longest of Paul's letters and the one in which his theology of justification by faith and the relationship between the old and new Israel is systematically unfolded, has recently acquired another theological significance as women recognize the importance of Romans 16 for them in their quest for new insights regarding their missionary role in the Christian community. Paul is thought to have written Romans from Greece between 57 and 58 C.E. to inform the Roman community that he intended to travel to Rome after he had visited Jerusalem, and from Rome make his way farther west to Spain. Paul did not establish a Christian community in Rome; and, according to the Roman historian Suetonius, the edict of the emperor Claudius expelling Jews from Rome in 49 C.E. also seems to refer to a dispute within the Jewish community over the identification of Jesus as the Messiah—a fact that would confirm the presence of Christians there prior to Paul's intended visit. Paul was seeking support from those Jewish and Gentile Christians as he prepared for his mission to Spain.

Romans 16:1-16 has acquired a special significance for women because Paul identifies women as deacons, as apostles, and as co-workers. Before showing the importance of Paul's portrayal of women in Romans, it is necessary to mention briefly and critique those who argue that Romans 16 is best understood as an addition. This position, most often associated with

British scholar T. W. Manson,[38] who wrote immediately prior to World War II, initially enjoyed support. A major plank in Manson's argument was that if Paul did not establish the church in Rome, then his greetings to numerous people become somewhat problematic. Furthermore, the personal quality of Romans 16 contrasts with the more impersonal and universalist quality of Romans 1-15. As Byrne argues, however, modern commentators are wary of embracing Manson's position and see "chapter 16, especially the long series of greetings, to be thoroughly integral to Paul's rhetorical purpose in writing to Rome."[39]

Phoebe is one of the women whom Paul knew and described as "sister" (*adelphē*), "deacon" (*diakonos*), and "benefactor/patron" (*prostatis*) in Romans 16:1-3. Phoebe belonged to the church at Cenchreae, a seaport seven miles distant from Corinth. Gillman observes that the name "Phoebe" is "an epithet for the goddess Artemis, [and] this suggests she must have been a Gentile since it is unlikely to have been given to a Jewess."[40] The three titles that Paul gives her merit further consideration because they are critical for our understanding of women's role in the mission of the Pauline communities.

"Sister" (*adelphē*) is a term that can identify a member of a missionary team because "the masculine equivalent of the term is a frequent designation for Paul's very important missionary collaborator, Timothy, [and] leaves little doubt about the respect bestowed by the title (e.g., Phlm 2; 2 Cor 1:1; 1 Thess 3:2)."[41] Phoebe is also called a deacon, another title frequently used by Paul as the name of an office holder in the Christian community (see Phil 1:1; 1 Cor 3:5; 1 Thess 3:2), and which can be appropriately translated as "servant." Schüssler Fiorenza states that "the word cluster, *diakonos, diakonia, diakonein* is found most often in 2 Corinthians and it characterizes the so-called pseudo-apostles who were charismatic missionaries, eloquent preachers, visionary prophets and Spirit-filled apostles . . . Phoebe has the same title as these charismatic preachers in Corinth. Yet she is not one of Paul's opponents, but has a friendly relationship with him."[42]

Phoebe is also referred to as patroness or benefactor (*prostatis*). In this instance, the masculine equivalent is *prostatēs*, and means "legal patron." This has led Ernst Käsemann to claim that Phoebe's designation as *prostatis* had no legal connotations such as those belonging to the male patron, *prostatēs*, and that Phoebe's role should be understood as one of personal

38. See T. W. Manson, "St Paul's Letter to the Romans—and Others," in *The Romans Debate: Revised and Expanded Edition*, ed. K. P. Donfried (Peabody, Mass.: Hendrikson, 1991).

39. Brendan Byrne, *Romans*, ed. Daniel J. Harrington (Collegeville, Minn.: Liturgical Press, 1996), 29.

40. F. M. Gillman, *Women Who Knew Paul* (Collegeville, Minn.: Liturgical Press, 1992), 59-60.

41. MacDonald, "Reading Real Women," 208.

42. Elisabeth Schüssler Fiorenza, "Missionaries, Apostles, Co-workers: Romans 16 and the Reconstruction of Women's Early Christian History," *Word and World* 6 (1986): 420-33.

ministry toward Paul and his male companions.[43] Schüssler Fiorenza vigorously refutes this:

> It is obvious that an androcentric perspective on early Christian history has to explain away the meaning of both words [*diakonos* and *prostatis*] because it does not allow for women in church leadership, or it can accord them only "feminine" assisting functions. Since this traditional interpretative model takes it for granted that the leadership of the early church was in the hands of men, it assumes that the women mentioned in the Pauline letters were the helpers and assistants of the male apostles and missionaries, especially of Paul. Such an androcentric model of historical reconstruction cannot imagine or conceptualize that women such as Phoebe could have had leadership equal to and sometimes superior to men in early Christian beginnings.[44]

Patronage was a critical aspect of Greco-Roman life.

> Patrons are elite persons who can provide benefits to others on a personal basis, due to a combination of superior power, influence, reputation, position and wealth. In return for these benefits, patrons (who were both men and women in the ancient Mediterranean world) could expect to receive honor, information, and political support from clients. Clients on the other hand, are persons of lesser status who are obligated and loyal to a patron over a period of time. In Roman society patronage/clientage was a clearly defined relationship between individuals of different status for their mutual benefit.[45]

This suggests that Phoebe was probably the leader of a well-known house church in Cenchreae, a woman with significant resources who journeyed from Cenchreae to Rome for a specific mission, perhaps to rally support for Paul as he planned for his mission to Spain. Therefore, her role was not one that was exercised primarily in the private or domestic realm.

Paul greets Prisca and Aquila, his co-workers in Christ, and who like Paul were tent makers (see Acts 18:2; 1 Cor 16:19; 2 Tim 4:19). Prisca and Aquila

---

43. Ernst Käsemann, *Commentary on Romans*, ed. G. W. Bromiley; trans. G. W. Bromiley (Grand Rapids, Mich.: Eerdmans, 1980), 411.

44. Elisabeth Schüssler Fiorenza, "The Apostleship of Women in Early Christianity," in *Women Priests: A Catholic Commentary on the Vatican Declaration*, ed. Leonard Swidler and Arlene Swidler (New York: Paulist Press, 1977), 137. Robert Jewett confirms Schüssler Fiorenza's argument in his "Paul, Phoebe and the Spanish Mission," in *The Social World of Formative Christianity and Judaism: Essays in Tribute to Howard Kee*, ed. Jacob Neuser et al. (Philadelphia: Fortress Press, 1988), 142-61.

45. K. C. Hanson and Douglas E. Oakman, *Palestine in the Time of Jesus: Social Structures and Social Conflicts* (Minneapolis: Fortress Press, 1998), 70.

may have been a married couple, as Acts 18:2 claims, or given that Prisca is named before Aquila in Acts, Romans, and 2 Timothy, but not in 1 Corinthians 16:19, she and Aquila may have been a missionary couple, in which case the position of her name suggests that the woman's role was not subordinate to that of the man. Although Paul had become acquainted with Prisca and Aquila in both Corinth and Ephesus, Romans makes it clear that by ca. 58, they were in Rome, and their house had become an important gathering place for Gentile Christians. The fact that Prisca and Aquila are associated with three cities, Corinth, Ephesus, and Rome, offers further evidence of the importance of itinerant missionaries in the primitive Christian community. Once again we see how the household church enabled women to move effectively and easily between the private and public realms.

Another important missionary couple were Andronicus and Junia. In the sixteenth century, interpreters and translators transformed the woman "Junia" into the man "Junias," no doubt because a patriarchal church was less than enthusiastic about the identification of a woman as an apostle. Even as late as 1946, the Revised Standard Version of the Bible refers to Junia as Junias. Although it is now widely accepted that Junia, disciple and missionary, was a woman, Castelli observes:

> Reference to Junia the *apostolos* in 16:7 has inspired remarkable interpretative contortions, resulting ultimately in sex-change-by-translation. The feminine name Junia is replaced in modern translations by the masculine name Junias, a name nowhere else attested in the ancient world. Once again the argument is a circular syllogism since, by definition, women cannot be apostles, when a woman is called an apostle, she is either not an apostle or she is not a woman.[46]

In 1 Corinthians 15:5-9, Paul defines what makes an apostle. It is the one who has "seen" the risen Jesus, and who has received a commission to witness to that event. Junia is one who shares responsibility for preaching the good news with Paul, indicating that she has seen the risen Jesus. Two other male-female missionary couples are mentioned: Pholologus and Julia, and Nereas and his sister (Rom 16:15). It is more difficult to ascertain the roles of these four people, but it is possible that they are leaders of household churches.

In Romans 16:12, Paul greets two women missioners, Tryphaena and Tryphosa, who are identified as "co-workers in the Lord." This missionary couple are women of some prominence in the early church, and so Paul, wanting to present his own credentials to the Christians in Rome, establishes a connection between himself and the two women. As Mary Rose D'Angelo points out, some male scholars, rather than confer the status of missionary

---

46. Elizabeth A. Castelli, "Romans," in *Searching the Scriptures: A Feminist Commentary*, ed. Elisabeth Schüssler Fiorenza, 2 vols. (New York: Crossroad, 1993, 1994), 2:280.

couple on the two women, have understood the two women as biological sisters or have argued that the similarity of their names persuaded Paul to link them together.[47] She continues, "the missionary couple constitutes a category that is well accepted by New Testament scholars,"[48] and therefore Tryphaena and Tryphosa should be recognized as a missionary couple in the same way that Paul and Timothy are acknowledged.

Schüssler Fiorenza believes that Paul has listed the people in Romans 16 according to their status and standing in the community. "It begins with the most important persons of the community—Prisca and Aquila—and ends with greetings to whole groups, and to 'all the saints belonging to them' (Rom 16:10-11)."[49] Romans 16 then informs the reader that women were engaged in the mission of the early Pauline churches, working as deacons/ministers, patrons, and apostles.

But a caution is warranted as feminists seek "to restore women to history and to restore our history to women."[50] Elizabeth Castelli summarizes some of the pitfalls for women who seek to restore women to history. First, Paul's letters were written to particular communities, and therefore we have to be wary about generalizing from the particular. Second, it is difficult twenty centuries later to claim that Paul's theology was normative for the couple of generations of Christians after the death and resurrection. Paul offers tantalizing glimpses of what might have been rather than a detailed historical overview.[51] But even taking into account such warranted cautions, we can see that Romans 16 constitutes an important text for women seeking to reframe their missionary role in the contemporary church.

In attempting to rewrite women back into the missionary story of the early church, I argue that it is possible to claim on the basis of references to women leaders in Paul's letters that they were an integral part of the expansion from Palestine and Asia Minor into Europe. When it comes to explaining how their involvement occurred, it is important not to turn Paul into a prototype feminist, engaging women to work with him. In the seven letters identified as genuinely Pauline, there appear to be conflicting messages. On the one hand, Paul affirms women as apostles, as deacons, as co-workers, and, on the other hand, if we accept that 1 Corinthians 11:3-7 and 14:33b-35 are gen-

---

47. See Mary Rose D'Angelo, "Women Partners in the New Testament (Rom 16:12; Phil 4:2; Luke 10:38-42; John 11:2, 12)," *Journal of Feminist Studies in Religion* 6 (1990).

48. Ibid., 73.

49. Schüssler Fiorenza, "Missionaries, Apostles, Co-workers," 420-33.

50. Joan Kelly, "The Social Relation of the Sexes: Methodological Implications of Women's History," in *Women, History and Theory: The Essays of Joan Kelly*, ed. Joan Kelly (Chicago: University of Chicago Press, 1984), 1.

51. See Elizabeth A. Castelli, "Paul on Women and Gender," in *Women and Christian Origins*, ed. Ross Shepard Kraemer and Mary Rose D'Angelo (New York/Oxford: Oxford University Press, 1999), 223.

uinely Pauline, then it becomes more difficult to identify Paul as feminist. Again, it is hard to decide if Paul's identification of women as leaders in the expanding Christian movements was driven by theological imperatives about equality or whether it reflected the more fluid social roles open to women in the more western parts of the empire. In all probability, Paul's attitude to women in the Christian communities with which he was associated probably flowed from a variety of causes, which would have included sensitivity to changing cultural contexts and, above all, to his belief that baptism in Christ brought about a new creation that should impact the way in which the newly baptized related to one another. At the same time, the minority status of the new religion prevented him from striving for structural or systemic change that today's liberation theologians or advocacy exegetes would favor. Paul's theology was eschatological rather than political, and he believed that the freedom Christians enjoyed through baptism in Christ would be more fully realized at the parousia.

Having said that, it is important to recognize that important developments occurred as the first Christians spread from Palestine to other parts of the empire. As his letter to the Galatians makes clear, once baptism was accepted as the primary rite of initiation, the Christian community was not one whose boundaries were defined by ethnicity or gender. Faith in the crucified and risen Jesus, rather than the biological factors of race and sex, is what would unite people to one another.

Paul's use of familial imagery, especially that of the generic "brother" and, hence by extension, "sister," and the repeated calls to love and unity, although not uncommon in other religious sects and communities of the time, were in contrast to the patriarchal and hierarchical structures existing throughout the empire. While it is not possible to argue categorically that it represents a turn toward egalitarianism, nevertheless, it suggests that hierarchical structures were not the defining characteristic of the earliest Christian communities.

After Paul's death, the ambiguities inherent in his seven letters concerning women's missionary role developed along two distinct lines. Those texts that became part of our canon and which probably come to us from followers of Paul—Colossians and Ephesians, 1 and 2 Timothy, and Titus—fail to generate the same excitement for women seeking to revision their missionary role in the contemporary church. They prescribe, for example, that women should be silent, that women are second in the order of creation, and that women will be saved by childbearing. In other words, the possibility of women's involvement in the public sphere is circumscribed. On the other hand, a more positive development occurred among another group of Paul's followers, so that the *Acts of Paul and Thecla* offer a picture that represents a positive development of Paul's understanding of women's involvement in the mission of the church. We will now turn to a more detailed consideration of these texts that come to us from some of the different post-Pauline communities.

# 2

## *Women as Homemakers in the Post-Pauline Letters*

As our study of those letters that have Paul as their author suggests, there are conflicting messages about the role of women in the first Christian communities. Despite some ambiguities, it is legitimate to argue that Paul favors women being actively involved as deacons, co-workers, and apostles with him in his proclamation of the Lord Jesus Christ, crucified and raised from the dead. After Paul, the situation changes as two oppositional trajectories developed. On the one hand, in those letters we designate as Deutero-Pauline—Colossians, Ephesians, 1 and 2 Timothy, and Titus[1]—the position of women seems to have altered quite remarkably, and the reader is soon aware that women's role as homemakers in the domestic realm is the main role open to Christian women as the first century draws to a close. On the other hand, in some of the apocryphal texts, women are depicted as still having an active and public involvement in the life of the community.[2] In this chapter, I wish to examine the reasons for and implications of the shifts that occur in the Deutero-Pauline letters. Then I will turn to one important non-canonical text that signifies a very different role for women.

---

1. The majority of contemporary New Testament scholars argue that the five letters are pseudonymous, that is, written some years after Paul's death in 64 C.E. by followers or disciples of Paul. See Raymond E. Brown, *An Introduction to the New Testament* (New York/London: Doubleday, 1997), 803-4. For an alternative view, see Luke Timothy Johnson, *Letters to Paul's Delegates: 1 Timothy, 2 Timothy, Titus* (Valley Forge. Pa.: Trinity Press International, 1996), 1-36. In his introduction, Johnson explains why he no longer believes that the Deutero-Pauline letters are pseudonymous. I will refer briefly to other non-Pauline letters, notably 1 and 2 Peter, James, and Jude.

2. See, for example, Karen L. King, "Prophetic Power and Women's Authority: The Case of the *Gospel of Mary* (Magdalene)," in *Women Preachers and Prophets through Two Millennia of Christianity*, ed. Beverly Mayne Kienzle and Pamela J. Walker (Berkeley: University of California Press, 1998); Maureen A. Tilley, "The Passion of Felicity and Perpetua," in *Searching the Scriptures: A Feminist Commentary*, ed. Elisabeth Schüssler Fiorenza, 2 vols. (New York: Crossroad, 1993, 1994), 2:829-58.

Before embarking on that task, it is important to mention arguments that favor understanding Colossians, Ephesians, 1 and 2 Timothy, and Titus as pseudonymous. Few contemporary scholars argue in favor of Paul's authorship of Ephesians, 1 and 2 Timothy, and Titus, although there is less unanimity regarding the pseudonymity of Colossians.[3] In discerning whether or not a letter should be designated as pseudonymous, Pauline scholars look at literary features of the letters—style, vocabulary, grammar—and identify how textual analysis points to significant differences. Second, the theological ideas located in the Deutero-Pauline letters represent a development that moves beyond the ideas located in the genuinely Pauline letters. Those in favor of Pauline authorship of the disputed letters argue that Paul wrote these five letters at a later date, and they reflect his changing thought. This is a difficult argument to sustain, given Paul's martyrdom in Rome probably in the summer of 64 C.E. during Nero's persecution. Finally, these letters seem to reflect a different historical context from that obtaining in the genuine Pauline letters. For example, the references to "apostles and prophets" (Eph 2:20; 3:5) as the church's foundation suggest that apostles and prophets belong to the past.

Pauline authorship of the Pastoral letters, 1 and 2 Timothy, and Titus has been questioned since the eighteenth century. The ecclesiology of these letters, which offers advice to bishops, elders, and deacons, points to more organized church structures that belong to the late-first- or early-second-century church life. Harris notes that "scholars believe that a single Pauline disciple—who possessed little of his mentor's fire or originality—wrote all three between about 100 and 140 C.E."[4] Arguing for or against the pseudonymity of these letters does not have any bearing on their canonical status, but favoring Paul's authorship makes it easier to label Paul as restrictive of women's role in the community. Furthermore, if these five letters are assumed to be non-Pauline and to have been written after the death of Paul toward the end of the first century or even in the early second century, this becomes important for us in identifying the social and theological developments that led to changing missionary roles for women in the early Christian community. I will examine these letters in their chronological order in an effort to see how the positive Pauline legacy with respect to women changed and developed.

## COLOSSIANS

This letter is addressed to "the saints," who included both Gentile and Jewish Christians living in Colossae in the Lycus Valley, the eastern part of

---

3. Maurya P. Horgan, "The Letter to the Colossians," in *The New Jerome Biblical Commentary*, ed. R. E. Brown et al. (Englewood Cliffs, N.J.: Prentice-Hall, 1990); P. T. O'Brien, *Colossians, Philemon* (Waco, Tex.: Word Books, 1982). Horgan favors pseudonymity while O'Brien defends Pauline authorship of Colossians.

4. Stephen L. Harris, *Understanding the Bible* (Boston: McGraw-Hill, 2003), 570.

the empire in what is now modern Turkey. As Colossians 2:8-23 indicates, the community was troubled by false teachers. Much scholarly attention has been expended in identifying who these opponents of Christianity might have been, and what their offense was. Recent research indicates that syncretism was a particular problem, "not understood here in any way as the corruption of 'pure' religious traditions, but instead as a combination of religious traditions"[5]—Christian, Jewish, pagan, Stoic, and Cynic.

There are two texts in Colossians that warrant further consideration if we are to better appreciate the role of women in the early church. In the final greeting and blessing, the author refers to "Nympha and the church in her house" (Col 4:16), which suggests that women still enjoyed a public role in the Christian community. However, Colossians 3:18-4:1, one of the "household codes," makes it clear that the authority invested in women as leaders of household churches is not as important as the power that is invested in the *paterfamilias*, the head of the patriarchal household.

> Wives, be subject to your husbands, as is fitting in the Lord. Husbands, love your wives and never treat them harshly. Children, obey your parents in everything, for this is your acceptable duty in the Lord. Fathers, do not provoke your children, or they may lose heart. Slaves, obey your earthly masters in everything, not only while being watched and in order to please them, but wholeheartedly, fearing the Lord. Whatever your task, put yourselves into it, as done for the Lord and not for your masters, since you know that from the Lord you will receive the inheritance as your reward; you serve the Lord Christ. For the wrongdoer will be paid back for whatever wrong has been done, and there is no partiality. Masters, treat your slaves justly and fairly, for you know that you also have a Master in heaven.

In approaching the household code in Colossians, its counterparts in other Deutero-Pauline letters (Eph 5:22-6:9; 1 Timothy 2:8-15; 6:1-2; Titus 2:1-10), and similar texts in early Christian writings dating from the first and second centuries (1 Pet 2:18-3:7; *Didache* 4:9-11; *Barnabas* 19:5-7; *1 Clement* 21:6-9; *Epistle of Polycarp to the Philippians*),[6] it is important

---

5. Margaret Y. MacDonald, *Colossians and Ephesians*, Sacra Pagina 17 (Collegeville, Minn.: Liturgical Press, 2000), 11.

6. A good example of a later household code occurs in the *Epistle of Polycarp to the Philippians*. Polycarp (66-155 C.E.) writes, "After that we can go on to instruct our womenfolk in the traditions of the faith, and in love and purity; teaching them to show fondness and fidelity to their husbands, and a chaste and impartial affection for everyone else, and to bring up their children in fear of God. Widows are to observe discretion as they practice our Lord's faith; they should make constant intercessions for everyone, and be careful to avoid any tale-bearing, spiteful tittle-tattle, false allegations, over-eagerness for money, or misconduct of any description." See Andrew Louth, ed., *Early Christian Writings: The Apostolic Fathers* (London: Penguin Books, 1987), 120.

that we have some awareness of the culture in which they were written. In the Greco-Roman world of the first century, the patriarchal household was hierarchically ordered, and according to the political thought of the period, the structure of superior and inferior roles was believed to be basic to the well-being of not only the household but also of society and of the state. In the patriarchal household, the husband, father, and master exercised power over wives, children, and slaves. Patriarchal culture believed that the experience of successfully managing a household was good preparation for male involvement in state management. As the Jewish philosopher Philo of Alexandria commented, "The future statesman needed first to be trained and practiced in house management, for a house is a city compressed into small dimensions, and a household management may be called a kind of state management."[7]

There are at least two reasons why the household codes were identified as important for Christian communities as the first century drew to a close. First, one of the problems that confronted the Christian communities was that if women's behavior was not in accord with the social conventions of the day, the young and numerically insignificant Christian communities might be regarded in a negative light. In turn, this could lead to the good news not being well received and the communities being regarded as subversive of the existing social order. In such a context, the household code was "part of a strategy for survival for Pauline Christians in a hostile environment."[8] Therefore, the equality among Christians was to be an "inner equality" (cf. Gal 3:28) rather than a visible, social equality that could subvert the structure of the patriarchal household.

At the same time, it is possible to locate in the New Testament evidence that suggests criticism of the patriarchal household, for example, in those Gospel texts that demonstrate that the faith community of those who follow Jesus (see Mark 3:31-35; Luke 11:27-28) has more importance for Jesus than his biological family. Discipleship is about relinquishing claims of power and domination that belonged to husbands, fathers, and masters in the patriarchal household (see Mark 10:45). The abdication of power these texts imply was perceived as a threat to the structure of the Greco-Roman household. Therefore, as the first century drew to a close, the potential disruption of the patriarchal household caused by the participation of women and slaves in the Christian missionary movement prompted a clamping down on women and slaves in an effort to foster good relationships with the wider pagan community. The texts from Colossians, Ephesians, 1 and 2 Timothy, and Titus, probably written after 70 C.E., represent an attempt to restrict the enthusiasm of women and slaves for social egalitarianism, and thus restore order to the patriarchal household.

---

7. D. L. Balch, "Household Ethical Codes in Peripatetic, Neopythagorean and Early Christian Moralists," *Society of Biblical Literature Seminar Papers* 11 (1977): 402, quoting from Philo of Alexandria, "On Joseph," 38-39.

8. MacDonald, *Colossians and Ephesians*, 166.

A second reason often suggested is that Paul's belief in the imminence of the parousia (see 1 Cor 7:25-31), and the fact that "the time is running out" (1 Cor 7:29), meant that normal societal customs such as getting married, raising a family, and establishing a household were no longer a pressing concern for new Christians. After Paul's death, however, it became apparent that the parousia was not imminent and that the Christian community would need to adapt to the mores of Roman imperial culture if it were to survive.

Commentators are divided as to the origins of the household codes, some attributing them to Greco-Roman cultural practices derived from Aristotelian philosophy,[9] and others looking to Palestinian and Hellenistic Judaism.[10] Sarah Tanzer warns of the risks involved in "blaming" either "pagans" or "Jews" for the household codes. As we have seen in chap. 1, the status of women throughout the empire varied considerably, and, generally speaking, women, particularly upper-class women, enjoyed more freedom in the western part. It is also problematic to refer to Jewish texts dating from the third century to explain the Jewish origins of the household codes. Locating the origins of the household codes in Greco-Roman and Jewish cultures may serve as a ploy whereby Christian commentators portray the situation of women in the worst possible light in order to show how Christianity improved their status.[11]

Whatever reasons lie behind the formation of the household codes, they reveal a "pattern of exhortation that characterizes the subordinate status of women, children and slaves."[12] D'Angelo states that "*patresfamiliae* (heads of families but not necessarily biological fathers) have power over the family, which is defined as wives/women, children, slaves and property; ultimate power resides in the emperor, who is the father (and savior) of his country (*patria*)."[13] If the household codes were to be the law by which the Christian communities ordered their lives and ministries, then the likelihood of women continuing to work alongside male disciples as co-workers or apostles

---

9. S. Moller Okin, *Women in Western Political Thought* (Princeton: Princeton University Press, 1979), 48. Okin cites Aristotle's *Politics* 1.1253b, "the smallest primary parts of the household are master and slave, husband and wife, father and children. We ought therefore to examine the proper constitution and character of each of the three relationships, I mean that of mastership, that of marriage and thirdly the progenitive relationship."

10. See Balch, "Household Ethical Codes," 405, who cites the Diaspora Jew Philo of Alexandria: "Organized committees are of two sorts, the greater which we call cities and the smaller which we call households. Both of these have their governors [*prostasian*], the government of the greater is assigned to men, under the name of statesmanship [*politeia*], that of the lesser known as household management to women. A woman then should not be a busybody, meddling with matters outside her household concerns, but should seek a life of seclusion" (*Special Laws* 3.7.14).

11. See Sarah J. Tanzer, "Ephesians," in *Searching the Scriptures: A Feminist Commentary*, ed. Elisabeth Schüssler Fiorenza, 2 vols. (New York: Crossroad, 1993, 1994), 2:328-32.

12. Mary Rose D'Angelo, "Colossians," in *Searching the Scriptures: A Feminist Commentary*, ed. Elisabeth Schüssler Fiorenza, 2 vols. (New York: Crossroad, 1993, 1994), 2:315.

13. Ibid.

became virtually impossible. Even if it is possible to locate continuity between the Pauline and Deutero-Pauline texts with respect to women's leadership of household churches (see Col 4:16), the prescriptions enshrined in the household code served to militate against those earlier Pauline initiatives that affirmed the position of women as co-workers with him in the work of the early Christian community.

## EPHESIANS

The letter to the Ephesians has as one of its main functions to explain how Paul's major teachings for the Christian community would function in a new and changing situation. As MacDonald says, "Ephesians constitutes the first interpretation of and guide to Pauline tradition in light of the disappearance of Paul. While in all likelihood Colossians was the earliest Deutero-Pauline writing, Colossians does not reflect the same sustained effort to summarize Paul's teachings as we find in Ephesians."[14] There is much discussion as to the intended recipients of this letter, and it would be wrong to assume automatically that it was intended for a Christian community at Ephesus. It is likely that it was written for more than one community because it lacks the specificity that we find in letters Paul has directly addressed to a particular community. While there is uncertainty regarding the geographical locale of the community, it is obvious enough that the community was primarily composed of Gentile Christians who were outnumbering Jewish Christians in the community (see Eph 2:11).

There are a number of theories regarding the purpose of Ephesians: first, it was a general letter written after Paul's death to different Christian communities living in the eastern part of the empire, summarizing and interpreting key elements in Paul's teachings that addressed the new situation in which Christians found themselves. Second, it was concerned with God's salvific plan whereby Jew and Gentile are united in the body of Christ. This plan had both a present and an eschatological dimension and was intended to end the disunity between God and humankind, and among humans, notably Jew and Gentile. Third, it was intended to rebut the teachings of Judaizing Christians and gnostic Christians that threatened unity. Finally, it addressed the danger that hostile spiritual powers represent for the young communities.

The household code in Ephesians 5:22-6:9 is strongly patriarchal and hierarchical although it is possible to identify traces of an ethos of mutuality (see Eph 5:31-32) more characteristic of Paul's letters.

Be subject to one another out of reverence for Christ. Wives, be subject to your husbands as you are to the Lord. For the husband is the head

---

14. MacDonald, *Colossians and Ephesians*, 16.

of the wife just as Christ is the head of the church, the body of which he is the Savior. Just as the church is subject to Christ, so also wives ought to be, in everything, to their husbands. Husbands, love your wives, just as Christ loved the church and gave himself up for her, in order to make her holy by cleansing her with the washing of water by the word, so as to present the church to himself in splendor, without a spot or wrinkle or anything of the kind—yes, so that she may be holy and without blemish. In the same way, husbands should love their wives as they do their own bodies. He who loves his wife loves himself. For no one ever hates his own body, but he nourishes and tenderly cares for it, just as Christ does for the church, because we are members of his body. "For this reason a man will leave his father and mother and be joined to his wife, and the two will become one flesh." This is a great mystery, and I am applying it to Christ and the church. Each of you, however, should love his wife as himself, and a wife should respect her husband. (Eph 5:21-33)

These verses occur within the context of the author's teaching on what unity in the body of Christ requires of the Christian community. The author argues that disunity occurs at different levels—cosmological, cultural or ethnic, and familial. In Ephesians 1:3-14 (the christological hymn) and 6:10-20 the author develops his cosmological theology, while in the household code, he provides a way whereby social and familial alienation can be overcome. While his purpose is praiseworthy, feminists recognize that the teaching in Ephesians 5:21-33 is predicated on women acknowledging that their status and role are defined by their relationship to their husbands on whom they are economically dependent and whom they must obey. The Christ/church metaphor is introduced to teach what the attitude of the husband to his wife should be—one of love and concern; and in return the wife should respect her husband. While it is possible to find teachings in this text that are commendable, nevertheless its passive presentation of the wife is not one that resonates with the aspirations of many contemporary Christian feminists, who want to exercise their ministry in the public realm.

In concluding this brief overview of the household codes in Colossians and Ephesians, Tanzer's insights are helpful. Although those letters judged to be genuinely Pauline offer a different perspective of women, it is possible to discern in them patriarchal tendencies, which become much more marked in the Deutero-Pauline corpus. Tanzer, following Elisabeth Schüssler Fiorenza, argues that just as first-century Judaism and "the Roman Empire included both emancipatory and patriarchal views of women, so too early Christianity had a variety of strains within it, including those which advocated a more emancipatory stance as well as those of the patriarchal persuasion."[15] In both

---

15. Tanzer, "Ephesians," 2:331.

Colossians and Ephesians, patriarchal culture was triumphing over an earlier emancipatory ethos, a process that would accelerate in the Pastoral letters.

## 1 AND 2 TIMOTHY AND TITUS

In assessing the import of 1 and 2 Timothy and Titus for women, it is as well to recall Luke Timothy Johnson's claim that these letters "are also not easy for contemporary readers in particular because the symbols and concepts of these letters may offend many sensibilities of the present age. Ours is an age that likes to think of itself as egalitarian and inclusive and nonsexist. Whatever else they are, these compositions are hierarchical, exclusive, and androcentric, if not actually sexist."[16]

Or, as Linda Maloney puts it, the challenge facing the contemporary interpreter is "how to approach the Pastoral letters in a way that will, without doing violence to them, render them productive for insight rather than destructive in practice."[17] In interpreting these letters, Maloney, who accepts their pseudonymous nature, believes that their androcentric and patriarchal character may in fact offer Christian feminists an entry point for a positive reading. Statements so restrictive of women's roles in the Christian community are not the statements of a strong and vigorous male leadership but rather the defensive posturing of authority figures who do not know how to respond to women's leadership of the community except through a hectoring and bullying tone.

In explaining the apparently misogynist nature of the Pastoral letters, we need to recall the community's need to maintain good standing in the pagan society of which they are part. There is evidence too that the church was threatened by heretical or false teachers whose ascetical impulse led them to deny the goodness of marriage (1 Tim 4:3), but whose gnostic teachings seemed to attracted adherents (1 Tim 6:20). These two factors meant that the male community leaders favored a strictly hierarchical structure as a way of controlling a difficult situation.

First Timothy contains two texts that present particular difficulty for women seeking to find an affirming scriptural foundation for their contemporary exercise of mission. The one that causes the most concern, and indeed anger, is 1 Timothy 2:8-15-3:1a:

> I desire, then, that in every place the men should pray, lifting up holy hands without anger or argument; also that the women should dress themselves modestly and decently in suitable clothing, not with their

16. Johnson, *Letters to Paul's Delegates*, vii.
17. Linda M. Maloney, "The Pastoral Epistles," in *Searching the Scriptures: A Feminist Commentary*, ed. Elisabeth Schüssler Fiorenza, 2 vols. (New York: Crossroad, 1993, 1994), 2:361.

hair braided, or with gold, pearls, or expensive clothes, but with good works, as is proper for women who profess reverence for God. Let a woman learn in silence with full submission. I permit no woman to teach or to have authority over a man; she is to keep silent. For Adam was formed first, then Eve; and Adam was not deceived, but the woman was deceived and became a transgressor. Yet she will be saved through childbearing, provided they continue in faith and love and holiness, with modesty. This saying is sure.

This is not a passage that generates enthusiasm among women. Chapter 2 of 1 Timothy is concerned with instructions about prayer, directed to both women and men. There is an emphasis on the need for the community to pray for "kings and all who are in high positions so that we may lead a quiet and peaceable life in all godliness and dignity" (1 Tim 2:2). First Timothy 2:1-15 appears driven by the concern of the Christian community to protect its future in the dominant pagan culture, hence the exhortation to live "a quiet and peaceable life." In particular, the author is concerned to outline a code of conduct that will ensure that the behavior of women does nothing to jeopardize the well-being of the community. Nothing about women's lives, whether it is their behavior, their speech, or their dress should attract public opprobrium or even attention. Most importantly, women are not to teach or have authority over men. The author of 1 Timothy locates scriptural legitimation for his position in his interpretation of Genesis 3, which is interpreted as meaning that Eve alone is responsible for humankind's fallen state. Women will be saved through childbearing, which, as Maloney claims "is a truly shocking statement, since it seems to say that Christ's redemptive work does not extend to women; rather, they must save themselves by a particular mode of conduct."[18] This soteriology is very different from Paul's teachings concerning justification by faith (see Gal 2:16; Rom 1:16-17).

The anthropology of Genesis 1:27, which teaches that both male and female are created in the image and likeness of God, does not influence the author of 1 Timothy, and therefore his interpretation of Genesis 3 is markedly different from Paul's found in the Corinthian correspondence. While Paul affirms that Eve was deceived by the serpent (2 Cor 11:3), he is also clear that it was through Adam that sin came into the world (1 Cor 15:21-22). In opting to blame Eve for humankind's sinfulness, the author of 1 Timothy is more influenced by Sirach 25:24, written about 180 B.C.E. ("From a woman sin had its beginning, and because of her we all die"). Jouette Bassler believes that "The saying is sure" (1 Tim 3:1a) more appropriately belongs to the author's teaching on women rather than to his teachings that follow on the role of bishops and deacons.[19] If Bassler is correct,

---

18. Ibid., 2:370.
19. See Jouette M. Bassler, "The Widow's Tale," *Journal of Biblical Literature* 103 (1984): 23-41.

then the prescriptive nature of the text for women is even more marked. In 1 Timothy 3:11, the author of the Pastoral letters continues to address the role and place of women in the community: "Women likewise must be serious, not slanderers, but temperate, faithful in all things." "Women" may refer to wives of deacons, given that the verse occurs in the context of teachings about the role of deacons, or it may refer to women deacons. If this is the case, then the role of women deacons is now "limited by the constraints put on women's behavior in 2:11-12,"[20] and represents a departure from the more positive role Paul assigns to Phoebe in Romans 16:1-2.

Titus 2:3-5 reads, "Likewise, tell the older women to be reverent in behavior, not to be slanderers or slaves to drink; they are to teach what is good, so that they may encourage the young women to love their husbands, to love their children, to be self-controlled, chaste, good managers of the household, kind, being submissive to their husbands, so that the word of God may not be discredited." These verses occur as a part of a list of virtues that highlight the value placed by the Christian community on the hierarchical structure of the Greco-Roman household. Thus Titus 2:2 refers to older men; 2:3-5, to older and younger women; 2:6-8, to younger men who are not exhorted to silence but told to use "sound speech that cannot be censured"; and 2:9-10 refers to slaves.

Once again, we find an emphasis on the behavior expected of women. In addition to being given injunctions against slander, women are cautioned against enslavement to drink and enjoined to be submissive to their husbands. Although older women are exhorted to teach, this teaching is to occur within the home and has as its purpose to train younger women to be submissive to their husbands. It should not be read as establishing teaching ministries for women within the community. Clare Drury argues that it is possible that "the 'opponents of sound doctrine' (Tit 2:1) taught that women could remain single and continue to lead a full Christian life and like Thecla become an itinerant preacher (see 2 Tim 3:1-9)."[21] The instructions to women about their relationships with their husbands are not complemented by instructions on the responsibility of husbands toward their wives.

There are also instructions in 1 Timothy 5:3-16 concerning another group of women—widows.

Honor widows who are really widows. If a widow has children or grandchildren, they should first learn their religious duty to their own family and make some repayment to their parents; for this is pleasing in God's sight. The real widow, left alone, has set her hope on God and continues in supplications and prayers night and day; but the widow

---

20. Clare Drury, "The Pastoral Epistles," in *The Oxford Bible Commentary*, ed. John Barton and John Muddiman (Oxford: Oxford University Press, 2001), 1225.
21. Ibid., 1232.

who lives for pleasure is dead even while she lives. Give these commands as well, so that they may be above reproach. And whoever does not provide for relatives, and especially for family members, has denied the faith and is worse than an unbeliever. Let a widow be put on the list if she is not less than sixty years old and has been married only once; she must be well attested for her good works, as one who has brought up children, shown hospitality, washed the saints' feet, helped the afflicted, and devoted herself to doing good in every way. But refuse to put younger widows on the list; for when their sensual desires alienate them from Christ, they want to marry, and so they incur condemnation for having violated their first pledge. Besides that, they learn to be idle, gadding about from house to house; and they are not merely idle, but also gossips and busybodies, saying what they should not say. So I would have younger widows marry, bear children, and manage their households, so as to give the adversary no occasion to revile us. For some have already turned away to follow Satan. If any believing woman has relatives who are really widows, let her assist them; let the church not be burdened, so that it can assist those who are real widows.

Different meanings are associated with the term "widows" in the New Testament. Widows emerge as an oppressed group of women, a tradition that is rooted in the Hebrew Bible (see 1 Kgs 17:9; 2 Kgs 4:18-37; Pss 94:6; 146:9). Mark 12:40 (par Matt 23:14; Luke 20:47) affirms widows, and Luke's parable of the unjust judge unfavorably compares the judge who neither fears God nor man with the widow. Because of their severely straitened circumstances, Christian widows in the ancient world relied on financial support from the Christian community, and they are to be distinguished from what appears to be the institutionalized order of widows who serve the community. Paul refers to widows in 1 Corinthians 7:8 but does not mention any particular office associated with widows, nor is an order of widows listed among the different charismatic ministries characteristic of the Corinthian community. First Timothy 5:3-14, however, contains detailed instructions concerning widows, because of the apparent increase in their number. Bassler suggests that this increase could be the result of the mortality rate of the times, but it could also have had its origins in married women who divorced their pagan husbands after converting to Christianity.[22]

The author makes a distinction between genuine widows, those who have no one on whom they can depend (1 Tim 5:6), and those who can be supported by family members (1 Tim 5:8). Only older women may be designated as widows—they must be at least sixty years old and have been married only once. Maloney contends that the author of 1 Timothy specifi-

---

22. Bassler, "The Widow's Tale," 35.

cally wishes to exclude "younger widows" who may not necessarily have been married, because the author refers to women who want "to marry" not "to remarry."[23] In other words, the order of widows might have been attracting celibate women who, remembering the freedom and equality of the first-generation Christian communities, believed that widowhood would have allowed them to assume public leadership roles in the community. Bassler writes that

> the church seems to have been caught in a disastrous feedback loop. The heresy problem combined with social pressure caused the church to move from a *communitas* structure challenging society's norms to a patriarchal structure embracing them. Increased patriarchalization of the church seems to have led to an increase in the size of the widows' circle where a degree of freedom from that structure was preserved through the celibate life style.[24]

Furthermore, "the increasing number of wealthy (especially male) converts [meant] the churches began to shape their organization and teachings to better fit with the normative, patriarchal Graeco-Roman social structures. Consolidation of power in the hands of the *paterfamilias* was one step along the way to consolidation of patriarchal, hierarchical structures in the churches."[25] This could be threatened by "the danger" that the ministry of widows, as distinct from ministry to widows, posed for the Christian community.

It is worth digressing here on the nature of leadership in first-century Christian communities. As the Synoptic and Johannine traditions, the Acts of the Apostles, and Paul's seven letters make clear, the dominant earliest Christian leadership was itinerant, modeled on Jesus' own ministry in the Synoptic Gospels. This itinerant model came to be complemented or rather superseded by a model that more appropriately might be called residential. David Horrell argues that

> it is legitimate to speak of a development or transformation from itinerant to resident leadership in early Christianity . . . there is evidence which reflects the tensions and difficulties which the diverse pattern of leadership caused, and that the transference of power from itinerant to resident leadership is a sociologically significant transformation which may be connected with the development of more socially con-

---

23. Maloney, "The Pastoral Epistles," 372.

24. Bassler, "The Widow's Tale," 39.

25. Sheila E. McGinn, "The Household Codes of the Later Pauline Traditions," *The Catechist* 37 (2004): 50.

servative patterns of ethical instruction (especially the "household codes").[26]

In addition to the contrasting itinerant/residential models of leadership to which Horrell refers, there is evidence of a contrast between celibate and married forms of leadership. The canonical texts indicate that both Jesus and Paul opted for a celibate leadership model. In the seven letters Paul wrote, we see that leadership could be exercised by women, some of whom were single. There is also evidence that women and men could share a ministry of leadership. The situation had changed significantly by the time of the non-Pauline-authored letters. Almost without exception, women have been restricted to the home, and their roles as wives and mothers take precedence over other roles that were formerly open to them, which indicates that a celibate, itinerant lifestyle for the sake of mission was not a possibility for women.

Christian feminists may find the Pastoral letters a daunting challenge, but perhaps there is some consolation in the fact that the constant emphasis on right behavior, on women's silence and submission suggests that women may have been an active and involved group who strenuously resisted attempts to restrict their influence and authority to the private and domestic realms.

## 1 PETER

Before moving on to consider more women-friendly developments associated with the post-Pauline years, it is helpful to briefly engage with 1 and 2 Peter, which like 1 and 2 Timothy and Titus are usually considered to be pseudonymous. Similarly, the letters of Jude and James are also thought by many scholars to be pseudonymous, perhaps written by Jewish Christians late in the first century. These four letters also add to our understanding of the role and place of women in first-century Christian communities.

First Peter, written in the last decade of the first century, was originally intended for Gentile communities in the northern Roman provinces of Asia Minor. These communities were harassed by the numerically stronger pagan peoples among whom they lived. This harassment included abuse of Christian slaves by their non-Christian owners (1 Pet 2:18), pressure on Christian wives to conform to the expectations of their non-Christian husbands (3:1), and abuse because of an unwillingness to participate in pagan ritual and cults (4:4). First Peter 2:13-17 instructs Christians to obey civil authorities, while 2:18-20 requires that slaves of pagan masters are to obey without complaint

---

26. David Horrell, "Leadership Patterns and the Development of Ideology in Early Christianity," *Sociology of Religion* 58 (1997): 323-41.

when and if they are treated unjustly. In this manner they are true followers of Christ who suffered through no fault of his own.

First Peter 3:1-7, another example of a household code, similarly exhorts wives to be obedient and to accept suffering without complaint.

> Wives, in the same way, accept the authority of your husbands, so that, even if some of them do not obey the word, they may be won over without a word by their wives' conduct, when they see the purity and reverence of your lives. Do not adorn yourselves outwardly by braid-ing your hair, and by wearing gold ornaments or fine clothing; rather, let your adornment be the inner self with the lasting beauty of a gentle and quiet spirit, which is very precious in God's sight. It was in this way long ago that the holy women who hoped in God used to adorn themselves by accepting the authority of their husbands. Thus Sarah obeyed Abraham and called him lord. You have become her daughters as long as you do what is good and never let fears alarm you. Hus-bands, in the same way, show consideration for your wives in your life together, paying honor to the woman as the weaker sex, since they too are also heirs of the gracious gift of life so that nothing may hinder your prayers.

Because the teachings of 1 Peter are similar to those found in the Deutero-Pauline letters, some scholars initially postulated a Deutero-Pauline author-ship, a position that no longer enjoys much support.[27] The opening verse indicates that Greco-Roman culture required that wives adopt the religious and social beliefs of their husbands so that the position of Christian wives married to pagan husbands was often untenable. Its message of enduring "'unjust suffering' at the hands of 'every social institution' after the manner of Christ has no doubt encouraged many Christian women throughout his-tory to submit quietly to the yoke of various unjust social institutions,"[28] an acceptance that historically has weighed heavily upon them, both in abusive marriage situations and in the church. While it is possible that the author's injunction that slaves and wives accept the authority of their masters and husbands was a successful first-century missionary strategy that allowed Christians to be accepted by Greco-Roman society, it reflects a real distance from Paul's attitude toward and reliance on women in his missionary prac-tice. Once again, we find a male author dictating what women should wear and how women should be submissive toward their husbands, calling them "lord." The author exhorts husbands to pay honor to women "as the weaker sex" (3:7), which "reflects a Greco-Roman perception that women were of

---

27. See Kathleen E. Corley, "1 Peter," in *Searching the Scriptures: A Feminist Commentary*, ed. Elisabeth Schüssler Fiorenza, 2 vols. (New York: Crossroad, 1993, 1994), 2:350.

28. Ibid., 349.

a lower order of humanity than men."[29] Obviously, imperial authorities would be concerned about religious movements that encouraged egalitarian and therefore subversive tendencies among women and slaves. However, the author's belief in the soteriological value of unjust suffering for slaves and women is given a missionary significance. He believes that conformity to pagan society's cultural mores will deflect criticism from the church. It is not an understanding of mission that resonates with contemporary women missionaries.

## JUDE AND 2 PETER

Most scholars believe that the shorter text of the Letter to Jude later became the basis for the longer second letter of Peter. Both letters, written in the late first or early second century, were probably composed by Jewish Christian authors for Christian communities riven by conflict over what constituted orthodox teachings. Neither letter makes any direct reference to women and therefore exemplifies "a patriarchal culture that excludes mention of women and renders women's presence, voice, contributions, and roles invisible."[30] In Jude, the author addresses internal divisions and theological disputes within the community by drawing on Hebrew tradition. While it is appropriate for church leadership to respond to presumed heterodoxy, women who through their baptism were attempting to model new ways of exercising leadership roles in the community often would have been the target of the author's teachings.

Second Peter understands the world as corrupt because of lust and therefore headed for destruction, and at the same time the Christian community to whom the author is writing is torn apart by internal dissension. Women are invisible in this letter, although the false prophets and false teachers to whom he alludes may well have included women whose idea of a community in Christ pointed to the continuing influence of Galatians 3:27. The author finds that Peter's presence at the transfiguration (2 Pet 1:16-20) mandates him to be a teacher and preacher. No women are recorded as being present at the transfiguration (see Mark 9:2-8, par Matt 17:1-8; Luke 9:28-36). Traditionally and contemporaneously, women have found a mandate for their exercise of mission in the appearance of the risen Jesus to Mary Magdalene and the other women at the tomb. Marie-Eloise Rosenblatt suggests that the assertions of the author "are designed to counter the foundational experiences of some women who claim to have seen and heard the

---

29. Ibid., 353.
30. Marie-Eloise Rosenblatt, "Jude," in *Searching the Scriptures: A Feminist Commentary*, ed. Elisabeth Schüssler Fiorenza, 2 vols. (New York: Crossroad, 1993, 1994), 2:393.

risen Jesus speaking in vision to them, for example, Mary Magdalene in the *Gospel of Mary*.[31]

## JAMES

Though the letter of James was purportedly written by James, the brother of Jesus (Matt 13:55; Mark 6:3; Gal 1:19), most contemporary scholarship rejects this possibility. Commentators agree, however, that the author was Jewish, familiar with the Jesus tradition, and able to write in fluent Greek. There is less unanimity as to when the letter was written, with Sophie Laws dating it between 70 and 130 C.E., while Peter Davids and Pedrito Maynard-Reid suggest an earlier date, possibly between 55 and 65 C.E. and perhaps revised some years later, around 75 C.E.[32] The author's concern for the economically marginalized is praiseworthy, and similarly James asserts the responsibility of the community toward widows and orphans (1:27); he invites a compassionate response toward "the brother or sister who is naked, and lacks daily food" (2:16), and he affirms Rahab, the prostitute (Josh 2:1-21) for her good works. While James does not advocate a public role for women in the mission of the early church, his concern for the marginalized and oppressed, his teaching that members confess their sins to one another (5:16), a teaching that seems to run counter to the prevailing patriarchal mindset characteristic of other non-Pauline letters, means that this letter can be considered as more positive for women. It also suggests that the earlier dating suggested by Davids and Maynard-Reid may be correct because the position and role of women became more marginalized as the century progressed.

In our reading of the Deutero-Pauline corpus—Colossians, Ephesians, 1 and 2 Timothy, and Titus—and the non-Pauline letters—1 and 2 Peter,

---

31. See the *Gospel of Mary* "4) [Peter] questioned them about the Savior: Did He really speak privately with a woman and not openly to us? Are we to turn about and all listen to her? Did He prefer her to us? 5) Then Mary wept and said to Peter, My brother Peter, what do you think? Do you think that I have thought this up myself in my heart, or that I am lying about the Savior? 6) Levi answered and said to Peter, Peter you have always been hot tempered. 7) Now I see you contending against the woman like the adversaries. 8) But if the Savior made her worthy, who are you indeed to reject her? Surely the Savior knows her very well. 9) That is why He loved her more than us. Rather let us be ashamed and put on the perfect Man, and separate as He commanded us and preach the gospel, not laying down any other rule or other law beyond what the Savior said. 10) And when they heard this they began to go forth to proclaim and to preach." See Karen L. King, *The Gospel of Mary of Magdala: Jesus and the First Woman Apostle* (Santa Rosa, Calif.: Polebridge Press, 2003).

32. See Corley, "1 Peter," 382, for a more detailed examination of the possible dating of James; she refers to Peter Davids, *The Epistle of James: A Commentary on the Greek Text* (Grand Rapids, Mich.: Eerdmans, 1982); and Pedrito U. Maynard-Reid, *Poverty and Wealth in James* (Maryknoll, N.Y.: Orbis Books, 1987).

Jude, and James—we need to remember that by opting for pseudonymous authorship of these letters, we presume that they were written after Paul wrote Romans, his last letter, with the possible exception of the letter to James. Therefore, the shifts regarding the roles of women found in post-Pauline letters reflect the changing historical circumstances in which the different early Christian communities found themselves. It appears as if church leaders collectively decided that their survival necessitated a degree of accommodation to the dominant culture.

## ACTS OF THECLA

We need to turn now to the other development that occurred in the Christian community after Paul's death. The post-Pauline writers' polemical texts against women probably had their origins in concern about the significant roles that women enjoyed in the community, a reality that was not only difficult for a male leadership to accept but also a danger to the ongoing life of the community. Some important noncanonical texts, however, were much more affirming of women, as our examination of Thecla, whose story we find in the *Acts of Paul and Thecla*,[33] indicates. The story of Thecla sometimes appears as a stand-alone story, the *Acts of Thecla* or as *The Martyrdom of the Holy Proto-Martyr Thecla*.

Most of us are not familiar with the story of Thecla, and so I offer this brief summary. Paul and his two male traveling companions, Demas and Hermogenes, journey to Iconium (modern southeast Turkey) on a preaching mission. Thecla, who is young and beautiful, is immediately converted and refuses to marry Thamyris. Thamyris and Thecla's mother, Theocleia, beg her to reconsider her decision but to no avail. Thamyris resorts to skullduggery and bribes Demas and Hermogenes to bring Paul before the Roman authorities, on false charges. Paul is then imprisoned but Thecla visits him, and she too is brought to trial with him. Paul is flogged and released, but the incensed Theocleia insists that Thecla be condemned to death on the pyre. There is a miraculous shower of rain that extinguishes the flames and Thecla leaves Iconium in search of Paul.

Eventually she finds Paul hiding in a cave with Onesiphorus's family and praying for her welfare. She relates her adventures and begs Paul to baptize her, which he refuses until she has more fully proven herself. More trials befall her as she and Paul journey to Antioch in Pisidia, where one of the imperial guards attempts to rape her. In defending herself, she violates the imperial symbol that Alexander wears by knocking off his ritual headdress, and, accused of sacrilege, is again condemned to death by being thrown to

---

33. R. A. Lipsius and M. Bonnet, eds., "Acts of Paul and Thekla," in *Acta Apostolorum Apocrypha,* vol. 1 (Hildesheim: G. Olms, 1959).

wild beasts. Fortunately, the female lioness refuses to eat her, and instead kills a bear. Then a lion is released, and again the lioness springs to the rescue. In her ensuing struggle with the lion, both lion and lioness are killed.

Because Paul has refused to baptize her, Thecla baptizes herself in a pool of ferocious seals, and once again evades the potentially death-dealing animals. She is again thrown to wild beasts, but women friends distract them by throwing flowers, spices, and perfumes into the arena. Her dastardly enemies are not yet daunted. They tie her to two bulls, which they goad by thrusting hot pokers onto their genitals. Fortunately, fire burns the ropes, and once again Thecla is spared. Queen Tryphaena, her patroness in Antioch, gives her money to care for the poor, and once again she sets off to find Paul. At last Paul thinks that Thecla has proven herself and commissions her "to teach the word of God." Dressed as a man, Thecla ministered in Seleucia where she taught, cared for the poor, healed the sick, and supposedly died. By the fourth and fifth centuries, however, a further development in the narrative occurs; Thecla has not died at all, but has been swallowed alive by the earth (or by a rock).

The *Acts of Paul and Thecla* is a second-century Christian apocryphal work that recounts the mission and death of the apostle Paul and his companions. Paul is described as traveling from city to city, preaching the good news to Gentiles, and emphasizing the need for sexual abstinence and other ascetical practices and disciplines. The *Acts of Paul and Thecla* was translated from Greek into Syriac, Armenian, and Ethiopic and appears to have circulated among the different Christian communities in the empire, particularly in the East. Sheila McGinn offers a useful summary of theories regarding the composition of this work. "(1) the *Acts of Thecla* was originally a literary work produced by an unknown presbyter of Asia Minor who composed the *Acts of Paul* as a whole. (2) A community of "widows" (continent Christian women who were supported by the institutional church) wrote the entire *Acts of Paul*, including the *Acts of Thecla*. (3) The *Acts of Thecla* had its origins in a legend tradition or oral folk story told by women, which subsequently took written form."[34] McGinn argues that the last theory is the most likely because it follows the pattern of composition we know from the canonical Gospels and Acts, while its emphasis on the leadership of women points to its origins in women's circles. A theory of origins in women's folk tales explains the significant variations in the different endings of *Acts of Thecla*.[35] It is possible that women's folk tales and their importance for women in first- and second-century Christian communities lies behind 1 Timothy 4:7, which warns, "Have nothing to do with profane myths and old wives tales." Perhaps such tales attest to women enjoying leadership roles in first- and second-century Christian communities.

---

34. Sheila E. McGinn, "The Acts of Thecla," in *Searching the Scriptures: A Feminist Commentary*, ed. Elisabeth Schüssler Fiorenza, 2 vols. (New York: Crossroad, 1993, 1994), 2:820.
35. Ibid., 803-4.

Though *Acts of Thecla* has never been condemned as heretical, nevertheless, its perspective on women stands in marked contrast to what we identified in Colossians and Ephesians and the Pastoral letters. There are two significant areas that allow us to see this more clearly: first, the lifestyle of Thecla and Paul; and second, the ministry of Thecla. In *Acts of Paul and Thecla,* there is an emphasis on the desirability of sexual continence, an emphasis that continues Paul's teachings in 1 Corinthians 7:8-9, 25-35. First-generation Christians had a highly developed eschatological awareness, and so social institutions such as marriage were regarded as less significant than the impending marriage to the heavenly bridegroom. As the first century drew to a close, Christian expectations concerning the parousia had changed, and Christian leadership recognized that such a radical Christianity needed to be reassessed. So 1 Timothy 4:1-3 rejects those who wish to abstain from marriage and affirms that women will be saved through childbearing, a position that sharply contrasts with the *Acts of Paul and Thecla* 2:16 and 4:2:

> Demas and Hermogenes replied, We cannot so exactly tell who he [Paul] is; but this we know, that he deprives young men of their (intended) wives, and virgins of their (intended) husbands, by teaching, "There can be no future resurrection, unless you continue in chastity, and do not defile your flesh." (*Acts of Paul and Thecla* 2:16)
>
> O governor, I know not whence this man cometh; but he is one who teaches that matrimony is unlawful. Command him therefore to declare before you for what reason he publishes such doctrines. (4:2)

While neither text reports the purported words of Paul, but rather the words of Paul's enemies (Demas and Hermogenes, former traveling companions of Paul in 2:16, and Thamyris, the thwarted bridegroom in 4:2) as they testify against Paul to the imperial authorities, they suggest that some Christians advocated a sexual continence that ran counter to the mores of patriarchal culture. "Understood as the reflection or articulation of a reality for some at least, Thecla has been seen as evidence for the ascetic appeal of early Christianity for women: Christianity authorized them to reject marriage and so to remove themselves from male control."[36] Judith Lieu rightly notes that after the fourth century, sexual asceticism allows women a certain self-determination and self-autonomy but that it is more difficult to locate it with the same certainty in second-century Christian literature.[37]

Ascetical practice was not restricted to the practice of sexual continence. Paul and Thecla also appear to have been vegetarians and teetotalers, perhaps "because of a cultural belief that meat and alcohol inflamed sexual pas-

---

36. Judith Lieu, *Neither Jew nor Greek? Constructing Early Christianity* (Edinburgh: T & T Clark, 2003), 96.
37. See ibid., 96.

sion. The author of I Timothy instructed, 'No longer drink only water, but take a little wine for the sake of your stomach and your frequent ailments' (5:23)."[38] Although the *Acts of Paul and Thecla* postdates the Pastoral epistles, the author of the latter teaches that those who abstain from sexual activity and from certain foods are influenced by "deceitful spirits and doctrines of demons" (1 Tim 4:1-3). In the *Acts of Paul,* those who became Christian also chose chastity.

Sexual continence was not an end in itself. It also allowed women to function in the Christian community as itinerant leaders. The *Acts of Paul and Thecla* was a text that African church father Tertullian (ca. 160-220) believed wrongly set out to legitimate women ministering as teachers and baptizers in the early church (see Tertullian, *De baptismo* 17).

> Thecla longed to see Paul, and inquired and sent everywhere to find him; and when at length she was informed that he was at Myra, in Lycia, she took with her many young men and women; and putting on a girdle, and dressing herself in the habit of a man, she went to him in Myra in Lycia, and there found Paul preaching the word of God; and she stood by him among the throng. But it was no small surprise to Paul when he saw her and the people with her; for he imagined some fresh trial was coming upon them. Which when Thecla perceived, she said to him: "I have been baptized, O Paul; for he who assists you in preaching has assisted me to baptize." Then Paul took her, and led her to the house of Hermes; and Thecla related to Paul all that had befallen her in Antioch, insomuch that Paul exceedingly wondered, and all who heard were confirmed in the faith, and prayed for Trifina's happiness [Trifina was Thecla's patron in Antioch]. Then Thecla arose, and said to Paul, "I am going to Iconium." Paul replied to her: "Go, and teach the word of the Lord." But Trifina had sent large sums of money to Paul, and also clothing by the hands of Thecla, for the relief of the poor. So Thecla went to Iconium. And when she came to the house of Onesiphorus, she fell down upon the floor where Paul had sat and preached, and mixing her tears with her prayers, she praised and glorified God in the following words: "O Lord the God of this house, in which I was first enlightened by thee; O Jesus, son of the living God, who was my helper before the governor, my helper in the fire, and my helper among the beasts; thou alone art God forever and ever. Amen." (*Acts of Paul and Thecla* 9:25-10:7)

In his study of Thecla, Stephen Davis traces the history of devotion to the saint from its inception in the second century through to the fifth century. He

---

38. Nancy A. Carter, "The Acts of Thecla: A Pauline Tradition Linked to Women. Conflict and Community in the Corinthian Church." Available at http://gbgm-umc.org/umw/corinthians/theclabackground.stm; accessed June 17, 2004.

explores the relationship of female sexual continence to itinerancy, and argues that the Thecla tradition influenced, and was influenced by, stories of wandering Egyptian transvestite nuns, thereby associating her with the contested practice of female itinerancy. For example, art work of Thecla adorns numerous churches in Syria, Rome, Spain, and Egypt, which suggests that she visited such places, and she is buried supposedly in at least three countries—Turkey, Syria, and Italy. Traditionally, Thecla and Paul traveled to Spain, where Paul's preaching persuaded some women to leave their husbands and follow Paul.

When we read the *Acts of Paul and Thecla*, we see that Thecla emerges as a more courageous example of Christian faith than Paul, who is prepared to leave Thecla to her fate while he is free to go. He opposes her baptism, her desire for a teaching ministry, and only toward the end of the narrative does he support her decision to go to Iconium to teach (not preach) the word of the Lord (10:4). *Acts of Paul and Thecla* is yet another ambivalent text for women aspiring to ministry in the public realm. The contemporary reader feels uncomfortable with the high value given to virginity and sexual continence, as it appears to denigrate marriage as an institution. There is evidence, however, that such a lifestyle encouraged women to assume itinerant and residential leadership positions in the early church. The narrator describes Thecla's dependence and fixation on Paul as follows:

> From whence, by the advantage of a window in the house where Paul was, she both night and day heard Paul's sermons concerning God, concerning charity, concerning faith in Christ, and concerning prayer. Nor would she depart from the window, till with exceeding joy she was subdued to the doctrines of faith. At length, when she saw many women and virgins going in to Paul, she earnestly desired that she might be thought worthy to appear in his presence, and hear the word of Christ; for she had not yet seen Paul's person, but only heard his sermons, and that alone. (2:2-4)

Theocleia's words to Thamyris, to whom Thecla is betrothed, can lead to uneasiness:

> Notwithstanding this, my daughter Thecla, like a spider's web fastened to the window, is captivated by the discourses of Paul, and attends upon them with prodigious eagerness, and vast delight; and thus, by attending on what he says, the young woman is seduced. Now then do you go, and speak to her, for she is betrothed to you. (2:8)

Nevertheless, as McGinn claims, "by presenting a Christian woman in the role of apostle, the *Acts of Thecla* opens possibilities for imagination and action among Christian readers today."[39]

---

39. McGinn, "The Acts of Thecla," 820.

This survey of the role and ministry of women in the canonical and non-canonical post-Pauline texts raises as many questions as it answers for contemporary women regarding their call to be missionary. How we interpret them depends to a significant degree on our particular socioeconomic location, our ethnicity, our denominational affiliation as evangelical or liberal Christians, to use two somewhat inadequate nomenclatures, and the ideologies that inform our thought. What we need to remember is that the biblical texts do not offer us a clear window through which we can view communities in the ancient Greco-Roman world. Authorial intention, so important for those committed to historical-critical methodologies, needs to be complemented by the insights of literary and rhetorical criticism which allow for multiple meanings to be derived from a particular text. As Paul says in 2 Corinthians 3:6, "the letter kills but the spirit makes alive" (see 2 John 12). Perhaps the principle of intertextuality will help us to better appreciate the polyphonous voices within the New Testament regarding the role and status of women. Rather than turning Galatians 3:28 or 1 Timothy 2:11-12 or the *Acts of Paul and Thecla* into slogans around which we rally the troops to our particular position, we recognize that these different texts, apparently so contradictory, do not permit us to take absolutist positions about their different interpretations.

# 3

# Women as Disciples and Prophets in the Canonical and Apocryphal Gospels and in the Acts of the Apostles

Today, a reliance on historical-critical methodologies for interpreting the biblical text is not without its difficulties. In particular, these methodologies can distance the reader from her contemporary context. Furthermore, even though historical-critical practitioners acclaim the presumed neutrality and objectivity of their methodologies, feminist biblical scholars point to its often androcentric nature and claim that it "serves masculine interests."[1] As Botswanian Musa W. Dube expresses it, "I have discovered that the privileging of the ancient historical setting in the academic interpretation of the Bible is a powerful tool that divorces my experiences and my questions from the field."[2]

Nevertheless, feminist biblical scholars often turn to historical-critical methodologies to subvert rather than to enhance masculine interests, and since I am interested in exploring the historical role of women in the mission of the early church, I will be relying primarily on historical-critical methodologies because I believe that they can help us to answer women's questions about the first missionary experiences of women in the canonical and apocryphal Gospels. The hermeneutical approach of New Testament scholar Elisabeth Schüssler Fiorenza is particularly helpful, for she argues that silence about women in the Gospels is not proof of absence but rather an indication of the androcentric interests that drove the Gospel writers. Feminist exegesis reveals that women were vital players in the Jesus movement, and therefore their stories deserve careful consideration.

---

1. Monika Fander, "Historical-Critical Methods," in *Searching the Scriptures: A Feminist Commentary*, ed. Elisabeth Schüssler Fiorenza, 2 vols. (New York: Crossroad, 1993, 1994), 1:206.

2. Musa W. Dube, "Toward a Post-Colonial Feminist Interpretation of the Bible," *Semeia* 78 (1997): 11-26.

## HOW ARE WE TO READ THE GOSPELS?

Before engaging with the Gospel texts from a feminist perspective, it is useful to discuss the origins of the Synoptic Gospels. Given that the Gospel of Mark, our earliest canonical Gospel, was written around 70 C.E., one of the more critical questions concerns the relationship of Jesus of Nazareth, who died around 30 C.E., to the canonical Gospels. As Raymond Brown asks, "Does the earliest canonical gospel derive from memories of what Jesus did and said in his lifetime, or is it mostly an imaginative creation retrojecting beliefs about the post-resurrectional Jesus into his lifetime?"[3] I would number myself among those who maintain that the canonical Gospels derive from the memories of what the historical Jesus of Nazareth said and did. At the same time, I would argue that the Gospel writers creatively interpreted these memories. To better appreciate this, it is necessary to briefly consider the historical processes that led to formation of our canonical Gospels.

The genesis of the Gospels is in the public ministry of Jesus in the third decade of the first century. Jesus appears to have worked as a tradesman or carpenter, perhaps one of the many Galileans involved in the construction of the Hellenistic city Sepphoris, not far from Nazareth, until he began his public ministry in Galilee around the year 30, a ministry that culminated in his passion and death in Jerusalem. Jesus' teachings, his miracles, his relationships with other Palestinians and in particular with his disciples were remembered by these disciples after his death and resurrection.

After the resurrection, Jesus' followers came to believe that he was indeed the Son of God, and they attributed to the deeds and words they had witnessed during Jesus' public ministry a new significance. Jesus, the Aramaic-speaking Galilean, was by the mid 50s being proclaimed as Son of God, as Paul's letters make clear, to urban-based Jews and Gentiles throughout the Greco-Roman world. Already, an interpretative process was underway, and this became more evident as important memories were liturgically ritualized, for example, as we find in 1 Thessalonians 1:1, 10 and Galatians 3:27-28.

The next important development in the formation of the Gospels occurred in the last four decades of the first century when the oral traditions evolved into the first written traditions, probably now lost. Mark is the first of the canonical Gospel authors to take these written traditions and creatively edit them so that his Gospel emerges as a new literary genre that reflects his indebtedness to the genre of both Hebrew and Greco-Roman biographical writing. In making such a claim, we need to recognize that ancient biographies are not to be confused with modern biographies with their emphasis on historical exactitude. The Gospels of Matthew and Luke, drawing on Mark and Q, a collection of sayings and teachings attributed to Jesus, plus

---

3. Raymond E. Brown, *An Introduction to the New Testament* (New York/London: Doubleday, 1997), 99.

other literary traditions that were significant for their particular communities, were probably written in the mid 80s. It is important to remember that the authors of the three Synoptic Gospels were not eyewitnesses of the ministry, death, and resurrection of Jesus, but more properly speaking, creatively interpreted the memories of Jesus of Nazareth that had assumed significance for the different communities that lay behind the formation of the Gospels.

Given the different interpretations of the Jesus tradition found in the Synoptic Gospels, it is apparent that they are not historical records of the life of Jesus of Nazareth. The Gospels are creative interpretations of the Jesus tradition for the early Christian communities of the Greco-Roman world mediated to the reader by male authors. Feminist biblical scholarship argues that this interpretative process, as it belonged to men, would have consciously and unconsciously been driven by the patriarchal mores of the time. Given this reality, women are right to regard them as androcentric texts. Furthermore, almost without exception until the mid-twentieth century, responsibility for both subsequent translation and interpretation of the biblical text has normally belonged to men. The traditional male ownership of this historical process has led to skepticism among Christian feminists regarding traditional biblical interpretation and has encouraged them to articulate methodologies that allow for movement beyond androcentric interpretations.

John's Gospel was probably written toward the end of the first century, and its geographical structure and story of Jesus' ministry are quite different from those of the Synoptic Gospels. Though John's Gospel may seem very different from the Synoptic Gospels, it follows them in focusing on the public ministry of Jesus and his death and resurrection. Just as Matthew creatively edits and interprets the traditions first used by Mark, so does the author of John interpret them even more radically to suit his particular theological purpose of proclaiming Jesus of Nazareth as the incarnate Word of God. In the first half of the twentieth century, it was thought that the fourth evangelist drew on nonhistorical sources, a position robustly rejected by Johannine scholar C. H. Dodd,[4] and as Brown points out, both "the Synoptics and the Gospel of John, then would constitute independent witnesses to Jesus, witnesses in which early tradition has been preserved."[5]

In this chapter, I will be guided primarily by feminist historical methodologies associated with Elisabeth Schüssler Fiorenza, Bernadette Brooten, and Luise Schottroff. Schüssler Fiorenza argues that the androcentric nature of the New Testament texts and the reality of the patriarchal culture in which they were written in their canonically received form, means that women, keen to learn more of women's role in the early church, must approach the

---

4. See C. H. Dodd, *Historical Tradition in the Fourth Gospel* (Cambridge: Cambridge University Press, 1963); idem, *The Interpretation of the Fourth Gospel* (Cambridge: Cambridge University Press, 1968).

5. Brown, *An Introduction to the New Testament,* 363-64.

texts with what she calls "a hermeneutic of suspicion."[6] Proponents of this process argue that silence in the texts about women's roles in the early church should not be interpreted as indicative of women's absence in the mission of the early church. The task of the feminist exegete is to read between the lines for clues about women's mission and ministry. Brooten also devotes attention to the canonical texts, and her realization of the absence of women's stories leads her to look at extrabiblical Jewish and Greco-Roman sources and inscriptions in order to arrive at a more rounded appreciation of women's roles.[7] Brigitte Kahl asks important questions concerning the social and historical contexts in the first-century Greco-Roman world, and is concerned to explore the reality of "the life and the struggles of ordinary people especially, as well as the functioning of domination, exploitation, and discrimination within the economic, political and ideological framework of society as a whole . . ."[8] Schottroff believes that "*feminist historical scholarship* demands that gender must takes its place next to the category of class as a social category at the centre of historical research."[9]

Through working with feminist interpretative processes, we can better appreciate the ministry of women in the primitive Christian communities. To better understand the missionary role of women in the Gospels and Acts of the Apostles, I propose to examine the passion and resurrection narratives in all four Gospels, Luke's infancy narrative, and selected passages from Acts, as this book continues the story of Jesus' disciples after the resurrection. I will conclude by briefly referring to some apocryphal and gnostic texts.

## WOMEN IN THE PASSION NARRATIVES

With varying emphases, the Synoptic Gospels and the Gospel of John affirm the centrality of women in the passion and resurrection narratives. The importance of these texts for women seeking to claim a public missionary role in contemporary society ought not to be underestimated. I will concentrate primarily on Mark, the earliest of our canonical Gospels, which Matthew follows closely, and on the Gospel of John.

---

6. See Elisabeth Schüssler Fiorenza, *In Memory of Her: A Feminist Reconstruction of Christian Origins* (New York: Crossroad, 1983); idem, *Bread Not Stone: The Challenge of Feminist Biblical Interpretation* (New York: Crossroad, 1986).

7. See Bernadette Brooten, "Feminist Perspectives on New Testament Exegesis," *Concilium* (1980); idem, "Early Christian Women and Their Cultural Context: Issues of Method in Historical Reconstruction," in *Feminist Perspectives on Biblical Scholarship*, ed. Adela Yarbro Collins (Chico, Calif.: Scholars Press, 1985).

8. Brigitte Kahl, "Toward a Materialist-Feminist Reading," in *Searching the Scriptures: A Feminist Commentary*, ed. Elisabeth Schüssler Fiorenza, 2 vols. (New York: Crossroad, 1993, 1994), 1:227.

9. Luise Schottroff, Silvia Schroer, and Marie-Therese Wacker, *Feminist Interpretation: The Bible in Women's Perspective* (Minneapolis: Fortress Press, 1998), 180.

Mark's passion narrative begins with the story of the woman who anoints the head of Jesus (Mark 14:3-9; cf. Matt 26:6-13). John's passion narrative is also prefaced by the story of Mary of Bethany (John 12:1-8), who anoints the feet of Jesus and wipes them with her hair, a text to which I return later. These stories can fittingly be described as parabolic actions. The actions of the unnamed woman in Mark suggest that, unlike the male disciples, she recognizes who Jesus is and what his mission is ultimately going to require of him. She anoints him for his task. In the Old Testament, Samuel anointed Saul as king of Israel and told him that "the Lord has anointed you ruler over his people Israel . . . and you shall save them from the hands of their enemies" (1 Sam 10:1-2). Therefore, it is possible to identify the woman as a prophet, as chosen by God to anoint God's chosen one, his son. Furthermore, the woman's actions are countercultural because they take place within the context of a meal at which a male host provides hospitality for a group of men. This meal is shortly to be followed by another significant meal text.

In Mark 14:17-25, the author begins his account of Jesus' last meal with his disciples, where we find the language of breaking, pouring, and blessing, language that recalls the woman's action in the earlier meal. Is it legitimate to read into the woman's action eucharistic overtones as she anoints the body of Jesus? Mark's Jesus tells us that "wherever the good news is proclaimed in the whole world what she has done will be told in remembrance of her." This language echoes that used by Paul in 1 Corinthians 11:24-25 when he recalls that the tradition was handed on to him and that the Christian community was to continue to remember the actions of Jesus at the Last Supper. A patriarchal church has been very careful to remember in word and action the deeds of Jesus by incorporating the words "Do this in memory of me" into the Catholic Church's eucharistic liturgies.[10] The earlier injunction of Jesus that the prophetic, eucharistic actions of the woman with respect to Jesus' body be remembered has been virtually ignored.

We have the second instance of a woman's prophetic actions being marginalized in the Johannine story of Mary of Bethany's anointing the feet of Jesus. Again this is a story that occurs immediately prior to the narrative of the Last Supper. Six days before the Passover, Jesus comes to Bethany to the home of Lazarus, whom he had raised from the dead. During the meal, Mary "took a pound of costly perfume made of pure nard, anointed Jesus' feet and wiped them with her hair" (John 12:3). Again Jesus affirms the action of Mary in response to Judas's criticism that Mary is wasting money. More importantly, Mary's action in anointing the feet of Jesus prefigures the action of service that occurs in John 13:5-10 when Jesus washes the feet of his disciples prior to the meal.

---

10. The words "Do this in memory of me" occur immediately after the words of consecration in the Catholic Church's Eucharistic Prayers I, II, III, and IV.

What do these two stories contribute to our understanding of women's role in mission? First, on the one hand, John's account describes an event that belongs very much to the domestic realm—the household of Martha, Mary, and Lazarus—and the setting for Mark's meal in the house of Simon the leper suggests a private event. But in its cultural setting, the meal was "open" to onlookers and in that sense was "public." On the other hand, as our study of household churches indicates, households for the early Christian communities were thresholds between the private and public domains, that place from which women could begin their journey toward creating new social roles for themselves in a patriarchal society.

Second, the prophetic actions of both the unnamed woman and of Mary of Bethany in anointing Jesus, through which they acknowledge their belief as to the true nature of his mission, stand in marked contrast to the actions of the objecting men. The Gospels differ as to who the objectors actually are. In Mark, it is simply some who were there; in Matthew it is Jesus' disciples; in Luke 7:36-50 it is Simon the host, and in John it is Judas alone. Given that, in Mark, Jesus is accompanied by his disciples in these last days, it is reasonable to assume that the Twelve constitute the majority of the guests in the house of Simon.

Earlier, in Mark 10:13-16, Jesus accompanied by the disciples, journeys toward Jerusalem, and we find another example of what R. T. France refers to as the disciples' "churlish disapproval which provokes Jesus to another subversive declaration that it is the last who are in fact first. It is not the self-righteous charity of the (presumably male) onlookers which will be remembered, but the rash extravagance of an unnamed woman whose devotion to Jesus leaves no room for pious calculation."[11] In fact, her action normally was not remembered until Elisabeth Schüssler Fiorenza's 1983 groundbreaking work *In Memory of Her*[12] was published. In Mark's account, the author, unlike the author of John, does not identify the characters, and France believes that this weakens the contrast between the unnamed woman and her critics. Mark's guests, however, would have included the Twelve, something that Matthew makes explicit.[13]

Third, as Jesus begins his journey to Jerusalem in the Synoptic Gospels, on three occasions he foretells his impending suffering, death and resurrection (Mark 8:31; 9:30-32; 10:33 and par). On each of these three occasions, the male disciples refuse to accept these prophetic statements of Jesus. Because the Gospels all speak of women disciples of Jesus who have followed Jesus from Galilee being present at his crucifixion (Mark 15:40-41; Matt 27:55-56; Luke 23:49; John 19:25), we can presume that Mark's unnamed woman

---

11. R. T. France, *The Gospel of Mark*, New International Greek Testament Commentary, ed. I. Howard Marshall and Donald A. Hagner (Grand Rapids, Mich.: Eerdmans, 2002), 549.

12. See Schüssler Fiorenza, *In Memory of Her*.

13. See France, *The Gospel of Mark*, 550.

was probably one of those faithful women disciples who followed Jesus, and who understood the import of his words.

Fourth, Mark's account ends with the words "Truly, I tell you wherever the good news is proclaimed, what she has done will be told in remembrance of her" (Mark 14:9), and John tells the reader that "the house was filled with the fragrance of the perfume" (John 12:3b). Mark's words have missionary overtones and direct attention to the future proclamation of the gospel to the whole creation (see Mark 16:15, part of what the NRSV calls "The Longer Ending of Mark"). Likewise, John's reference to the fragrance of perfume filling the house also has missionary overtones, as "the spreading of the odor is a symbol of the spread of the message throughout the Gentile world."[14] Both women are depicted as faithful disciples and believers, praised and commended by Jesus who will soon be betrayed by the male disciples. Their stories are told in ways that identify their actions as missionary, proclaiming who Jesus really is.

Another important instance of women's missionary significance in the passion narrative occurs in Matthew's story of Pontius Pilate's wife, who intercedes for Jesus (Matt 27:19).[15] As Elaine Wainwright states,

> she is given a voice in the narrative even though she is introduced embedded in the patriarchal structure. Her words, like those of the two servant girls, place her on the side of Jesus and of the truth; but like them, she has no power in or against the male world which surrounds her and which has power over life and death even on the basis of falsehood. In the narrative these female voices are drowned by male voices of denial and condemnation.[16]

Pilate's wife says that she has "suffered a great deal because of a dream about him [Jesus]."

---

14. Moloney writes "that some scholars following a rabbinic tradition and Clement of Alexandria (cf. *Eccles. Rab.* 7:1; *Song Rab.* 1:22; Ignatius, *Eph* 17:1; Clement of Alexandria, *Paedogogus* 2:8, MPG 8:466-490) understood this remark as the Johannine version of Mark 14:9; the spreading of the odor is a symbol of the spread of the message throughout the Gentile world . . . [others] take this further, understanding the whole incident as a symbol of the Gentile church receiving the gospel message at the feet of Jesus." See Francis J. Moloney, *The Gospel of John*, Sacra Pagina 4 (Collegeville, Minn.: Liturgical Press, 1998), 357.

15. See James F. Forcucci, ed., *Relics of Repentance: The Letters of Pontius Pilate and Claudia Procula* (Lincoln, Neb.: Issana Press, 1990). This contains a first-century letter supposedly written by Pilate's wife, which was translated from an ancient Latin manuscript found in a monastery in Bruges, Belgium, and which is now referenced in the Vatican archives. The Coptic Church celebrates the memory of Pontius Pilate and Claudia on June 25, while the Greek Church assigns her a feast on October 27. The belief that she became a Christian goes back to the second century.

16. Elaine Wainwright, *Towards a Feminist Critical Reading of the Gospel according to Matthew* (Berlin: de Gruyter, 1991), 137.

She recognizes that her word of truth will never be believed in the context of an unjust condemnation of the just man. Her witness to the truth is important in at least two ways: on the one hand, it situates her in the tradition of the Old Testament prophets who witnessed to Yahweh's truth, and, on the other, her status as a Gentile woman makes it clear that the proclamation of good news of Jesus belongs to Jew and Gentile alike.

The final important stories of women occur in the context of Jesus' death on the cross (see Mark 15:40-41; Matt 27:55-56; Luke 23:49; John 19:25:26). The Gospels all attest to the presence of the Galilean women at Jesus' crucifixion and death. They remind us that when Jesus set his face toward Jerusalem (Luke 9:51), he was accompanied by women disciples. As the Synoptic passion narratives make obvious, the men finally deserted him, and at the crucifixion (Mark 15:39-41), the centurion is alone, apart from the women who stood some distance off. It is improbable that the centurion was alone, but his solitary presence serves Mark's literary purpose of accenting Jesus' isolation at the moment of death. Matthew refers to the centurion and those who were keeping watch with him, which is a more likely scenario, and to the many women who were also there; Luke's crucifixion scene points to the presence of the centurion, the crowds, and Jesus' "acquaintances, including the women who had followed him from Galilee" (23:49). There is nothing to indicate that these "acquaintances" are disciples, but they are presumably male. Jane Schaberg believes that the author of Luke is concerned to present the male disciples in a more positive light than Mark does, and this is achieved through appending the women among "his [Jesus'] acquaintances."[17] Earlier, in the Last Supper narrative, Luke has indicated that the Twelve are the foundational leaders of the eschatological community (Luke 22:28-30).

John's Gospel states that "standing by the cross of Jesus were his mother, and his mother's sister, Mary the wife of Clopas, and Mary Magdalene" (19:25). Moloney warns against attributing exaggerated Mariological significance to this text,[18] and writes that at such a dramatic moment in the narrative, it "cannot simply mean that the Beloved Disciple is to look after the widowed mother of Jesus once her only son dies."[19] What we have at the climax of the crucifixion scene is the author pairing together a woman and a man as examples of faithful discipleship, as members of the new family of Jesus committed to continuing his mission. Australian Johannine scholar Margaret Beirne indicates that the "new family of disciples established by the Johannine Jesus is genuinely inclusive of women and men."[20]

17. See Jane Schaberg, "Luke," in *The Women's Bible Commentary*, ed. Carol A. Newsom and Sharon H. Ringe (Louisville, Ky.: Westminster John Knox, 1992), 289.
18. See Moloney, *The Gospel of John*, 504.
19. Ibid.
20. Margaret M. Beirne, *Women and Men in the Fourth Gospel: A Genuine Discipleship of Equals* (Sheffield: Sheffield Academic Press, 2003), 11.

It is important to note that "the mother of Jesus," the Johannine preferred name for Mary, is present at two key moments in the life of Jesus, the beginning of his ministry in John 2:1-11, the wedding feast at Cana, and again at the crucifixion of Jesus. In both scenes, she emerges as the faithful disciple, although in the first instance, Jesus tells her that his hour has not yet come even if the subsequent miracle suggests otherwise; and she is there at his final hour. In the Cana narrative, Jesus, in response to his mother's request, "did this the first of his signs, in Cana of Galilee and revealed his glory; and his disciples believed in him" (John 2:11). The "mother of Jesus" appears as one whose faith is not dependent on Jesus' working signs but on her belief in Jesus. Jesus' work "started and ended with his mother. For John, as for Luke, perseverance is a mark of a disciple. Initial faith may depend on miracles and signs. But in the end, faith involves 'staying with,' remaining with Jesus."[21] Given the prominence of women in the passion narratives, I turn now to a consideration of the resurrection narratives to explain how that faithful presence at the moment of crucifixion becomes a joyful awareness in the resurrection narratives.

## THE RESURRECTION NARRATIVES
## IN THE CANONICAL GOSPELS

In Mark's resurrection narrative, which initially ended at 16:8, we learn that the women (Mary Magdalene, Mary the mother of James, and Salome) "went out and fled from the tomb, for terror and amazement had seized them, and they said nothing to anyone, for they were afraid."[22] It is easy to be critical of the women's silence, but it is also possible to interpret their fear and silence as evidence of human limitations in the presence of mystery, rather than as typical signs of weakness and fallibility.[23] In the absence of the body, the three women recognize the presence of the holy.

In seeking to explain the women's fear and silence, it is helpful to examine Mark 16:1-8 as both a historical and a theological statement. If we look at Mark's resurrection narrative from a historical perspective, it is obvious that the women were not permanently or universally silent, because the good news of the resurrection of Jesus was proclaimed to all (see Acts 2:5-47). In Mark's resurrection narrative, it is important not to critique the women's silence in terms of what is extrinsic to the Markan text—for example, what

---

21. Mary Ann Getty-Sullivan, *Women in the New Testament* (Collegeville, Minn.: Liturgical Press, 2001), 230.

22. Such an abrupt ending explains why both the New Revised Standard Version and the *New Jerusalem Bible* have extended notes that state that the first Christians added both a shorter ending and a longer ending (Mark 16:9-20).

23. In explaining the women's actions in Mark 16:1-8, I have been helped by Gerald O'Collins, "The Fearful Silence of Three Women," *Gregorianum* 69 (1988): 489-503.

we know of the resurrection from Paul and Acts, where the male disciples
speak extensively about the resurrection. In the context of Mark's Gospel,
women are more often than not silent.[24]

It is perhaps easier to locate a reason for the women's silence by looking
at the theological significance of silence in Mark's narrative. Mark's Gospel
is characterized by injunctions to silence (1:40-45; 3:11-12; 8:25-26, 30);
such injunctions occur after Jesus' healing miracles, or in the case of 8:30
after Jesus' revelation of his identity to the disciples. The women in 16:1-8
are the women who stand near the cross (15:40-41) and who are at Jesus'
burial (15:42-47). The women's presence contrasts favorably with the pro-
gressive failure of Jesus' male disciples, which began in 6:52 when after the
miraculous feeding of the five thousand we read that "they did not understand about the loaves, but their hearts were hardened." Such failure reaches
its climax with Judas's betrayal and Peter's denial. The women take over the
role that one might have expected of the men. Is their failure to speak, then,
really a sign of the failure of Jesus' mission?

In Mark 15:40-47, the author emphasizes the women's fidelity; so why
would Mark want to cancel it in 16:8? Perhaps the women's silence is best
understood by trying to appreciate what sort of fear the women experience.
The fear that the women experience is fear of the divine in their midst. The
resurrection language of "alarm" (16:5), "terror and amazement, afraid"
(16:8) are expressions paralleled elsewhere in Mark (1:22; 2:12; 4:35-41;
5:14, 42; 9:32). Such emotional states serve as fitting responses to manifes-
tations of the divine (see Dan 7:28; Ezek 3:26; Luke 1:20; 2 Cor 12:4). The
mystery of the resurrection, communicated by the heavenly messenger, causes
amazement, terror, and fear.

Therefore, should the women's silence be interpreted as disobedience to
the angel's commands or religious awe when confronted by divine mystery?
Does their flight parallel the male disciple's flight in 14:50 ("All of them
deserted him and fled"), or does it express an initial awe, a fear of God, at
divine intervention in human history? Does Mark want his readers to take a
negative or a positive view of the women's silence, fear, and flight? It is incon-
ceivable that Mark intended to finish his Gospel on a negative note. Instead,
the women's initial response is understandable and appropriate. The Twelve
have revealed themselves as rocky ground, whereas the women's silent
fidelity and watchfulness suggests that they represent the good earth (see
Mark 4:2-9), that fruitful minority whose faithfulness demonstrates recep-
tivity to the meaning of Jesus' death.

The influence of Mark's resurrection narrative on Matthew 28:1-8 is obvious, but Matthew's redaction of Mark 16:8 reads, "So they [the women] left
the tomb quickly with fear *and great joy, and ran to tell his disciples*" (ital-

---

24. See Susan Lochrie Graham, "Silent Voices: Women in the Gospel of Mark," *Semeia* 54
(1991): 147-58.

ics added to show Matthew's addition). Matthew 28:1-10 affirms that the first people to be commissioned by the risen Jesus were the women who had remained faithful to Jesus in his hour of need (see Matt 27:55-56). Some contemporary male scholarship, however, seems unaware of the importance of Matthew 28:1-10 for women and ministry. Thus, Daniel Harrington includes Matthew 28:1-10 in a larger section, 28:1-15, which he entitles "The Empty Tomb," as does Douglas Hare.[25] Neither author critically analyzes the role of "Mary Magdalene and the other Mary." After briefly comparing the Matthean account with the Markan and the Johannine texts, it appears as if 28:1-10 serves as a prelude to the important appearance of Jesus to the eleven disciples. Conversely, Raymond Brown argues that although the women are not called "disciples," nevertheless they are "rewarded for their initiative in coming to see the sepulcher by being made the first human proclaimers of the resurrection and the intermediaries through whom the faith of the disciples will be rekindled."[26]

In his study of the Matthean passion and resurrection narrative, John Paul Heil alludes to the positive role attributed to the women as witnesses, in contrast to the male guards who become "as if dead" (Matt 28:4). Furthermore, the women are no longer to be regarded as passive witnesses (27:55-56; 27:61) but rather as active messengers of the good news. The former passivity is to be resolved and transformed:

> The angel commissions the women with the divinely authorized activity of "going" and "telling" the disciples that Jesus "has been raised from the dead," and that in fulfillment of his previous promise (Matt 26:32), he is going before them to Galilee, where they will see him. As substitutes for the disciples who have been absent, the faithful Galilean women serve as the reliable intermediaries who are to link the disciples with the reality of Jesus' death, burial and resurrection. Empowered by the divine authority of the angel, the previously passive women actively begin to fulfill their role as authentic messengers of Jesus' resurrection.[27]

The text emphasizes the women's movement away from passivity; they left "the tomb *quickly* with fear and great joy and *ran* to tell his disciples" (Matt 28:8, italics added). The risen Jesus, whom they meet, "reinforces the commission of these faithful women to direct the disciples back to Galilee in

---

25. See Douglas Hare, *Matthew* (Louisville, Ky.: John Knox Press, 1993); Daniel J. Harrington, *The Gospel of Matthew* (Collegeville, Minn.: Liturgical Press, 1991).

26. Raymond E. Brown, "The Resurrection in Matthew 27:6 2- 28:20," *Worship* 20 (March 1990): 157-68.

27. John Paul Heil, *The Death and Resurrection of Jesus: A Narrative-critical Reading of Matthew 26-28* (Minneapolis: Fortress Press, 1991), 101.

order to see him (Matt 28:10)."[28] Heil emphasizes the missionary task entrusted to the women.

Writing more recently, Warren Carter argues that Matthew 28:1-10 "makes an important contribution to the resurrection narrative as well as to the Gospel's presentation of discipleship and of women."[29] In Matthew 28:1, the women go "to see the tomb." Carter writes that "to see" is to be understood literally and metaphorically. It is used metaphorically to denote "people's insight into and comprehension of God's purpose."[30] Matthew's decision to use "to see" indicates that he intends the women to be more than witnesses. The women are blessed with insight and comprehension as to the true meaning of the events that have taken place. The fact that the two women do not come to the tomb to anoint Jesus suggests that they have learned from Jesus' teaching that "God's purposes do not end with Jesus' death but continue through the resurrection on the third day."[31] Their coming to the tomb is not primarily expressive of grief but signifies their faith in the reality of Emmanuel—"God-with-us." Such faith makes it fitting that they be commissioned as the bearers of good news to the male disciples. Furthermore, it is appropriate that such a role should be entrusted to the two women because Matthew has earlier indicated that women have a significant role in his Gospel in crossing gender and ethnic boundaries, as we see in the story of the Canaanite woman (Matt 15:21-28) and Pilate's wife. Carter concludes that the women

> did not come with grief or to ensure that premature burial has not taken place. They come because of their insight and expectation that, as with Jesus' death, his words about resurrection will also be reliable. This statement of the purpose in 28:1, then, denotes their comprehension and contributes an integral element to the resurrection narrative's presentation of the women as models of comprehending, faithful and active discipleship at the close of the gospel (cf. 7:24-27; 12:46:50).[32]

Janice Capel Anderson notes that the women are "last at the cross and first at the tomb,"[33] and believes the women's fidelity means they are the first commissioned to bring the good news of the resurrection to the male disciples, although she argues that the gendered culture of the Matthean com-

---

28. Ibid., 102.

29. Warren Carter, "'To See the Tomb': Matthew's Women at the Tomb," *Expository Times* 107 (1996): 201-4.

30. Ibid., 202. "'Seeing the star' (Matt 2:2) means insight into more profound realities since it activates a search for the one who is 'King of the Jews' (2:2) and Christ (2:4-6), for the purpose of worshiping him (2:2)." Other texts that point to Matthew's metaphorical use of seeing include 4:16; 5:8; 5:16; 9:27-31; 13:13-17; 27:54. Note that the opponents of Jesus are referred to as "blind" (15:14; 23:16).

31. Ibid., 204.

32. Ibid., 204.

33. Janice Capel Anderson, "Matthew: Gender and Reading," *Semeia* 28 (1983): 3-27.

munity does not allow women more than "subordinate and auxiliary positions."[34] Yet Matthew 28:1-10 reveals the women as important faith models for the Christian community, something that Matthew has already alluded to earlier in his Gospel (see 9:20-22, the woman suffering from the hemorrhage, and 15:21-28, the Canaanite woman. Both women, transgressors of Jewish cultural mores, exhibit initiative and faith, and therefore "see" Jesus as Lord and Messiah.)

Elaine Wainwright's use of a feminist hermeneutics of suspicion means that this subversive story "can function deconstructively in relation to the androcentric perspective and patriarchal structures within the text."[35] In Matthew's infancy narrative, the author refers to four women—Tamar, Rahab, Ruth, the wife of Uriah—whose presence among the male ancestors of Jesus highlights their subversive role in a patriarchal culture (1:3-7). For Wainwright, Matthew's Gospel ends as it begins. "Female power and female presence function to subvert the patriarchal constructs and androcentric worldviews that both frame the narrative and find expression throughout."[36]

The emphasis on the women coming "to see the tomb" in Matthew highlights their role as witnesses, a theme begun in Matthew 27:55. Unlike the guards who become "like dead men" (28:4), the women, fearful because of the apocalyptic nature of the events that they are witnessing, are also filled with "great joy" (28:8), as they run to tell the disciples what they have witnessed. The Matthean language, "left quickly," "ran," contrasts the women to the guards, who are "like dead men." Not only do the women proclaim life; they are also filled with life. The first proclamation of the angel to the women is to prepare "the readers for the divine origin of the resurrection proclamation to follow with Matthew specifying that this divine revelation is given specifically to women."[37] The women are told by both the angel and Jesus to go to Galilee, where the risen Jesus, in fulfillment of the earlier prophecies (16:21; 17:23; 20:19), will be found. The sense of urgency characteristic of the faithful women is very apparent.

The words of commission given to the women to go to the disciples (28:7) are complemented in the commission given to the disciples to go to all nations (28:19). Matthew, like Mark, restricts the women's role to bringing the good news of the resurrection to the disciples. Wainwright asks if such a limitation reflects a later tradition and in fact might there not be an earlier tradition "which linked the ancient Easter kerygma to the angel's commissioning of the women."[38]

---

34. Ibid., 21.
35. Elaine Wainwright, "The Gospel of Matthew," in *Searching the Scriptures: A Feminist Commentary*, ed. Elisabeth Schüssler Fiorenza, 2 vols. (New York: Crossroad, 1993, 1994), 2:667.
36. Ibid., 665-66.
37. Wainwright, *Towards a Feminist Critical Reading of the Gospel according to Matthew*, 305.
38. Ibid., 307.

In Matthew the women do not fail to recognize Jesus (cf. Luke 24:16; John 20:14; 21:4). They approach Jesus, take hold of his feet, and worship him, and so, in contrast to some of the male disciples who doubted (Matt 28:17), model what discipleship means: faith in the risen Jesus. Their fidelity to the crucified Jesus and their faith in the risen Christ allow them to be ministers of reconciliation between "the risen Jesus and his unfaithful disciples."[39] The story of the two women possibly points to an early tradition that hints at a more egalitarian and inclusive understanding of community in which women, like men, were called to discipleship and apostleship (see Rom 16:1-15). The final redaction represents an attempt by Matthew's community to forsake the radicality of the earlier traditions in favor of those that reflected a subsequent patriarchal rehabilitation of the male disciples.

Luke's resurrection narrative is more ambivalent regarding the role of the women. Women are more active in Luke than in Mark in preparing the body of Jesus for anointing. The narratives about burial and empty tomb form a single sequence. The women do as much as they can as quickly as they can, without breaking the Sabbath. Even before sunrise they return to the tomb with fragrant oils, prepared on the burial day, to undertake the woman's work of anointing the body, a task that is unnecessary.

Their role is reduced to being intermediary, transient bearers of the news of resurrection to the male disciples. This is a spontaneous action on their part, without any heavenly commission to go tell the disciples that Jesus is risen and to tell the male disciples to meet him in Galilee (cf. Mark 16:7; Matt 28:7). Instead, they are reminded that Jesus told them that the Son of Man must be handed over to sinners, be crucified, and rise on the third day (see Luke 24:6-7). The women are the first to learn that the prophetic words of Jesus have been fulfilled. They are those who have heard the word and "held fast to it in an honest and good heart and [have borne] fruit with patient endurance" (Luke 8:15). The exhortation to remember what Jesus told them echoes earlier statements about hearing the word and taking it to heart (see Luke 2:19; 11:28; 14:35). In fact, although the word "remember" does not appear as such, Luke's resurrection narrative consistently invites the community to recall earlier teachings given to the disciples (24:25f., 32, 44f.).

John 20:11-18 has become a key text for women in understanding their missionary role. Even though the four canonical Gospels vary regarding the names and number of women gathered at the tomb, all attest to the presence of Mary Magdalene.[40] John's Gospel has earlier signified that women exer-

---

39. Ibid., 312.

40. Despite her prominence in the resurrection narratives in the four Gospels, more confusion exists about Mary Magdalene than about any other character in the Gospel. She is confused with the sinful woman of Luke 7:36-50, the woman taken in adultery (John 7:53-8:11), and even with the Samaritan woman (John 4:7-42). This confusion occurs because of the unwarranted identification of Mary Magdalene as a prostitute. There is no scriptural text for such an appellation. Mary Magdalene is also confused with Mary of Bethany, sister of Martha and Lazarus (John 11:1-44; 12:1-8).

cised missionary roles in the primitive Christian community, and the story of Mary Magdalene serves as the climax to these earlier stories.

For example, the Samaritan woman exercises a real missionary function. After acclaiming Jesus as the Messiah, she returns to her village and invites its inhabitants to return to see the Messiah, many of whom "believed in him because of the woman's testimony" (John 4:39). Prior to that, in 4:38, we find the verb *apostellein*, "to send," a term that occurs in such important Johannine missionary texts as 17:20 and 20:21, again perhaps signifying the woman's missionary significance. A further indication of the missionary significance of the Samaritan woman can be located in the "harvest" language, which is similar to that found in Matthew 9:37-38 ("Then Jesus said to his disciples, 'The harvest is plentiful, but the laborers are few, therefore ask the Lord of the harvest to send out laborers into his harvest.'") The narrative suggests that her testimony has borne fruit insofar as the townspeople come to Jesus because of it. Although the text indicates that it is the male disciples who were sent to harvest, the woman's role is an essential component in that total mission. Therefore, her missionary presence in the Johannine narrative serves to modify the thesis that male disciples were the only important figures in the primitive Christian community.

That women had apostolic or even quasi-apostolic roles in the community is even more apparent in John 20. Paul had earlier stipulated that the essential characteristics of being an apostle were having seen the risen Jesus and having been sent to proclaim him (1 Cor 9:1-2; 15:8-11; Gal 1:11-16). This leads to an important emphasis on Peter as the first one to have seen the risen Jesus (1 Cor 15:5; Luke 24:34), thus confirming him as leader of the post-Easter community. More than any other Gospel, John revises that tradition about Peter.

In John 20:2-10, Simon Peter and the Beloved Disciple go to the empty tomb and do not see Jesus, although the Beloved Disciple, recognizing the significance of the burial cloths, comes to believe in the resurrection (20:8), but with Simon Peter returns home. Instead, Jesus appears to Mary Magdalene, instructing her to go and tell his brothers of his ascension to the Father. In Mark 16:5-7 (Matt 28:5-7; Luke 24:5-7), angelic figures appear to tell the women that Jesus has been raised from the dead, but in John (and in Matt 28:10, after the angel's earlier appearance), Mary Magdalene is sent by the risen Lord to proclaim the standard apostolic announcement of the resurrection: "I have seen the Lord." Her mission is not to the whole world, but Mary Magdalene comes close to meeting the basic Pauline requirements of an apostle. As we shall see, this explains why in some gnostic communities, Mary Magdalene, rather than Peter, emerges as the most prominent witness to the resurrection of the Lord.[41]

---

41. In the Latin Catholic tradition, she receives the honor of being the only woman (beside Mary) on whose feast the creed is recited, precisely because she was considered to be "the apostle to the apostles."

It is possibly Mary Magdalene's dominant position in the primitive Christian community that led to an epilogue being added to John's Gospel. Chapter 21 is intended "to explain the relationship between the Beloved Disciple and Peter, and between the Church of the Beloved Disciple and the greater church Peter represents and which looked to John's community with a certain suspicion and uncertainty."[42] It indicates the need to affirm the primacy of Peter in the primitive Christian community.

There are at least four reasons why we can identify Mary Magdalene as a disciple and apostle, and therefore as missionary. First, Jesus teaches that the disciple's grief will be turned into joy (John 16:6, 20) and Magdalene's weeping is turned into joy (20:18). Second, throughout John's Gospel, the disciple is the one who seeks (see John 1:39; 5:44; 7:34; 11:56; 12:20; 13:22; 18:4). John 20:11-18 describes a woman seeking what she has lost, and through that process of seeking finding what she has lost. Third, Jesus calls his sheep by name, and his sheep know his voice (10:1-5). Magdalene recognizes Jesus when he calls her by name (20:16). Finally, like the Samaritan woman and the male disciples before her (1:40-45; 4:28-30), Mary Magdalene bears witness about Jesus to others (20:17-18).

## PROPHETIC WOMEN IN LUKE'S INFANCY NARRATIVE

Both Matthew and Luke preface their Gospels with the "infancy narratives." While both the Matthean and Lukan infancy narratives give us important historical data—the parentage of Jesus, the birthplace of Jesus, the return to Galilee—both authors basically use narrative to teach their belief in Jesus as the Christ, the Son of God, whose birth had been foretold by the prophets and who has come to save his people. In Luke's infancy narrative three women—Elizabeth, Mary, and Anna—are accorded a significance that is not paralleled elsewhere in Luke's Gospel. As noted above, feminists often do not regard Luke's Gospel as favorably disposed toward women. Turid Karlsen Seim points out that some feminists hold that Luke's Gospel represents "a programmatic androcentrism that pleads the subordination of women,"[43] while Mary Ann Getty-Sullivan writes that "scholars debate whether Luke is promoting women by giving them special attention or denigrating them by portraying them only as models of submissive service."[44] On the negative side, it could be argued that the activities of Mary and Elizabeth are restricted to the household; for example, the angel Gabriel appears to Mary in her Nazareth home, but visits Zechariah in the Temple. The Spirit

---

42. Getty-Sullivan, *Women in the New Testament*, 185-86.
43. Turid Karlsen Seim, "The Gospel of Luke," in *Searching the Scriptures: A Feminist Commentary*, ed. Elisabeth Schüssler Fiorenza, 2 vols. (New York: Crossroad, 1993, 1994), 2:728.
44. Getty-Sullivan, *Women in the New Testament*, 5.

is poured on Mary and Elizabeth in the privacy of their homes, and again at Pentecost the Spirit comes upon the eleven who were "devoting themselves to prayer together with certain women, including Mary, the mother of Jesus" while gathered in an upstairs room (Acts 1:14). Anna "never left the temple but worshipped there with fasting and prayer, day and night" (Luke 2:37). On the other hand, "Luke opens what is for him the most important chapter of salvation history with the least important people in society: a barren wife, a young peasant girl, and an elderly widow."[45] All three women are referred to by name, and all three offer important examples of discipleship in action through their faith, prayer, and obedience to God's will, and therefore are actively involved in God's saving plan for humankind.

Elizabeth emerges as one who has waited in faith for God's mysterious plans to be revealed, and she is compared favorably to Zechariah, who despite the appearance of the angel refuses to believe. Furthermore, she proclaims the blessedness of Mary and the child she has conceived. Like Elizabeth, Mary too is a faith-filled woman, whom Gabriel greets as "blessed among women" even before she learns of the role that God will entrust to her. Mary's response to Gabriel, far from being seen as a negative reaction, places her firmly in the tradition of great Old Testament figures such as Moses (see Exod 4:10 and 13), Jeremiah (see Jer 1:6), and Isaiah (see Isa 6:5). Mary should not be regarded as creating obstacles but rather as seeking direction in order that she may fulfill the mission entrusted to her.

Mary begins the long and tiring journey from Nazareth in Galilee to Judah, where she meets Elizabeth, and then breaks into song, the "Magnificat." This song has served as a charter or mandate for liberation theologians and for those who understand mission as reversing situations of political and economic disenfranchisement experienced by so many. As Joel Green explains, "two motifs are held in balance throughout Mary's Song. The first is the portrait of God as the divine warrior who accomplishes deliverance . . . At the same time God is the merciful God of the covenant. He looks with favor on, and 'lifts up the lowly,' extends mercy to those who fear him, 'fills the hungry' and helps Israel."[46] It is fitting that this song belongs to Mary through whose agency salvation has decisively begun. Mary's song proclaims that the proud will be scattered, the powerful vanquished, the rich impoverished. Throughout the remainder of the Gospel the powerful and wealthy are opposed to Jesus and the good news of salvation. Mary's song functions as a prelude to the Gospel narrative.

The third prophetic woman to figure in Luke's infancy narrative is Anna, the daughter of Phanuel, of the tribe of Asher.[47] The Old Testament names

---

45. Ibid., 8-9, referring to Barbara E. Reid, *Choosing the Better Part? Women in the Gospel of Luke* (Collegeville, Minn.: Liturgical Press, 1996), 94-95.

46. Joel B. Green, *The Gospel of Luke*, ed. Ned B. Stonehouse, F. F. Bruce, and Gordon D. Fee (Grand Rapids, Mich.: Eerdmans, 1997), 102.

47. Anna's membership in the tribe of Asher is important for Luke's thematic development

four women as prophets (Miriam, Exod 15:20; Deborah, Judg 4:4; Huldah, 2 Kgs 22:14; 2 Chr 34:22; and Isaiah's wife, Isa 8:3). Generally speaking, the New Testament authors are reticent in naming women as prophets (but see Acts 2:17; 21:9; 1 Cor 11:5), and even though Anna is labeled as "prophet," there is no reference to the Spirit empowering her. In this respect, "she is dramatically overshadowed by Simeon, thrice anointed with the Spirit (2:25, 26, 27), whose mouth pours forth 'amazing' words of praise and prophecy to the young Jesus and his parents in the preceding scene (2:28-35)."[48] Unlike Simeon, Anna receives "her identity through her descent (v. 36a), age (36b), and her social and religious position (36c-37). This literary distinction probably reflects the difference of status between men and women in contemporaneous Judaism."[49] Like Mary, Zechariah, the shepherds, and Simeon, Anna praises God for his intervention in human history and speaks "about the child to all who were looking for the redemption of Jerusalem" (Luke 2:38).

## PROPHETIC WOMEN IN THE ACTS OF THE APOSTLES

The Acts of the Apostles continues the story of salvation as the Spirit-empowered disciples proclaim the good news of Jesus to the uttermost ends of the earth. In particular, Acts highlights first the postresurrection ministry of Peter, and from chap. 13 onward, the story of Paul and his companions.

The genre of Acts may best be described as "theological history," a type of historical monograph. Not an actual, thoroughgoing "factual history" of Christian beginnings in the modern sense but a continuation of the story begun in the Third Gospel, Acts sets forth a "sacred history" showing how the divine purposes were fulfilled in the birth and progression of the Christian church on the world scene.[50]

Unfortunately, women figure in a very minor way in this story. Clarice Martin suggests that the contemporary reader must approach Acts first with a hermeneutics of suspicion, assuming that its author was primarily interested in the missionary work of his male protagonists and so neglected to describe women's activities, which also contributed to the growth and well-being of

---

of Jesus as the one who is concerned about the poor and the outcast. "As a descendant of the exiles of the tribe of Asher [a northern tribe], Anna ensures that the community represented in the narrative is Israel as a whole, northern tribes as well as southern, exiles as well as inhabitants of the land." See Richard A. Bauckham, *Gospel Women: Studies of the Named Women in the Gospels* (Grand Rapids, Mich.: Eerdmans, 2002), 98.

48. F. Scott Spencer, "Out of Mind, Out of Voice: Slave Girls and Prophetic Daughters in Luke-Acts," *Biblical Interpretation* 7 (1999): 133-35.

49. François Bovon, *Luke 1: A Commentary on the Gospel of Luke 1:1-9:50*, ed. Helmut Koester; trans. Christine M. Thomas (Minneapolis: Fortress Press, 2002), 105.

50. Clarice J. Martin, "The Acts of the Apostles," in *Searching the Scriptures: A Feminist Commentary*, ed. Elisabeth Schüssler Fiorenza, 2 vols. (New York: Crossroad, 1993, 1994), 2:765.

the Christian community. Second, she favors a hermeneutic that assesses and critiques the androcentric ideologies that informed the writer's perspective, thus promoting a reductionist approach to women's contributions. Third, if the nonmarginal nature of women's missionary efforts is to be better appreciated, then it is imperative that texts other than the canonical are also studied. This would entail a study of nonbiblical and apocryphal texts, classical literary sources, art, funerary remains, and inscriptions.[51]

Given the prophetic utterances of Elizabeth, Mary, and Anna in Luke 1-2, I propose now to examine Acts 21:8-9, where we read that Philip the evangelist had four unmarried daughters[52] who had the gift of prophecy. As we have seen in Luke's infancy narrative, Elizabeth, Mary, and Anna all speak of the mystery of God present in their midst, but Philip's four daughters are curiously silent prophets, though in Acts 21:10, the male prophet Agabus speaks. While the reference to the daughters as prophets fulfills the prophecy of Joel (Acts 2:17-21), Luke "silences" them, and "women prophets never utter an actual prophetic utterance in Acts—and therefore within the early Christian missionary enterprise."[53] On the other hand, the church historian Eusebius (ca. 260-341) ascribed significance to Philip's daughters and states that the churches in the Asian provinces derived their apostolic origin from them.[54] As Ephesians 2:19-20 makes clear, however, the church is "built upon the foundation of the apostles and prophets [some of whom would be women], with Christ Jesus himself as the cornerstone."

As our examination of Mark, Matthew, Luke-Acts, and John indicates, no clear picture emerges regarding the missionary role of women during the public ministry of Jesus and in the life of the early church. However, women emerge as key characters in the passion and resurrection narratives, even when we take into consideration the negative perceptions regarding women that so many feminist scholars find in Luke. Feminist scholars argue that this is because the texts come from a patriarchal culture in which androcentric norms prevail. It would be foolish to assume that silence about women be equated with assuming the absence of women from the missionary life of the different communities that lie behind our texts.

## WOMEN IN APOCRYPHAL AND GNOSTIC GOSPELS

As Elisabeth Schüssler Fiorenza has demonstrated, women undoubtedly would have been active in the mission of the early church, even though the

---

51. Ibid., 773-76.

52. According to Eusebius, one of Philip's daughters was married. See G. A. Williamson, ed., *Eusebius: The History of the Church from Christ to Constantine*, rev. ed. (New York: Penguin Classics, 1990), 3.30.1.

53. Martin, "The Acts of the Apostles," 786-87.

54. See C. F. Crusé, ed., *The Ecclesiastical History of Eusebius Pamphilus* (London: G. Bell & Sons, 1897), 3.39.7-17.

New Testament male authors refer only fleetingly or even negatively to their contribution.[55] Some contemporary feminist scholarship argues that both apocryphal and gnostic texts suggest more active roles for women than the canonical texts allow. The New Testament canon represents the triumph of patriarchy and hierarchy over Schüssler Fiorenza's claim that the first Christians lived as a "discipleship of equals." Sociological interpretations of early Christianity suggest that

> the Jesus movement stands in conflict with the dominant patriarchal society and is "heretical" with respect to its dominant religious community. The earliest Jesus traditions expect a reversal of all social conditions through the eschatological intervention of God; this is initially realized in the ministry of Jesus . . . In distinction to other Jewish renewal movements, such as the Qumran community, the Jesus movement was not exclusive but inclusive; it made possible the solidarity of those who would not be accepted by some other Jewish renewal groups because of religious laws and ideologies.[56]

Because such androcentric texts became the canonical texts, and those which reflected a more positive attitude toward women were at best noncanonical or at worst heretical, the history of the Christian movement became a patriarchal movement that effectively obscured the contribution of women. Many of these noncanonical texts originated in gnostic sects. Gnosticism is an umbrella term that refers to religious groups that appeared in the eastern parts of the empire in the late first and second centuries. Initially, our knowledge of gnosticism came from the antignostic writings of second-century Christian apologists such as Irenaeus. Gnostics thought of themselves as "people in the know," whose personal enlightenment enabled them to attain ultimate knowledge so that they were freed from the created world and able to return to the spiritual world of God. This emphasis on personal enlightenment put them on a collision course with church leaders who claimed that obedience to right teaching was a privileged path to personal salvation, and who rejected the antimaterialist nature of gnosticism, identifying it as capable of subverting the doctrine of the Incarnation.

Gnostic texts such as the *Gospel of Thomas*, the *Gospel of Mary*, and the *Gospel of Philip*, discovered at Nag Hammadi[57] in 1945, are sometimes thought to be more tolerant and sympathetic toward women than the canonical texts. Finnish New Testament scholar Antti Marjanem claims that these

---

55. See Schüssler Fiorenza, *In Memory of Her*.

56. Elisabeth Schüssler Fiorenza, *Discipleship of Equals: A Critical Feminist Ekklesia-logy of Liberation* (New York: Crossroad, 1993), 176.

57. Near Nag Hammadi in upper Egypt is the Jabal al-Tārif, a mountain honeycombed with more than one hundred and fifty caves, in which Egyptian peasants discovered a number of ancient Coptic manuscripts in 1945.

texts have persuaded some contemporary Christians that gnostic movements "adopted a favorable stand toward women's engagement in leadership roles in religious groups, whereas 'mainstream' Christianity radically tended to limit female participation in the church."[58] Or as Pheme Perkins puts it, the "*Gospel of Thomas, First Apocalypse of James,* and *Gospel of Mary* affirm the authority of women disciples over the male apostles said to be the founders of the orthodox tradition."[59]

It is beyond the scope of this chapter to explore in detail the stories of apostolic women in either the apocryphal or gnostic texts, but a brief consideration of the references to Salome and Mary Magdalene in the *Gospel of Thomas,* and to Mary Magdalene, who figures prominently in the Gospel named after her, the *Gospel of Mary,* and in the *Gospel of Philip* will serve to illustrate the different attitudes found in the canonical and noncanonical Gospels regarding the role of women.

The name "Salome" appears in Mark 15:40 ("There were also women looking on from a distance; among them were Mary Magdalene, and Mary the mother of James the younger and of Joses, and Salome") and Mark 16:1 ("When the sabbath was over, Mary Magdalene, and Mary the mother of James, and Salome bought spices, so that they might go and anoint him"). She is also referred to in the *Gospel of Thomas* saying 61:

> Jesus said, "Two will recline on a couch; one will die, one will live." Salome said, "Who are you mister? You have climbed onto my couch and eaten from my table as if you are from someone." Jesus said to her, "I am the one who comes from what is whole. I was granted from the things of my Father." [Salome's response] "I am your disciple."[60]

In Mark's Gospel, we know nothing else about the woman identified as Salome, a common name among Jewish women. Not that the *Gospel of Thomas* contains much more information, but what it does reveal is that Salome is participating in a communal meal with men, and her reference to Jesus as "Mister" rather than as "Lord" hints at a certain equality. In a 1999 article, Kathleen Corley provides a helpful entry point into understanding the social context to which this saying refers. She believes that the *Gospel of Thomas* originated in Syria and that this saying is possibly a reference to those Syrian women ascetics who "could be described as 'becoming like men' due to their practice of asceticism as their ascetic practice reflected the

---

58. Antti Marjanem, "The Mother of Jesus or the Magdalene? The Identity of Mary in the So-Called Gnostic Christian Texts," in *Which Mary? The Marys of Early Christian Tradition,* ed. F. Stanley Jones (Atlanta: Society of Biblical Literature, 2002), 31.

59. Pheme Perkins, *Gnosticism and the New Testament* (Minneapolis: Fortress Press, 1993), 167.

60. Stevan Davies, *The Gospel of Thomas Annotated and Explained,* ed. Stevan Davies (Woodstock, Vt.: Skylights Paths Publishing, 2002).

achievement of a higher level of 'masculine' spirituality . . . Here Salome is admitted to the table fellowship of the Thomas community due to her 'undivided' and 'male' status."[61] While Galatians 3:28 teaches that in Christ, "there is no longer male and female," for gnostics this implied that ascetical women became like men through renouncing their sexuality. In this perspective, "maleness" rather than "femaleness" becomes the best expression of being human, something that neither Paul nor the communities to which he wrote countenanced.[62]

Another saying in the *Gospel of Thomas* that emphasizes the superiority of maleness over femaleness is the following: "Simon Peter said to them, 'Mary should leave us because women are not worthy of the life.' Jesus responded: 'Look, I'll lead her in order to make her male so that she can become a living spirit as you males are. For each woman who makes herself male will enter the Kingdom of Heaven'" (*Gospel of Thomas* saying 114). This saying was probably added to the *Gospel of Thomas* at a later date and is decidedly ambiguous. On the one hand, Jesus rebukes Peter for his misogynist attitudes, and, on the other hand, Jesus argues that women will be saved when they cease to be women and become male. Though the language of Jesus is gentler than that of Peter, "nevertheless it conceals the same thought: women as such cannot enter the kingdom of heaven."[63]

Perhaps the gnostic text that most obviously hints at tensions in the primitive Christian community between male and female leadership is located in the *Gospel of Mary*,[64] a second-century Greek text later translated into Coptic in the fifth century. The text pits Mary Magdalene against Peter. Mary informs Peter and Andrew of her vision of the Lord and of his revelation to her. Andrew rejects this, "say what you (wish to) say about what she has said. I at least do not believe that the Savior said this," while Peter wondered if the savior did "really speak with a woman without knowledge and not openly? Are we to turn about and all listen to her? Did he prefer her to us?"[65] Peter and Andrew represent the orthodox position that we have already located in the Pastoral letters and which denies women a teaching

---

61. Kathleen E. Corley, "Salome and Jesus at Table in the *Gospel of Thomas*," *Semeia* 86 (1999): 85-97.

62. Bentley Layton argues that gnosticism's dependence on common Platonizing clichés means that the realm of matter "to which the body belongs and to which it will return is 'shadow,' a 'cave,' a realm of 'sleep.' It is 'female' and 'femininity'—for according to a philosophical cliché, shape-giving form is called in Greek 'male,' while passive constituent matter is 'female.'" See Bentley Layton, ed., *The Gnostic Scriptures: A New Translation with Annotations and Introductions* (New York: Doubleday, 1987), 18.

63. Giovanni Filoramo, *A History of Gnosticism*, trans. Anthony Alcock (Oxford: Basil Blackwell, 1990), 177.

64. W. Schneemelcher, "The Gospel of Mary," in *New Testament Apocrypha: Gospels and Related Writings* (London: Lutterworth Press, 1963), 340-43.

65. J. M. Robinson, ed., *The Nag Hammadi Library in English* (New York: HarperCollins, 1988), sayings 17-18.

role in the community. Another disciple, Levi, warns against the males' rejecting Mary, and the Gospel ends with the men going to preach the good news and Mary rejoicing that God "has prepared us and made us into men."

Similarly, Mary Magdalene is affirmed in the *Gospel of Philip* where we read:

> The disciples said to him "Why do you love her more than all of us?" The Savior answered and said to them, "Why do I not love you like her? When a blind man and one who sees are both together in darkness, they are no different from one another. When the light comes, then he who sees will see the light, and he who is blind will remain in darkness."[66]

Such references to Mary Magdalene certainly suggest that she enjoyed an important status in the early church, an honor she lost at the end of the sixth century when Pope Gregory I identified her as a prostitute whose former sinfulness was contrasted with the sinlessness of the Virgin Mary. Despite the brevity of our consideration of gnosticism, the *Gospel of Thomas* indicates that the reference to Salome means that women were allowed to join men at communal meals, and that even if it did not encourage, it tolerated an equality that was inadmissible in the orthodox Christian community as the first century drew to a close. The *Gospel of Mary* and the *Gospel of Philip* make it obvious that Mary Magdalene was a key figure in the early church. It seems, however, to be a big jump from claiming an important role for Mary Magdalene to asserting that gnosticism was friendly to women. Most of the gnostic teachers appear to have been men. What seems to have happened is that gnostic teachers sought support from wealthy women patrons. This in turn may have meant, as Perkins concludes, that the "essentially private structure of gnostic texts as well as their need of influential patrons may have provided opportunities for women as teachers and leaders that the more public and formally ordered orthodox churches denied them. Such activities could easily become a lightning rod for anti-Gnostic polemic."[67]

As our study of the Gospels indicates, the contemporary reader is faced with ambiguities and ambivalences regarding the mission of women that were also present in our reading of the Pauline and Deutero-Pauline letters. There are texts that are encouraging for women seeking legitimation for greater missionary scope in the public realm as the story of the Samaritan woman in John, the story of Pilate's wife in Matthew's Gospel, and the women's proclamation of the good news of Jesus' resurrection make clear. At

---

66. "The Gospel of Philip" in *The Nag Hammadi Library in English*, 339.
67. Perkins, *Gnosticism and the New Testament*, 175.

the same time there are other texts that seem to militate against such involvement by women. The challenge lies in holding these conflicting texts in a creative tension that allows women to respond to new missionary challenges in a manner that reflects awareness of the insights that feminist hermeneutics offer.

# Part II

# WOMEN STRUGGLING TO BE MISSIONARY

# 4

# Missionary Women from the Second to the Fifteenth Century

Our study of women in the canonical and noncanonical Christian literature of the first century reveals that some women actively sought a public role in the young community's proclamation of the good news. It was a story of success, as some Pauline and Gospels texts reveal, and it was a story of failure, as a patriarchal culture, albeit Christian, sought to relegate women to the domestic sphere as the first century drew to a close. In this chapter, I will attempt to outline the major developments that occur in the next fourteen centuries, that period of Western European history that begins at the conclusion of the apostolic era and continues to the end of the Middle Ages. I will restrict my study to the story of representative missionary women in the Western church, referring to the story of women in the Eastern church insofar as it explains or clarifies developments in the West. I undertake this task with some trepidation because it seems wrong to limit such an engrossing story to one chapter. However, scholarly works that cover some or all of this period from a feminist perspective are numerous and merit careful reading.[1]

In order to reclaim the story of women's mission in the life of the church, obscured or lost in androcentric readings of history, I intend to refer, first, to some striking examples of women who were martyred; second, to women who embraced virginal or chaste lives for the sake of the gospel prior to the Edict of Milan (313); third to those chaste women who followed either the eremitic or cenobitic ways of life; and fourth, to the emergence of women as abbesses and administrators in the West between the sixth and eighth centuries. The success of these abbesses was such that during the Carolingian era, there was a concerted effort to limit their authority. Fifth, by the eleventh

---

1. See Anne Jensen, *God's Self-Confident Daughters: Early Christianity and the Liberation of Women*, trans. O. C. Dean (Louisville, Ky.: Westminster John Knox Press, 1996), 84; Jo Ann Kay McNamara, *Sisters in Arms: Catholic Nuns through Two Millennia* (Cambridge, Mass.: Harvard University Press, 1996); Patricia Raft, *Women and the Religious Life in Premodern Europe* (New York: St. Martin's Press, 1996).

and twelfth centuries, there is clear evidence of an extraordinary revival of women's monastic life; and finally in the thirteenth century, the emergence of the Beguines and tertiaries, both committed to the *vita apostolica*, represented an important development in the involvement of laywomen in mission.

As the second century opened, the Roman Empire seemed to be at the height of its power and influence. Church growth was steady but not spectacular, and as the Christian community was distancing itself, and being distanced, from Judaism, it began to "impinge on the life of the empire and come to the notice of authorities independently of Judaism."[2] Along with the seven churches of Asia referred to in the Book of Revelation, Rome had emerged as a leading Christian community whose authority was recognized outside of Italy, as the First Letter of Clement to the Corinthian Christian community suggests.

W. H. C. Frend claims that by the second century Christianity was not a subversive cult, and its adherents included some wealthy individuals, even a member of the emperor Domitian's household, Domitilla, as well as freedmen in the houses of Roman aristocracy. Such people, while well aware of their responsibility toward the poor, were usually averse to subverting important social institutions such as slavery (see *Didache* 4.11). Under the influence of early church leaders such as Irenaeus (d. ca. 90-110), Ignatius (d. ca. 98-117), and Cyprian (d. 258), the development of ecclesial offices such as *episcopoi*, orthodoxy in belief, and a certain uniformity in liturgical practice and organization were emphasized. However, the more organized structure and growing numerical strength of the young Christian church eventually was perceived as threatening by the Roman authorities, and, as the second century progressed, so too did persecution of the community, as the stories of Blandina, the young slave girl martyred in Lyon, and Perpetua and Felicity, killed in Carthage, North Africa, demonstrate.

## WOMEN IN THE EARLY CHURCH

The sufferings of Blandina (d. 177), along with those of her three companions, are described in some detail in book 5 of Eusebius's *Church History*.[3] Blandina is a slave, but her importance in the Christian community at Lyon is highlighted by the original author's omission of the name of her mistress. Instead, Blandina's importance as a "mother" of the community is emphasized: "But the blessed Blandina, last of all, having, as a noble mother, encouraged her children and sent them before her victorious to the King,

---

2. W. H. C. Frend, *The Rise of Christianity* (Philadelphia: Fortress Press, 1984), 121.

3. See C. F. Crusé, ed., *The Ecclesiastical History of Eusebius Pamphilus* (London: G. Bell & Sons, 1897).

endured herself all their conflicts and hastened after them, glad and rejoicing in her departure as if called to a marriage supper, rather than east to wild beasts."[4] Not only is she described as a "mother" of the Christian community, but she is likened to Christ, for at one stage she is

> suspended on a stake, and exposed to be devoured by the wild beasts who should attack her. And because she appeared as if hanging on a cross, and because of her earnest prayers, she inspired the combatants with great zeal. For they looked on her in her conflict, and beheld with their outward eyes, in the form of their sister, him who was crucified for them, that he might persuade those who believe on him, that every one who suffers for the glory of Christ has fellowship always with the living God.[5]

Paul Johnson claims that Blandina, "a mystic and a prophetess, [was] probably a Montanist."[6] His opinion is not shared by missiologists and church historians, and the fact that Blandina has always been counted among the saints of the Catholic tradition suggests this is not the case. A more positive assessment of Blandina argues that "the history of the Christian movement is one that is often inaugurated through suffering and blood,"[7] as the willingness of Blandina to publicly profess her faith and die demonstrates.

Two other women martyrs in the Latin church were Perpetua and Felicity, martyred in Carthage in 203. These two women catechumens, Perpetua, young wife and member of the patrician class, her slave, the pregnant Felicity, and three male catechumens, along with their teacher, Saturus, were martyred by being forced to battle with wild beasts. The story of Perpetua, Felicity, and her companions has come down to us in *The Passion of Saints Perpetua and Felicitas*.[8] Perpetua records not only her experiences but also her four visions. In these dreams, we see that the recently baptized Perpetua recognizes the important relationship between baptism and martyrdom or, as Anne Jensen explains "through this interaction, *martyrdom appears as the fulfillment of baptism*, and at the same time *baptism is the interpretation of martyrdom*."[9]

The deaths of Blandina, Perpetua, and Felicity are important not only to women but also to the wider ecclesial community for several reasons. First,

---

4. Eusebius, *Church History*. Available at http://www.newadvent.org/fathers/250105.htm; accessed March 28, 2005.

5. Ibid.

6. Paul Johnson, *A History of Christianity* (New York: Touchstone, 1976), 73.

7. Dale T. Irvin and Scott W. Sunquist, *History of the World Christian Movement* (Maryknoll, N.Y.: Orbis Books, 2001), 1:84. See also Stephen B. Bevans and Roger P. Schroeder, *Constants in Context: A Theology of Mission for Today* (Maryknoll, N.Y.: Orbis Books, 2004).

8. See H. Musurillo, ed., *The Acts of the Christian Martyrs* (Oxford: Oxford University Press, 1972).

9. Jensen, *God's Self-Confident Daughters*, 101.

these stories apparently describe Christian communities where ecclesiastical or socioeconomic status counted for little. In the story of Blandina, we have an account of a slave woman who is given more prominence than her mistress, and who is acclaimed as "mother" of the church. Perpetua, the patrician wife, stands side by side with her slave, Felicity, after the first attack of the wild cow. Second, these women are Christ-like figures who defeat their adversaries. Blandina is described as hanging as if on a cross, and, like Jesus on the cross, these women martyrs forgive those who have persecuted them. Third, if the martyr is one who witnesses publicly to her faith, even to death, then these women through their martyrdom are also witnessing to their belief in the resurrection of Jesus, and their witnessing takes on an apostolic or proclamatory character. Finally, martyrs, male and female, represented Christ most fully, and it "was not the eucharistic celebration that was the holiest place of the 'real presence,' but the arena in which the witness of faith was sealed in a life-and-death struggle."[10]

The stories of these three women are ambivalent regarding female sexuality. By her death on the cross, Blandina is thought to embody the male, crucified Jesus, and like him, she blesses her companions and assures them that they will be saved. On the night before her execution, Perpetua dreams that she will be stripped before entering the arena to fight and will be transformed into a man, while Felicity in her dreams understands her spirituality and victory in male terms. This suggests that women believed they were sanctified insofar as they transcended their womanly nature. Rosemary Rader argues against the idea that a woman must become a man in order to reach salvation, "for Perpetua is a man only during the contest; as victor she is greeted by the referee as 'daughter.'"[11] Jensen believes that because martyrs "were considered successors of the apostles . . . [these women] stood in competition with the bishop."[12] The stories of these women martyrs indicate a community in which socioeconomic divisions seem vanquished, but this eradication was limited to the exceptional situation of the arena and not characteristic of the ordinary Christian community in which bishops were assuming more and more power.

Another development for women who sought a public role in the life of the community occurred among those women who embraced lives of virginity and chastity, a development that ran counter to the prevailing social mores of both Jewish and Greco-Roman culture. It was a development that subverted the importance of the patriarchal family in Greco-Roman society.

---

10. Ibid., 124. Jensen adds that if "the Roman Catholic Congregation of the Doctrine of the Faith today bases its exclusion of women from the priesthood on the idea that only a man can represent the male Jesus, it really cannot substantiate this argumentation by appealing to early church tradition."

11. Rosemary Rader, *Breaking Boundaries: Male/Female Friendship in Early Christian Communities* (Ramsey, N.J.: Paulist Press, 1983), 9.

12. Jensen, *God's Self-Confident Daughters*, 114.

In Mark's Gospel we read that the two sons of Zebedee, James and John, left their father to follow Jesus (1:20), and soon after, Jesus makes it clear that biological and familial relationships are subordinate to faith and obedience to the will of God in identifying those who qualify as members of Jesus' community (3:34). Paul commends the unmarried state over the married because this allows the unmarried to devote themselves entirely to the work of the Lord (1 Cor 7:32-40). These developments constituted a break with both Jewish and Greco-Roman traditions with their family-centered cultures. The implications of this for women were significant. "Unknown disappointments or hopes led women from every rank and economic condition to answer Jesus' call to break old family ties and follow after him. Women and men traveled in chaste partnership, forging a new religion and a new social vision. This apostolic life, transcending gender in pursuit of the kingdom of heaven, gave them the foundation of chaste celibacy on which an autonomous identity could arise."[13]

Ecclesial culture, however, was suspicious of women who sought a religious identity for themselves that did not depend on their relationship to men as mothers, wives, or daughters. The lives of those women who chose virginity or widowhood illustrate some of the difficulties women faced in their efforts to forge an autonomous religious missionary identity. Such difficulties led some women to embrace gnosticism, which appeared to offer the possibility of freedom from the patriarchal family. For example, the Encratites, an extreme gnostic sect, forbade its members to engage in any potential procreative activity. Such freedom from familial roles propelled women members of the sect into leadership roles. The combination of women rejecting first their traditional prescribed roles, and, second, opting for leadership and ministry in the community was not always appreciated by church leaders. There was also concern about syneisactism, or chaste women and men working together as equals for the sake of the kingdom of God. The practice of "male and female prophets to travel together and to regard one another as equals in the prophetic life, became a tentative indicator of heresy."[14]

Initially, the option for virginity was limited to urban women, usually of the upper class. "Virgins were neither appointed nor ordained, but simply recognized: 'a virgin does not have an imposition of hands, for personal choice alone is that which makes a virgin' (*Apostolic Tradition* [*of Hippolytus of Rome*, ca. 215], xiii)."[15] Urban women who opted for virginity, or in

---

13. McNamara, *Sisters in Arms*, 1.

14. Ibid., 27.

15. Francine Cardman, "Women, Ministry and Church Order in Early Christianity," in *Women and Christian Origins*, ed. Ross Shepard Kraemer and Mary Rose D'Angelo (New York: Oxford University Press, 1999), 307, quoting from Gregory Dix and Henry Chadwick, eds., *The Treatise on the Apostolic Tradition of St. Hippolytus of Rome*, 2nd rev ed. (London: Alban, 1992), xiii.

the case of widows, for chastity, seemed to have gathered together in homes where they prayed and studied together and practiced charity toward the poor. Church leaders such as Tertullian (160-225 C.E.) feared that these women might try and exercise a sacramental ministry in the church. The example of Thecla, who lived in the first century, was the companion of Paul, and who baptized people, offered an important but disturbing model for such women.

As the role of the bishop developed and the subsequent movement toward a hierarchical form of government in the young church became more pronounced, there were questions raised about women's public ministries in the Christian community. Even though virginity as a way of life for both women and men was gaining importance, the idea of male and female virgins being co-workers was increasingly problematic for a church that was increasingly governed by hierarchical mores. One way of resolving the problematic nature of chaste or virginal women's ministry was to insist that virgins, as spouses of Christ, be veiled, as were married women. Thus their virginity was linked to their sexual nature, whereas those women who had embraced a life of virginity understood it as something that enabled them to transcend their gender for the sake of their ministry. "The imposition of the veil came to entail a liturgy of consecration that gave virginity and widowhood institutional definition . . . Virginity lost its transformative power when virgins were thus reduced to allegorical brides."[16] Women's choices for the asceticism of virginity could be interpreted by ecclesial and patriarchal culture as an unacceptable exercise of female power, a rebellion against social expectations that women were meant to be subject to men and to be childbearers.

Some virgins sought to be admitted to the order of widows. There are two meanings associated with the word "widow." First, "widow" in the technical sense refers to those women whose husbands have predeceased them. Within this group, we need to distinguish between true widows, who were elderly and relied on the community for support; those who were not enrolled as widows because they had some independent means; and younger widows who chose not to remarry. If the last group did not remarry, they were required to follow the legal and social requirements appropriate to their situation so that the good name of the Christian community was preserved. Second, an order of widows was instituted so that widows could serve the community through prayer, pastoral ministry to the poor and through collecting and preparing of food that would be eaten communally in different houses (see Acts 6:1). Virgins who did not wish to marry sometimes sought admission to the order of widows. However, to be enrolled in the order of widows, the woman was supposed to be over sixty years old (and given the much lower life expectancies for women in the second and third centuries, such an age requirement would have drastically reduced the number of wid-

---

16. McNamara, *Sisters in Arms*, 44.

ows for whom the church should assume responsibility), the wife of one husband, and the community had to attest to her good works, service, and compassion.[17] We need to ask if women were turning "to celibacy to find freedom from the inequalities imposed by marriage. Celibacy was required in the widows' circle but women were thereby freed from patriarchal norms."[18] Even though widows were one of the official orders of the church, financial support for them was limited in comparison to that provided for their male confreres. As Bonnie Thurston notes, "of those officials (bishop, deacon, deaconess, widow, elder) only the widows are limited with regard to support, finances, and sexual continence."[19]

Throughout the second and third centuries, widows played an important role in the ministry of the early church. That this angered some of the male leaders is obvious in the injunction directed against widows in the third-century church manual the *Didascalia*. "We do not advise that a woman baptize, nor that anyone allows themselves to be baptized by a woman, for it is a transgression of the commandment and a great danger for the one who is baptized and the one who baptizes" (*Didascalia* 15).[20] Such prohibitions suggest that widows held important ministries in the early church and were even regarded as members of the clergy. "In the same polemic, the writer tries to dissuade widows from exercising *public* ministries by urging them to return to *private* (italics added) spaces: 'Let a widow know that she is the altar of God. And let her constantly sit at home. A widow must not therefore wander or run about among houses for those who are roving and have no shame cannot stay quiet even in their houses' (*Didascalia* 15)."[21]

Surprisingly, given the opposition of male clergy to virgins and widows having ministries in the early church, the public ministry of deaconesses was approved. As Francine Cardman notes, "the *Didascalia* approves of the public ministry of deaconesses. It is not possible to determine where and how the role of deaconesses developed during the second and third centuries, but by the time of the *Didascalia*, it is a recognized office at least in the eastern churches."[22] Perhaps deaconesses were accepted because they were part of the ministerial hierarchy and thus more easily subject to the bishop's control. Their subordinate role in that ministerial hierarchy was emphasized by argu-

---

17. Bonnie Thurston, *The Widows: A Woman's Ministry in the Early Church* (Philadelphia: Fortress Press, 1989), 46.

18. Ibid., 39.

19. Ibid., 53.

20. See Karen Jo Torjesen, "Reconstruction of Women's Early Christian History," in *Searching the Scriptures: A Feminist Introduction*, ed. Elisabeth Schüssler Fiorenza, 2 vols. (New York: Crossroad, 1993), 1:292, quoting from the *Didascalia Apostolorum* 15. See R. Hugh Connolly, ed., *Didascalia Apostolorum* (Oxford: Clarendon Press, 1929). The *Didascalia Apostolorum* is a pastoral treatise containing pseudo-apostolic church laws. It was composed in north Syria in the third century.

21. Torjesen, "Reconstruction of Women's Early Christian History," 1:292-93.

22. Cardman, "Women, Ministry and Church Order," 312.

ing that like the Galilean women who followed Jesus and served him and his disciples (see Luke 8:1-3) they were to serve bishops, the representatives of Jesus. Further evidence of their subordination to male clergy was that deaconesses were not provided with as much support as were male officeholders and even widows.[23] The ministry of deaconess was restricted to ministry to other women that was considered inappropriate for male deacons, such as the anointing of women with oil after baptism had been administered by bishops, presbyters, or deacons. "Deaconesses are needed to instruct newly baptized women and to visit the sick among Christian women who live in 'heathen' households. Thus they have an approved but circumscribed and subordinate role, in teaching and baptizing, ministries that the *Didascalia* forbids to widows."[24] As the *Apostolic Constitutions* puts it, "just as the Comforter says or does nothing without Christ, so the deaconess should say or do nothing without the deacon" (*Apostolic Constitutions* 2.4.28).

The male authors of the *Didascalia* and the *Apostolic Constitutions* appear to have legitimated such prescriptions against women's ministry by drawing on the authority of those Deutero-Pauline texts that restricted women's role to the home. Women, whether deaconesses, widows, or virgins are to be obedient to male clergy and to restrict their ministry primarily to women and children, and to good works among the poor. Later, in 441, the Council of Orange forbade the ordination of deaconesses. As we shall see, however, women persisted in their struggle to be missionary, holding fast to the belief that a missionary vocation had its origin in the sacrament of baptism rather than ordination.

## WOMEN IN THE CONSTANTINIAN CHURCH

One of the most significant events in the life of the young church occurred early in the fourth century when the emperor Constantine began the process of transforming Christianity from a persecuted minority religion into a recognized religion of the empire. This process was initiated in 313 with the Edict of Milan, which guaranteed freedom of religion for all subjects in the empire. Though there is ongoing debate as to whether the edict (and Constantine's baptism in 324) was a ploy to ensure imperial unity or a genuine conversion, there is no dispute about the edict's irrevocably altering the position of the church in society, a position that was confirmed in 370 when the emperor Theodosius decreed that "Christian uniformity became the official policy of the empire."[25]

Christianity's status as the official religion of the empire had positive and negative effects for the church. Positively, Christianity's official status encour-

23. Ibid., 313.
24. Ibid., 312.
25. Johnson, *A History of Christianity*, 104.

aged church growth and provided a security that allowed for the construction of churches and basilicas, the development of organizational structures, and more study of the scriptures. On the other hand, the respectability and status now enjoyed by the church appeared to contribute to a loss of fervor, a perception that led some women and men to embrace a more radical, evangelical life. As early as the third century, increasing numbers of women and men lived either an eremitic or cenobitic life not only in the deserts of Egypt, Palestine, and Syria but also on the edges of the great urban centers. "The desert" was understood either metaphorically or literally, and, given Europe's changing political realities, often it made more sense for women to live closer to cities rather than in isolated rural or desert locales. This enthusiasm for a more radical living of the gospel was one of the many factors leading to the emergence of the monastic movement, a development of immense significance for Christian mission.

Jerome (347-420) records that by 340 Athanasius had successfully started monastic communities in Rome, and prior to 340, "no lady of noble birth knew the monk's way of life."[26] However, there is evidence that some women may have been living a type of monastic life before that. Knowledge about such women is sparse, and comes to us primarily through their male contemporaries. It appears as if there were Christian women, often of high birth who withdrew from family life, from the household of the *paterfamilias*, to follow an ascetical, chaste lifestyle and to minister to the poor. Some women chose to live a solitary life while others opted for communal living with other like-minded women. The arrival of Christianity as the official, imperial religion with its great churches and basilicas diminished the importance of house churches, in which women previously had exercised quite important ministries. However, women who embraced a more evangelical and chaste life found in the embryonic monastic-type communities of which they were part the opportunity to devote their lives to prayer, study, and good works.

These early expressions of monastic living appear to have been egalitarian, for wealthy women founders, when they "disposed of their wealth, . . . offered to the household including their slaves, the opportunity of gaining freedom, or of joining in the practice of the evangelical life."[27] It is unfortunate that much of our information about such communities concentrates on wealthy patrician women founders rather than on the lives of lower-class women who were part of such communities. One important patrician woman was Paula (347-404), who, widowed at thirty-two, devoted her life to prayer, study, and good works, along with other women of similar dispo-

---

26. Joan M. Petersen, ed., *Handmaids of the Lord: Contemporary Descriptions of Feminine Asceticism in the First Six Christian Centuries* (Kalamazoo, Mich.: Cistercian Publications, 1996), 22, quoting from Jerome's letter in I. Hillberg, ed., *Epistulae* (Vienna, 1912), *Ep.* 107.10.

27. Mary T. Malone, *Women and Christianity*, vol. 1, *The First Thousand Years* (Maryknoll, N.Y.: Orbis Books, 2001), 1:140. Malone refers to "a younger contemporary of Paula's, Melania the Younger [who] disposed of eighty thousand slaves in this way."

sition. Paula and the women associated with her gathered with Marcellina, the sister of Ambrose of Milan, in the house of Marcella (325-410), another prominent Roman woman, who was later killed by the Goths in 410. In 382, Jerome arrived in Rome to serve as papal scripture scholar and secretary to Pope Damasus. Marcella invited Jerome to come and teach scripture to the women, an invitation that Jerome accepted with alacrity; and he records that his "lectures led to frequent meetings, [and] through their meetings intimacy grew and their intimacy inspired mutual confidence."[28] The spirituality of these women was nourished by their communal spirit, prayer together, love of scripture, and asceticism. Such spirituality, rooted in their chaste and ascetical lifestyles, their prayer, and study, complemented and modeled an alternative to those spiritualities associated with the priesthood, which were more sacramentally focused.

These women believed that marriage limited their ability to identify and embrace new ways of Christian discipleship. Their chaste lifestyles, renunciation of wealth, enthusiasm for an egalitarian way of life, and ministry to the poor marked an important development in women's story of mission in the Western church. But their enthusiasm for virginity, as an alternative to married life, proved problematic for Ambrose, Augustine, and Jerome, whose writings subsequently have proved so influential in forming Christian anthropology. Women's "disturbance of the natural order was profoundly troublesome to the all-male church leaders while at the same time, they felt compelled to laud the practice of asceticism."[29] Social pressure on women to marry was considerable, because having children was regarded as a social duty. Church leaders coped more easily with those women who opted for a life of virginity in the deserts of the Middle East. It was a case of out of sight, out of mind, but it was more difficult dealing with large, well-resourced groups of urban-based women who chose a virginal and communal way of life in the city.

It was difficult for church leaders to criticize the choice for virginity because the Gospels suggest that Jesus himself opted for such a life. But they thought that women who chose such a life should be controlled so that they did not constitute a threat to a clericalized church. Women who opted for virginity were to be brought under the control of a male-dominated church that believed that women, as daughters of Eve, were always prone to temptation and were sources of temptation for men. Women's virginity was to be protected by obedience, submission, extreme asceticism, and silence. Ambrose, Jerome, and Augustine used their considerable intellectual gifts to marshal support for such a negative understanding of women. Ambrose contributed to the debate through his writings on Mary the Virgin. Prior to his contribution, both women and men had opted for a life of virginity in imitation of

---

28. Ibid., 136. Malone's translation of the *Letters of Jerome*, Letter 45.
29. Ibid., 146.

Jesus, but because of the influence of Ambrose, women were required to imitate not Jesus but Mary. Mary Malone states that Ambrose "invented, almost single-handedly, the doctrine of the perpetual virginity of Mary."[30] For Ambrose, Mary was the one who "stayed at home all day and rarely ventured forth. She shunned the company of men. She worked like a honeybee. She prayed to God, constantly, and let no bad thoughts take root in her heart. She was never bold or hard-hearted and always kept her voice low."[31] It is not surprising that the most popular Gospel text concerning Mary was Luke 1:38: "Here I am, the servant of the Lord, let it be with me according to your word." The importance of Ambrose's emphasis on this text for future generations of Catholic women, particularly Catholic sisters, should never be underestimated. Augustine also turned to Luke's Gospel to support his claim that Mary chose a life of perpetual virginity. Mary's choice lies behind her question to the angel, "How can this be since I am a virgin?" The developing theology of the virginity of Mary became a privileged weapon in the male arsenal to ensure that women were submissive, silent, and obedient to men. Because it was feared that women virgins could be considered superior to clergy, who were not required to live celibate lives at this time, although it was strongly recommended, the importance of celibacy for priests assumed more significance. Gender difference was emphasized, and men were to follow the example of the virginal Jesus, whose virginity freed him for his public ministry, while women were to follow the example of Mary, whose virginity restricted her to the domestic realm.

## MISSIONARY ABBESSES OF THE "DARK AGES"

As the fifth century drew to a close, so too did the Roman imperial world begin to disintegrate, and after 476 there was no longer a Roman emperor in the West. The fifth to the eighth centuries are often referred to as the Dark Ages in Western history, but the collapse of the Classical Age seemed to offer new hope for women. As the wars of the twentieth century have demonstrated, times of great cultural and political shifts often mean new opportunities for women. The first Christians, particularly Paul, had succeeded in bringing the good news of Jesus Christ to the Greco-Roman world. By the fifth century, the Christian church in the West was engaged in another great missionary task—bringing the good news to the Celtic and Germanic tribes. Prior to the fifth century, Celtic tribes had settled in the most isolated parts of Western Europe, and by the sixth century, the different Germanic tribes were moving across Europe. Christian mission faced a new challenge as it came face to face with peoples whose culture and traditions were oral rather

---

30. Ibid., 157.
31. Ibid., 167, quoting from Mary T. Malone, *Who Is My Mother? Rediscovering the Mother of Jesus* (Dubuque, Ia.: Wm. C. Brown, 1984), 25.

than literary. The collapse of traditional structures and institutions associated with the empire meant the emergence of many smaller kingdoms determined by tribal affiliations. These kingdoms were often at war with one another, and it is in this context that monastic life assumed more importance. Monasteries were often built and owned by aristocratic families, and leadership of the monastery belonged to members of such families. Given this situation, rulers tended to favor monasteries rather than dioceses whose bishops might attempt to subvert feudal claims to authority. Monasteries had several important roles: a missionary role in the sense that they were often people's first introduction to Christianity; pastoral, because nuns and monks ministered to the people; economic, because monasticism transformed forests into pastoral and arable land; and educational, because of their promotion of learning, particularly of the scriptures, and the classical and patristic authors.

From the sixth to the ninth century, a number of important Benedictine nuns emerged, and I now turn to their contributions to mission.[32] I propose to refer briefly to three English women and wish to make it clear that my choice is representative rather than exhaustive. Again, our information regarding saintly nuns comes to us from the writings of men, particularly from hagiographical stories, but this latter phenomenon should not obscure the historical significance of these women.

## Hilda of Whitby (614-680)

Hilda, named after one of the Valkyries of pagan Scandinavian mythology and baptized in her teens in 627 by Bishop Paulinus, was a Northumbrian princess. She lived the first part of her life as a married woman and the second as a nun, eventually becoming abbess of Whitby. Bede writes: "So great was her knowledge of affairs that not only ordinary people but kings and princes sought and received her advice. She compelled all those under her to devote much time to the study of the scriptures. All who knew Hilda called her 'Mother.'"[33] What did Hilda do to merit such affirmation from Bede? Prior to becoming abbess at Whitby, she had become famous through her leadership of Hartlepool, another significant Northumbrian abbey. In addition to her undoubted intellectual gifts, she was renowned for her charity and humility. During her time as abbess, Whitby became a center of great learning, and at least five bishops received their theological education at Whitby. The long-standing dispute between Celtic and British Christianity

---

32. Celtic monasticism was also an important feature of the Western church at this time, but apart from St. Brigid (453-523), women do not figure prominently in the story of Celtic monasticism.

33. B. Colgrave and R. A. B. Mynors, eds., *Bede: Ecclesiastical History of the English People* (Oxford: Oxford University Press, 1969), 4.23, 409-10.

concerning the date of Easter was resolved by a synod at Whitby, presided over by Hilda—evidence of the importance of Hilda and Whitby. Jo Ann Kay McNamara indicates that Hilda "assumed a prestige usually reserved for bishops when she presided over the synod where Irish and Roman churches competed for the allegiance of the Northumbrian king."[34]

Hilda was the abbess in what are called "double monasteries," that is, monasteries in which women and men were domiciled, although in different quarters. At this time, monasticism was much more of a lay than a clerical movement. A sufficient number of priests were ordained to provide for the basic sacramental needs of the community. *Opus Dei,* or the nonsacramental liturgical task of chanting the Divine Office, was the most important religious task of nuns and monks. Nonordained monks were responsible for heavy outside work, while women were responsible for domestic work. This reduced the significance of the clergy. As an aristocratic woman with both wealth and status, Hilda "enjoyed many of the prerogatives associated with bishops."[35] The story of Hilda's monastery at Whitby provides us with a good example of centripetal mission, that is, people were drawn to the monastery because it was perceived as a holy place in which love of God was manifested through works of charity, through study of the scriptures and the patristic writings, and through its life of prayer. The other important way in which nuns and monks exercised mission is perhaps best described as centrifugal, that is, nuns and monks "went out" to minister among those who had not yet heard the good news. I now turn to the stories of Leoba and Walburga as examples of centrifugal mission.

### Leoba (ca. 700-780)

The Benedictine nun Leoba was a co-worker of Boniface in the mission to Germanic tribes. Again, we learn about her important contribution to the German mission from male hagiographers, but this does not mean that we should be dismissive of their accounts. As Catherine Wybourne argues, "good hagiography is not necessarily bad history, nor is a consciously literary style evidence of distortion or falsification, but they do indicate that not every story can be accepted at face value."[36] Leoba was a nun at Wimbourne, another double monastery, and sometime in the 740s Boniface asked the

---

34. McNamara, *Sisters in Arms,* 127.
35. Ibid., 127.
36. Catherine Wybourne, "Leoba: A Study in Humanity and Holiness," in *Medieval Women Monastics: Wisdom's Wellsprings,* ed. Miriam Schmitt and Linda Kulzer (Collegeville, Minn: Liturgical Press, 1996), 82. It is instructive to compare Malone's assessment of Leoba with that of Peter Brown, whose only reference to her is limited to a detailed account of a local village's anger at Leoba and her community. See Peter Brown, *The Rise of Western Christendom: Triumph and Diversity A.D. 200-1000,* 2nd ed. (Oxford: Blackwell, 2003), 425.

abbess, Tetta, for nuns to join him in his German mission. In particular, he requested that Tetta allow "Leoba to join him as a comfort to him in his exile and the mission entrusted to him."[37] Leoba was appointed abbess at Bischofsheim, a monastery enjoying a special prominence. Like Hilda before her, Leoba's monastery focused on sound learning, good works, particularly hospitality, and prayer. Her importance to Boniface in the Anglo-Saxon mission to Germany is clear from Boniface's wish that they should be buried together. At their last meeting before his martyrdom in 754, he gave her his cowl and asked that she continue the German mission. Leoba died in 780, and, as Malone writes, "the death of Leoba signaled the end of an era. She was one of the last of an extraordinary group of Anglo-Saxon nuns whose labors created the Europe we know today. From the great monastery of Wimborne, thirty nuns had moved to the German mission-fields, where they had labored side by side with the monks."[38]

### Walburga (710-799)

Our third missionary nun is Walburga, an Anglo-Saxon princess, niece of Boniface, and sister of two other important missionaries, Willibald and Wunnibald. Walburga was another who was formed by the abbess Tetta at the great double monastery of Wimbourne for the mission to the Germans. Eventually she joined her brother Wunnibald at the monastery in Heidenheim in Bavaria, and, on his death in 781, became abbess. Many extraordinary tales and miracles stories are associated with Walburga, and although they may seem excessive in their claims to the contemporary reader, there is little doubt that they witness in a powerful way to her holiness, love of learning, and missionary enthusiasm.

When we consider the lives of such women as Hilda, Leoba, and Walburga, we should not be surprised by Joan Morris's claim that such women enjoyed a status equivalent to that of bishops.[39] These abbesses came from the aristocratic classes, and part of their success in managing large monasteries had its origins in their management of large households. However, they were also rightly honored for their spiritual and intellectual gifts. Additional support for the view that such women enjoying a status comparable to that of bishops is provided in an informative and stimulating article by Gary Macy. He explores "the use of the terms *ordination*, *ordinare*, and *ordo* in regard to the commissioning of women"[40] in the early Middle Ages, and

---

37. Wybourne, "Leoba," 88.

38. Malone, *Women and Christianity*, 1:215.

39. See Joan Morris, *The Lady Was a Bishop: The Hidden History of Women with Clerical Ordination and the Jurisdiction of Bishops* (New York: Macmillan, 1973), 130.

40. Gary Macy, "The Ordination of Women in the Early Middle Ages," *Theological Studies* 61 (2000): 481-507.

argues that "neither liturgies, nor popes, nor bishops had a problem referring particularly to deaconesses and abbesses, or to nuns, as persons entering into an ecclesiastical order through a ritual of ordination."[41] Obviously
these three words had meanings that were more inclusive and open-ended
than the meanings associated with them today. In particular, abbesses were
responsible for functions associated with ordination such as hearing the
nuns' confessions, baptizing children brought into the monastery, preaching,
distributing the blessed bread during the liturgy, excommunicating nuns from
either table or the Divine Office, blessing people, and consecrating women
who entered their monasteries.[42] By 1210, such activities had been condemned by Pope Innocent III, who was concerned that "[a]bbesses . . . bless
their own nuns, hear their confessions of sin, and reading the Gospel, presume to preach publicly."[43] What emerges from even a brief consideration of
the so-called Dark Ages is that they were less than dark for women or at
least for those aristocratic women who emerged as great abbesses at this
time. Their successful management and administration of great double
monasteries, their call to be part of the English missionary movement in Germany, their love of learning, and their devotion to prayer suggest that they
were pivotal figures in the church of their time. But their very success was
threatening to political and church leaders.

Efforts to suppress women's public role in the life of the church picked up
momentum as the eighth century drew to a close. Much of this suppression
can be attributed to the church reforms of Charlemagne, the Frankish king
who reigned from 768 to 814. Charlemagne did not set out to hinder the
mission of women, but he did set out to forcibly convert the Saxons as he
pushed his empire further east. This policy of forcible conversion under pain
of death was a missionary strategy that did not actively involve women. The
subsequent church legislation of Charlemagne reflected his indebtedness to
the Ten Commandments rather than to the Sermon on the Mount. His law
making led to bishops becoming more important than abbots and abbesses,
and increasingly nuns were subjected to episcopal authority. As early as 755,
the Council of Verneuil had begun the process of reversing monastic autonomy. Nuns and monks were placed under episcopal jurisdiction, and
attempts to impose a strict enclosure on nuns became more frequent. Increasingly monks were ordained, and the older, more egalitarian relationship
between nonordained monks and nuns began to disappear, as moves to physically separate nuns from monks meant that segregated living rather than
"double" living became normative. As the ninth century began, restrictive
laws with respect to women became more onerous. The Council of Chalon

---

41. Ibid., 485.
42. See Macy, "The Ordination of Women," 497.
43. Macy, "The Ordination of Women," citing *Corpus Iuris Canonici, Decretales* 1.5, t.38,
chap. 10, ed. E. Friedberg (Graz: Akademische Druck, 1959), 2. cols. 886-87.

in 813 stipulated that canonesses with their weak and unstable minds had to
lead a more austere life than male canons.[44] "They were to be strictly cloistered and management of their private property was relegated to an outsider.
Moreover, they had to veil their faces in church and be carefully guarded
from any contract with men. Even their communication with priests was limited; they could make a confession only within sight of the sisters."[45] Nuns
were no longer allowed to accept young boys into their monasteries as students. Much of this so-called reform was initiated by the different Carolingian kings, who "in an effort to consolidate and unify their territory . . .
attempted to make all monasteries, male and female, into royal abbeys."[46]
Carolingian monastic reform meant that women's communities were subject
to the wishes of secular and ecclesiastical leaders, "and as the women had
lost an influential voice in society, they had very little recourse to remedy
their situation."[47] As McNamara rightly claims, "all this legislation had but
one purpose for women: the imposition of external controls over them combined with internal claustration. The reformers seem to have been largely
indifferent to what they made of the life that resulted. Yet they set the pattern for the church's treatment of nuns in every major reform thereafter."[48]

Such efforts to control women's call to a public missionary role, however,
were soon to be challenged, initially through the patronage and support that
various English queens began to offer to monasteries in the tenth century.
Abbesses and abbots met at Winchester in 972 to draw up an agreement that
would be binding for nuns and monks. Together, they then assisted at the
coronation of the king. Change was slower to occur in France, which was
more directly influenced by the Carolingian reform, but the collapse of Carolingian rule meant the relaxation and even the disappearance of some of
the legislation that had been so restrictive of nuns. Strong abbesses, again
from the aristocratic classes, with significant managerial and administrative
skills emerged to assume responsibility for large monasteries. This was particularly the situation in Germany because monastic life had arrived there
later and had not been so affected by the Carolingian reforms. As the tenth
century drew to a close, monasteries were once again introducing young
women to the study of scripture, classical and patristic writings, the production of artistically decorated manuscripts and vestments, as well as to the
more mundane domestic arts. A greater political stability throughout West-

---

44. From the early Middle Ages, "canonesses" provided a quasi-religious alternative to
monastic life for aristocratic women. Canonesses did not make vows, retained their right to
private property, and were free to leave their convents when they wanted. Therefore they lived
"irregular" rather than "regular" lives.

45. Suzanne Fonay Wemple, "Women from the Fifth to the Tenth Century," in *Silences of
the Middle Ages*, vol. 2, *A History of Women in the West*, ed. Georges Duby and Michelle
Perrot (Cambridge, Mass.: Belknap Press, 1992), 2:190.

46. Raft, *Women and Religious Life*, 33.

47. Ibid., 33.

48. McNamara, *Sisters in Arms*, 162.

ern Europe, the growing strength of the papacy, and the initiation of monastic reforms led to the founding of Benedictine monasteries for women throughout Europe as the Christian faith spread, including one founded in Iceland in 1186.

## WOMEN IN THE LATE MIDDLE AGES

We have already seen how the transformation of Christianity from a minority sect into the official imperial religion in the fourth century contributed to a loss of fervor that a minority of Christians sought to redress through living more ascetical lives as cenobitic or eremitic nuns and monks. Something similar happened in the late Middle Ages. The greater cultural cohesiveness, political stability, and economic growth characteristic of Western Europe from the eleventh century onward meant the development of a middle class. It was from this class that some of the great reformers of the late Middle Ages emerged. In particular, laypeople concerned about the state of the priesthood embraced what came to be called the *vita apostolica,* a lifestyle that emphasized the practice of voluntary poverty modeled on the example of Jesus and his first disciples. Women and men were choosing to live an eremitic life, or one that combined elements of the solitary and the communal. At least two such wandering charismatic eremites, Robert of Arbrissel (1060-1116), and Norbert of Xanten (1081-1134), founded monasteries for men and women at Fontevrault and Prémontré respectively. Heloise and Peter Abelard, in their old (and reformed) age, brought to birth a new community for women, the Order of the Paraclete.

By 1121, the Premonstratensians had adopted the Rule of Saint Augustine and were living in a double monastery at Prémontré; other Premonstratensian foundations quickly followed in northeastern France and Germany. Both women and men engaged in apostolic works, notably care of the sick in hospices, although this situation was frustrated by the second abbot, Hugh, who by 1141 was actively seeking to dismantle Prémontré as a double monastery. In 1198, Pope Innocent III approved legislation forbidding the admission of women to the order. Such new non-Benedictine foundations did not minimize the importance of Benedictine monasticism, as the stories of Hildegaard of Bingen and Elisabeth of Schönau demonstrate.

### Hildegaard of Bingen (1098-1179)

Despite the emergence of "new" orders such as the Premonstratensians, the older model of Benedictine monasticism was still important. Hildegaard emerges as one of the most apostolic of all Benedictine women. Her undoubted intellectual brilliance, deeply mystical spirituality, and creativity confirm her as "the first acknowledged Western female teacher in the church; she fulfilled the roles of preacher and exorcist, roles usually reserved to men; she was a prophet revered by the leaders of the day."[49] She initially decided to live as an anchorite, but she later became a member of a Benedictine community that had gathered around Jutta, an aristocratic German woman. After the death of Jutta in 1136, Hildegaard became abbess of the monastery, and her fame spread throughout the Rhineland first and then through Europe. "As a prophetic reformer, she undertook four preaching tours which included such cities as Bamberg, Trier, Cologne, and Zweifalten,"[50] and, like Lady Wisdom, she raised her voice in the streets and in the public places. Constance Furey suggests, however, that often the men who came to her for advice chose not to regard her as educated and their intellectual equal, "but as a living temple of God, a chosen vessel,"[51] whom God had blessed in a unique way that allowed her to transcend her womanly deficiencies.

### Elisabeth of Schönau (1129-1165)

Elisabeth, thirty years younger than Hildegaard, was a nun in the double monastery at Schönau, where she began to have visions when she was thirty-three. She recognized that her visions had a public as well as a private import, and they conferred on her a prophetic role. In particular, she preached against the Cathar heresy and the failings of the clergy. Her sermons in *Viarum Dei* chastised ecclesiastical leaders "for their neglect of their flocks, for their public shows of piety and their private iniquities, for their willingness to buy and sell sanctification (simony), for their disregard of traditions, for their worldliness, and above all for their failure to combat Catharism."[52]

Both Hildegaard and Elisabeth had important preaching ministries, but they were not alone in this ministry. "Perhaps the most surprising expression of the presence of women in the 10th-12th centuries was their participation in itinerant preaching."[53] Women and men who had embraced the *vita apostolica* claimed the right to preach; they argued that their lives, lived in imitation of Jesus and open to the interior impulses of the Holy Spirit, enabled them to engage in such a ministry. In other words, their preaching ministries flowed from charism rather than from office, from the gift of prophecy rather

---

49. Raft, *Women and the Religious Life,* 58.

50. Hildegaard Ryan, "St. Hildegaard of Bingen (1098-1179) and Bl. Jutta of Spanheim (1084-1136): Foremothers in Wisdom," in *Medieval Women Monastics: Wisdom's Wellsprings,* ed. Miriam Schmidt and Linda Kulzer (Collegeville, Minn: Liturgical Press, 1996), 158.

51. Constance Furey, "'Intellects Inflamed in Christ': Women and Spiritualized Scholarship in Renaissance Christianity," *Journal of Religion* 84 (2004): 15-16.

52. Anne Beard, "The Visionary Life of Elisabeth of Schönau: A Different Way of Knowing," in *Medieval Women Monastics,* 173.

53. A. Valerio, "Women in the 'Societas Christiana': 10th–12th Centuries," *Theology Digest* 33 (1986): 155-58.

than from a theological education. The Cathari and Waldensian movements offer important examples of laypeople engaging in preaching ministries— this despite a long and official history of women being forbidden to preach.[54] That these preaching ministries were not appreciated by ordained ministers is obvious. Geoffrey of Auxerre, who followed Bernard as abbott of Clairvaux, likened Waldensian women preachers to Jezebel, and reiterated that the woman's place was in the home. He reaffirmed the teachings of the *Apostolic Constitutions*, written some six centuries earlier: "A woman, no matter how learned and holy, should not dare to teach men in assembly" (canon 37).[55] Despite this and other such prohibitions, a belief that preaching flowed from the power of the Holy Spirit present in chosen individuals rather than from ordination ensured that lay women and men continued to preach. This led to the condemnation of Cathari, Waldensian, and Humiliati preachers, although the Humiliatis' women's branch, who cared for lepers, persisted much longer. The Fourth Lateran Council (1215), however, severed the connection between preaching and charism and definitively linked preaching ministry to ordination.[56]

### *Women and the* Vita Apostolica

As the twelfth century drew to a close, the phenomenon of women and men choosing the *vita apostolica* became more marked. Such choices were partially motivated by a deep concern among laypeople about the institutional church because of the moral laxity and lack of theological formation of so many ordained ministers. Responsibility for renewal in the church was moving from the monastery to laypeople, and lay leadership was not always welcomed by a hierarchical church. As Simon Tugwell perceptively notes, "The tragedy of the church was that a real movement of evangelical fervor which should have been revitalizing the church from inside, was being pushed to and beyond the fringe by a combination of lack of effective under-

---

54. Catharism and Waldensianism were thirteenth-century French movements that believed in a dualistic notion of matter and spirit. At the same time, given their anticlericalism and criticism of a powerful and worldly church, they were perceived by the institutional church as dangerous. Women were prominent in both movements and lay women and men had important preaching ministries. The kings of France and England considered them to be subversive of the established order, and by 1184 had joined forces with the church in instituting the Inquisition in order to eradicate them. The Humiliati were another penitential order founded in the twelfth century initially for men, and then wives of the first Humiliati formed a women's branch. The male branch was suppressed in 1571, but the women's branch, whose members cared for lepers, persisted much longer.

55. Mary Catherine Hilkert, "Women Preaching the Gospel," *Theology Digest* 33 (1986): 423-40, citing the *Apostolic Constitutions* canon 37, in *Les Statua Ecclesia Antiqua, Edition-Etudes Critiques,* ed. Charles Munier (Paris: Presses Universitaires de France, 1960), 86.

56. For an excellent survey of women's preaching in the Middle Ages, see Beverly Mayne Kienzle and Pamela J. Walker, eds., *Women Preachers and Prophets through Two Millennia of Christianity* (Berkeley: University of California Press, 1998).

standing and leadership on the part of the official clergy and a serious lack of doctrinal formation on the part of the people."[57] We have already referred to the appearance of the Cathars and Waldensians, both of whom were condemned by the church, but there were other groups who contributed significantly to Christian reform, and women were often key players in such attempts at reform.

The story of women attempting to live the *vita apostolica* was a story of success and failure. Prominent among the failures is Clare of Assisi's efforts to ensure that the Poor Clares lived like the first Christian community (see Acts 2:44-47), ministering in the towns and villages in the daytime, often in the local hospices, and returning at night to their dwelling in order to pray and contemplate.[58] However, it was not long before strict enclosure was imposed on Clare and her community, and even Francis of Assisi, her mentor, ended up not supporting her wish for apostolic work. The Dominicans, on the other hand, never seemed to have visualized anything other than an enclosed, contemplative lifestyle for the women who sought admission, and Dominic himself understood the role of Dominican women as similar to that of Mary, while the men's more active preaching role meant they were likened to Martha (see Luke 10:38-42).

Two important expressions of the *vita apostolica* were the Sisters of the Common Life, founded by Dutchman Geert Grote (1340-1384), the founding father of the *devotio moderna*, an important reform movement in the Netherlands and northern Germany, and the Beguine movement. The Sisters of the Common Life were a nonmonastic community who adopted "neither vows nor habits, working for a living and pursuing a common life of service to God."[59] Their prayer too was an individual exercise, and their spirituality emphasized "inward emotions and direct communication with God inspired by reading Scripture rather than studying formal theology, while retaining a scrupulous orthodoxy in regard to sacraments and indulgences."[60] The importance of the Sisters of the Common Life for understanding women's missionary role is threefold: first, they were part of the wider reforming movement characteristic of the church in the later Middle Ages; second, they were nonmonastic and therefore noncloistered; and, third, they contributed to a growing number of spiritual and theological works written in the vernacular. But their importance in deepening our understanding of women's evolving missionary role is perhaps not as significant as that of the Beguines.

Prior to the second half of the twentieth century, Beguines barely warranted a mention in church history, but, more recently, there has been a

---

57. Simon Tugwell, ed., *Early Dominicans: Selected Writings* (Ramsey, N.J.: Paulist Press, 1982), 9-10.
58. See Raft, *Women and the Religious Life*, 65-66.
59. McNamara, *Sisters in Arms*, 391.
60. Ibid., 390.

wealth of publications about these laywomen who figured so prominently in the life of the church, particularly in northern Europe.[61] It is difficult to pinpoint the origins of the Beguines, who successfully combined a contemplative life with a mission to the poor. Sociological causes are offered as a reason. In this scenario, a surplus of women in northern Europe is responsible, but others offer more religiously grounded reasons, such as a desire among women to embrace more fervently lives of evangelical poverty and chastity. Another suggestion is that Beguines were nuns *manquées* (failed nuns), or that many women wanted to embrace the *vita apostolica* but not in already-existing religious communities with their strict enclosure. Beguines could live alone or in community. The importance of the *vita apostolica* for the Beguines is apparent in their sharing of "their inheritances or endowments with their companions. Since they lived by their own rules, they had greater latitude in choosing companions and living conditions."[62] Their apostolic activities were many and varied; they cared for the sick, including lepers, became caretakers of more isolated chapels and oratories, and acted as bankers for the poor, often enough to safeguard them from the unscrupulous behavior of money lenders.

Beguine spirituality was incarnational and sacramental, and devotion to the eucharist was a Beguine characteristic; Beguines are largely responsible for the establishment of the feast of Corpus Christi.[63] More importantly for the subsequent development of an authentic lay spirituality, they prayed and wrote in their vernacular languages. After some initial suspicion on the part of the church, Pope Gregory IX approved of them in 1233. As Patricia Raft points out, this was a mixed blessing: on the one hand, while approval meant that they were no longer regarded as heretical, on the other hand, it meant a more formal relationship with local bishops and priests. This was not necessarily negative, but it did allow for an interference that was not always beneficial. In 1317, however, Pope John XXII's decree *Cum de quibusdam* was more negative, and referred to the Beguines as those women who "promise no one obedience and neither renounce property nor live in accordance with an approved rule and consequently in no wise can be considered religious."[64] By the fifteenth century, it was apparent that the influence of the Beguine movement was waning.[65]

---

61. See Mary T. Malone, *Women and Christianity*, vol. 2, *From 1000 to the Reformation* (Maryknoll, N.Y.: Orbis Books, 2001), 2:124-49. Walter Simons offers a more developed account of the Beguine movement (*Cities of Ladies: Beguine Communities in the Medieval Low Countries, 1200-1565* [Philadelphia: University of Pennsylvania Press, 2001]).

62. McNamara, *Sisters in Arms*, 241.

63. In 1246, Robert de Torote, bishop of Liège, ordered the feast celebrated in his diocese. Prior to that, the Beguines and other women had sought such a celebration.

64. Elizabeth Makowski, "*Mulieres Religiosae*, Strictly Speaking: Some Fourteenth-Century Canonical Options," *Catholic Historical Review* 85 (1999): 1-14, citing *Cum de quibusdam*, the Clementine decree, *Clem* 3.11.1

65. See Raft, *Women and the Religious Life*, 73.

Raft's conclusions regarding the importance of the Beguines deserve to be fully quoted.

> In their immediate world the Beguines offered women an orthodox equivalent to heretical *vita apostolica* groups. Second, they were groups that women themselves directed. They were outside the bounds of monastic control, and originally, of diocesan control; Beguines were independent women. Third, some Beguines were powerful beyond their own circle of women. [Belgian] Mary of Oignies [1167-1213] was the supporter and director of many clerics and a voice of authority among the laity. Fourth, they offered women a type of religious life that was adaptable to the new urban development of the day. In southern Europe the male mendicants met this need, but it was female Beguines who supplied the solution in the north. Last, the Beguine movement was at its birth and remained until its final days a *via media*, a life for women somewhere between that of a nun and a laywoman. Future generations often used the Beguine movement as a model when they set out to create their own variation of religious life.[66]

Furthermore, "the development of the Beguine movement was part of the desire to 'democratize' religion. The desire to bring God to the people, into the market place, flowed from the dawning realization that Christianity was properly a way of life accessible to all, not just a series of rites performed by an inner circle of initiates."[67] Elizabeth Makowski claims that alongside "the narrow canonical definition of the *mulier religiosa* there existed a broader, popular definition which had been gaining currency since the twelfth century. According to that definition, devotion, piety, and striving for Christian perfection, a *vita apostolica*, not permanent vows and cloistered spaces, made a woman religious,"[68] but there was less enthusiasm for apostolic women who retained control of their property and who were not bound by canon law.

As the thirteenth century drew to a close, this lack of enthusiasm for women exercising a public ministry was evident in the stricter laws concerning nuns that Pope Boniface's decree *Periculoso* (1298) legislated for their strict enclosure. "Proper" nuns made solemn vows and were cloistered, which ensured greater episcopal control over conventual life. For example, one of the advantages of the solemn vow of poverty for the monastery was that if a nun were to leave, she could not take her dowry or possessions with her. One of the most comprehensive studies of the significance of *Periculoso*

---

66. Ibid., 74.

67. Saskia Murk-Jansen, *Brides in the Desert: The Spirituality of the Beguines* (Maryknoll, N.Y.: Orbis Books, 1998), 112.

68. Makowski, "*Mulieres Religiosae*," 3.

is Elizabeth Makowski's *Canon Law and Cloistered Women.*[69] She argues that the decree assumed that sexual difference between women and men equated to women's inferiority, and therefore eroded the equality that had existed between nuns and monks in the early Middle Ages. The consequences of such legislation included undermining the administrative and economic freedom of that earlier period, for it brought nuns more strictly under episcopal control and prevented them from instructing young women and girls who previously had come to their monasteries. This threatened the monastery's economic well-being and limited the spiritual, intellectual, and social importance of nuns in the wider community. It sharply delineated between nuns, who often came from the upper classes, and lay groups such as the Beguines who were more often from the middle and lower classes. It implicitly postulated gender and class differences as the prerequisite for such legislation. The decree was promulgated to malign female preachers and the presumed threat they posed for a hierarchical, clerical church, and to encourage nuns in their all-important task of preserving their chastity, a task they supposedly found difficult given their many deficiencies. In effect, this meant that "enclosure had already become an end in itself, to which other values of religious life were increasingly subordinated."[70] *Periculoso* affected women's missionary outreach in two ways: on the one hand, while traditional monastic communities remained important and respected, there was an increasing emphasis on the cloistered nature of such life; on the other, more apostolical, noncloistered communities of women found their capacity to respond in an innovative fashion to the extraordinary changes that were occurring in Europe restricted.

The third orders or tertiaries represent yet another development for women seeking to pursue a mission-focused life. Third orders emerged as a way of life for lay women and men who wished to live a religious missionary life, and at the same time maintain their secular status. Such laypeople sought to follow an evangelical life through living simply, prayer, fasting, and a ministry to the poor. Given the difficulties that the Beguines had experienced in obtaining ecclesiastical approval for their movement, it made sense for women who wished to live a *vita apostolica* to adopt a rule such as the *Third Rule of St. Francis* because the protection offered by an official rule spared them many of the difficulties that the Beguines had experienced. Indeed, some Beguines decided to become tertiaries. As Raft comments, "the development of third orders was advantageous to women, for it gave them a type of protection by affiliation and a way of life that enabled them to make the most of their abilities."[71] Some prominent tertiaries include Cather-

---

69. See Elizabeth Makowski, *Canon Law and Cloistered Women: Periculoso and Its Commentators, 1298-1545* (Washington, D.C.: Catholic University of America Press, 1997).

70. Ibid., 127.

71. Raft, *Women and the Religious Life,* 84.

ine of Siena (1347-1380), a Dominican tertiary, intellectual, mystic, and church reformer, whose brilliance, according to her male contemporaries, attested to "the scope and force of the sacred that could speak through the voice of the lowly";[72] Margaret of Cortona (1247-1297), a Franciscan tertiary who in 1286 founded a hospital called the Hospital of Mercy; Mary of Cervello (d. 1290), who belonged to the third order of the Order of Our Lady of Ransom and who worked to ransom Christian slaves from the Muslims; Angela of Foligno (1248-1309), a Franciscan tertiary and a married woman; and Juliana Falconieri (1270-1341), a Servite tertiary who eventually lived with like-minded women. Servite tertiaries engaged in social work and "because of their strenuous work they wore short sleeves; the nickname given to them because of this, 'mantellate,' became a term synonymous with all women tertiaries."[73] Even royal women embraced the tertiary life; Isabel of Portugal (1271-1336), for example, used her position and wealth to found an orphanage, a hospital, and a home for reformed prostitutes. It was a time of extraordinary growth of women's religious communities, both contemplative and active. Craig Harline in his microstudy of women's religious communities in Belgium, records that between 1120 and 1559, there were 235 female houses for nuns and 44 beguinages. About half of these houses were noncloistered, but even in the contemplative and enclosed communities, nuns reclaimed their educational ministry to young women.[74]

Our story of missionary women in the Middle Ages is indeed an extraordinary one, and one that until recently has been rarely alluded to in ecclesiastical histories written by males. Such histories have concentrated on male-initiated and male-dominated events, such as the appearance of Islam, the Hildebrandine reforms, the various Benedictine reforms, the Crusades, the emergence of the mendicant orders, or the dominance of Scholastic theology as the Middle Ages drew to a close. Such events, so formative for the development of Christianity in the West, deserve careful study from a feminist perspective, because almost without exception they are characterized by serious lacunae concerning the role of women. These women, whose journey across the pages of history we have briefly touched on, emerge as lights in the so-called Dark Ages, and again as beacons in the so-called high Middle Ages when the church was coming to grips with the reality of urbanization, and its corollary, the emergence of an articulate middle class. These women appear as mystics, as theologians whose writings in the vernacular reflect the importance of women's experience as the starting point in theological reflection, as great administrators and managers, as courageous missionaries who served and ministered to the poor, the sick, and the outcasts. While their

---

72. Furey, "Intellects Inflamed in Christ," 16.

73. Raft, *Women and the Religious Life*, 84.

74. See Craig Harline, "Actives and Contemplatives: The Female Religious of the Low Countries before and after Trent," *Catholic Historical Review* 81 (1995): 547.

efforts to be missionary were sometimes acknowledged and even supported by monks, the institutional church sought to curb the influence of such women, arguing that women's roles should be eliminated from public ministry and be restricted to the privacy of the home. As we will now see, although the Renaissance meant the end of the Middle Ages, it did not mean that new ways of understanding women's missionary roles were allowed to surface. If anything the situation worsened when Tridentine reforms were initiated.

# 5

# Missionary Women in the Sixteenth, Seventeenth, and Eighteenth Centuries

The end of the fifteenth century ushered in the early modern age, the period in European history that encompassed the sixteenth, seventeenth, and eighteenth centuries. The discovery of the Americas in 1492, the dawn of the Renaissance, and both the Protestant and Catholic Reformations led to seismic shifts in Europe and in those parts of the world that European powers sought to colonize and evangelize. Columbus's discovery of the Americas made missionary practice into an expansionist project to which both church and state were committed. Renaissance scholars and artists sought to reclaim and to continue the great achievements of the classical world through an intense celebration of the human as an artistic creation, as Michelangelo's *David* demonstrates. The Reformation was a complex process by which religious, intellectual, social, and political forces brought about the disintegration of Christianity as a monolithic reality in western Europe. While it is customary to attribute the Reformation to the reforming genius of Martin Luther (1483-1546), Huldrych Zwingli (1484-1531), and John Calvin (1509-1564), its causes were much more complex. The Western Schism, that period in the history of the church from 1378 to 1417 when there were first two, and later three, rival popes, the corruption of the Renaissance papacy, the divorce of piety from theology, and of theology from biblical and patristic traditions, and the rise of the nation state were all significant causes of the Reformation.[1]

As the story of missionary women in the early modern age begins, it is important to discover if these events—the discovery of the Americas, the Renaissance and the Reformation—so momentous for men, were equally important for women. The discovery and colonization of the New World significantly influenced the subsequent development of mission. Opinions vary about the consequences of the Renaissance for women. Joan Kelly-

---

1. See Richard P. McBrien, *Catholicism*, 2 vols. (East Malvern, Vic.: Dove Communications, 1980), 2:631.

Gadol asks if women had a renaissance, and believes that the answer is no,[2] as women's experiences differ substantially from those of men. Her analysis, restricted to the nobility and upper bourgeoisie, claims that the Renaissance strengthened the division between the domestic and the public realm, a process that culminated in the loss of economic, political, and cultural power for noble women. "All the advances of Renaissance Italy, its protocapitalist economy, its states, and its humanistic culture, worked to mould the noble-woman into an aesthetic object: decorous, chaste and doubly dependent— on her husband as well as on the prince."[3] Caroline Bynum Walker, on the other hand, believes that opportunities for women increased significantly in the sixteenth century.[4] As we shall see, although mission in the early modern era was a male event, by the seventeenth century, French women were seiz-ing the opportunity to go to Canada as missionaries.

William Monter argues that neither the Protestant nor the Catholic Ref-ormation encouraged new ideologies about the place and status of women in society or in the church. Rather, both reformations reaffirmed patriarchal dominance in church and in the home. He believes that the witch hunts of the sixteenth century pointed to the basically misogynistic climate of the time, and that improvement in the position of women began in the mid-sev-enteenth century when the horror of witch hunts was abating.[5] Of particu-lar import for Catholic women who wished to be involved in missionary work was Tridentine legislation concerning the cloister. As we saw earlier, the papal bull *Periculoso* responded to jurisdictional rather than missionary issues, and effectively deprived women of their right to be involved in mis-sionary activity through its insistence on the cloister. Trent, motivated by an ideology that argued that nuns, more than monks, needed the safeguard of the cloister to protect their chastity, reaffirmed such discriminatory legisla-tion. In 1566, Pius V decreed that strict enclosure was required of tertiaries; thus even those who had not made solemn vows had to be cloistered.

These decrees, in both their original and Tridentine promulgations, were intended to protect women from their presumed deficiencies and weaknesses, although Jo Ann Kay McNamara is probably correct in stating that "the real reason was not cloistering but clerical control."[6] There is little argument about the laxity, and on occasion, sexual immorality associated with con-vent life in the late Middle Ages and early modern era, and this persuaded

---

2. See Joan Kelly-Gadol, "Did Women Have a Renaissance?" in *Becoming Visible—Women in European History*, ed. Renate Bridethal, Claudia Koonz, and Susan Stuard (Boston: Houghton Mifflin, 1987), 174-201.

3. Ibid., 197.

4. See Caroline Bynum Walker, *Holy Feast and Holy Fast: The Religious Significance of Food to Medieval Women* (Berkeley: University of California Press, 1987).

5. See William Monter, "Protestant Wives, Catholic Saints, and the Devil's Handmaid: Women in the Age of the Reformation," in *Becoming Visible*, ed. Bridethal et al., 202-19.

6. Jo Ann Kay McNamara, *Sisters in Arms: Catholic Nuns through Two Millennia* (Cam-bridge/London: Harvard University Press, 1996), 461.

the council to restrict nuns' contact with society to a minimum. But Ruth Liebowitz points out that it was not only ecclesial pressure that led to such legislation but also the social mores of the time, because "families of upper-class nuns had an interest in preventing their daughters in convents from disgracing their family name . . . For unmarried women, honor was synonymous with virginity, and to protect it, families favored a form of seclusion for young, unmarried girls at home, as well in the convent."[7]

We need now to turn to the story of those women whose lives and work identify them as missionary, despite discriminatory church legislation and the cultural mores of the time. In this and the following chapters, I will limit my study to the story of Catholic women. This is not intended to minimize the extraordinary contribution that Protestant women have made to Christian mission, but the Protestant story has received much greater coverage than the story of Catholic missionary women, so it is to the latter I now turn.

It is often assumed that the Reformation began with a bang in October 1517, when a disillusioned Augustinian German monk, Martin Luther, nailed his ninety-five theses on the church door at Wittenberg. The Reformation began long before that, however, and its origins lay in Catholicism as well as in what later was termed Protestantism. It is now recognized that the Catholic Church in the century before Luther's posting of his theses was not as "corrupt and ineffective as Protestants have portrayed it, and that it generally satisfied the spiritual needs of late medieval people."[8] American Jesuit John O'Malley sees "both the Protestant Reformation and its Catholic counterpart as two different expressions of the same reforming impulse that ante-date 1517."[9] In other words, Catholic reform predated the Council of Trent (1545-1563). That council was preoccupied with church discipline, particularly insofar as it related to formation for, and exercise of, ecclesial office. The council "hoped to accomplish its moral and pastoral goals principally through canonical discipline."[10]

It is against the background of the discovery of the Americas, the Renaissance, and the Reformation that I propose to explore and critique the contributions that women made to Catholic mission. Again, my choice is representative rather than exhaustive, and will include Teresa of Avila, Angela Merici, Mary Ward, Jeanne de Chantal, Louise de Marillac, and two

---

7. Ruth P. Liebowitz, "Virgins in the Service of Christ: The Dispute over an Active Apostolate for Women during the Counter-Reformation," in *Women of Spirit: Female Leadership in the Jewish and Christian Traditions*, ed. Rosemary Ruether and Eleanor McLaughlin (New York: Simon & Schuster, 1979), 140.

8. Diarmaid MacCulloch, *Reformation: Europe's House Divided 1490-1700* (London: Allen Lane, 2003), xxiii.

9. See John O'Malley, "Was Ignatius Loyola a Church Reformer? How to Look at Early Modern Catholicism?" in *The Counter-Reformation*, ed. David M. Luebke (Malden, Mass.: Blackwell, 1999), 67.

10. Ibid., 69.

French women, Ursuline Marie Guyart and Marguerite Bourgeys, who went as missionaries to the New World.

## TERESA OF AVILA, 1515-1582

Teresa of Avila was not a missionary per se. Her vocation was as a contemplative Carmelite of the strict observance, but her high public profile as she embarked on her reform of Carmel means that we cannot ignore her contribution to the mission of the post-Reformation church as it sought to resist the inroads that Protestantism was making. To better appreciate her importance, it is necessary to understand something of the religious and political context of Spain in the first half of the sixteenth century, particularly with regard to women. Two important institutions made a significant impact on Spanish Catholicism, and therefore on Teresa's efforts to reform. The first of these, the Inquisition, addressed problems posed by groups whose presence threatened the institutional church—the *judaizantes, luteranos,* and *alumbrados.* The *judaizantes,* Jewish converts to Catholicism, were accused of still observing certain Jewish rituals. Teresa's grandfather was one of the *judaizantes.* While there is no disputing Teresa's Jewish ancestry, it is more difficult to determine how much she knew about it, how she regarded it, and how much it influenced her.[11] Similarly, there was an ecclesial nervousness about *luteranos,* those who had actually embraced Lutheranism, and more importantly those Catholics thought to favor certain aspects of Lutheranism, such as its antipapal sentiments or reductionist approach to the sacraments. Finally, the *alumbrados,* those men and women who claimed that their mystical prayer opened them to special enlightenment and even revelation from God, were another group in whom the Inquisition was particularly interested. For the *alumbrados,* knowledge and experience of God were not primarily mediated through ecclesial authorities but through the personal promptings of the Holy Spirit. Although the nomenclature, *alumbrados,* was used of both men and women, it was more commonly applied to women and pointed to an alternative, often feminine, but authoritative source of knowledge about God, something that an increasingly patriarchal and clerical church found hard to accept.

The second important institution was the Index of Prohibited Books, the child of the Inquisition, first issued in 1559 by Fernando Valdés and revised along more rigorous lines in 1583-1584. The Index was intended "to limit the scope of religious speculation and to define religious faith and practice very narrowly as the province of an educated elite whose task was not spec-

---

11. See Rowan Williams, *Teresa of Avila,* ed. Brian Davies (London: Geoffrey Chapman, 1991), 34-38. Williams provides a helpful summary of the influence of Teresa's Jewish ancestry on her life and work.

ulation but transmission of doctrine."[12] The invention of printing in the mid-fifteenth century and the subsequent appearance of books in the vernacular concerned the church, as it allowed for people other than Latin-educated clerics to access more readily theological and spiritual writings. "It changed the religious and intellectual history of Christendom."[13]

The Inquisition and the Index, coupled with clerical concern about *alumbrados*, meant that women reformers were often enough on the receiving end of the church's disciplinary efforts. Spanish women were characterized as *mujercitas*, "'little women,' a term that signaled women's political, social, and spiritual powerlessness."[14] As Dominican Martín de Córdoba, writing in the late fifteenth century stated, "Reason is not so strong in them [women] as in men, and with their greater reason men keep carnal passions in check; but women are more flesh than spirit, and therefore are more inclined to the passions than to the spirit."[15] Men assumed that women were their intellectual inferiors and were more "easily confused and deceived by visionary and revelatory experiences."[16] Knowledge of the divine that was experiential, mediated through mystical prayer and therefore less controllable, was considered inferior to intellectual knowledge that belonged to Latin-educated ordained ministers. Church authorities sought to diminish the influence of women who claimed mystical experiences by stressing their moral and intellectual inferiority, and therefore their need to be obedient, humble, and ascetical, and preferably cloistered.[17]

In 1554, after having been a Carmelite for twenty years, Teresa committed herself to founding new and reformed Carmels for women who wanted to pursue holiness through the practice of mystical prayer and virtue. Her reforming zeal also points to her missionary zeal, for "according to her contemporaries, Teresa . . . wished she had the freedom to travel to other countries to speak stirring words and convert Protestants back to Catholicism."[18]

---

12. Gillian T. W. Ahlgren, *Teresa of Avila and the Politics of Sanctity* (Ithaca, N.Y.: Cornell University Press, 1966), 17. Ahlgren's work assesses Teresa's significance within the context of sixteenth-century Spain.

13. Owen Chadwick, *The Early Reformation on the Continent*, ed. Henry and Owen Chadwick (Oxford: Oxford University Press, 2003), 1. By 1500 there were some 27,000 printed titles, nearly three-quarters Latin books, but there were also vernacular books of piety and prayer. The printers' chief object was the Bible—94 Latin Bibles by 1500, 16 German Bibles by 1522, and usually printed with a commentary.

14. Ahlgren, *Teresa of Avila*, 7.

15. Ibid., citing Martín de Córdoba, *Tratado que se intitula Jardin de las nobles doncellas*, ed. Fernando Rubio (Madrid, 1946), 91.

16. Ahlgren, *Teresa of Avila*, 8.

17. See ibid., 145-66. Ahlgren argues that Teresa, the reforming Carmelite who struggled against the Inquisition and the Index in order to claim a teaching and reforming role for herself in sixteenth-century Spain, was transformed by the Tridentine canonization process into a humble, obedient, and ascetical daughter of the church. Tridentine reformers were more interested in obedient daughters than prophetic women.

18. Ibid., 36.

For a woman this was an almost impossible task, and instead, "Teresa established as one of the Discalced Carmelites' special missions the support of the efforts of friars and priests through their prayers."[19] Catholic women, like their male counterparts, believed wholeheartedly in the reforming and evangelizing mission of the Tridentine church, but, given that their opportunities were limited, they sought other ways of expressing that missionary spirit, hence Teresa's desire to "transform the cloister into a missionary field, using the image of the mystical body of Christ."[20]

Even though Teresa could not travel throughout Europe, she could engage in a teaching ministry directed to her Carmelite nuns. She believed that if her sisters were to become contemplatives and mystics, then it was important that they had access to spiritual and religious books, not only the spiritual classics such as Augustine's *Confessions* and Thomas à Kempis's *Imitation of Christ*, but to contemporary Christian treatises designed to help women embrace a life of mystical prayer and virtue. Such contemporary treatises, written in the vernacular, were usually prohibited by the Index, and Teresa was forced to become a writer and teacher herself. Her first work was the autobiographical *Book of Her Life*. This was "a defense of her way of prayer, her vocation and her entire persona,"[21] and was written to establish her credibility in a church where women's experiences were suspect. The normal meaning and context of prayer in the early sixteenth century was community, or group, prayer, specifically, the Divine Office, and the sacrifice of the Mass. Personal "contemplative" prayer was a novelty, and often regarded as subversive of ecclesial authority. Teresa's *Life* was followed by *The Way of Perfection, The Book of Foundations,* and *The Interior Castle: The Mansions.*

From 1570 onward, there were investigations by the Inquisition of her works because her detractors sought to discredit her. Typical of her detractors' thinking was the criticism by the papal nuncio, who described Teresa as "a troublesome, restless, disobedient, and stubborn female, running around outside the cloister against the order of the Tridentine Council and prelates, instructing like a teacher in defiance of what St. Paul taught, who ordered women not to teach."[22] Although some officers of the Inquisition were negatively disposed toward her writings, others recognized her positive significance, and Teresa's oft-repeated promises of obedience to ecclesial authorities succeeded in allaying their fears.

Gillian Ahlgren argues that Teresa employed a variety of rhetorical strategies in her writings in order to profess her obedience and allegiance to ecclesial authorities. This led to Teresa's adopting a strategy of subordination to

---

19. Ibid.

20. McNamara, *Sisters in Arms*, 493.

21. Ahlgren, *Teresa of Avila*, 42.

22. Ibid., citing Francisco de Santa María, *Reforma de los descalozos de Nuestra Señora del Carmen de la primitiva observancia, hecha por Santa Teresa de Jesús* (Madrid, 1644-55), 1:556.

authority, which emphasized her humility and ignorance. At the same time, she believed that her mystical experiences meant that God spoke to her directly. Therefore, even though she was supposedly an ignorant, non-Latin-educated woman, her teachings merited attention because God revealed important truths to her. Ahlgren argues that this strategy of subordination to authority was a literary ploy used by Teresa to ensure that her reforming message was accepted. Similarly, Marie Anne Mayeskie refers to Teresa's literary strategy for gaining acceptance as a "rhetoric of protection,"[23] thereby highlighting the tactics Teresa used in order to gain, if not approval, then at least acceptance for her mystical theology.

That Teresa's strategy worked is apparent in the decision by the church to beatify her in 1614. At the same time even this honor led to an outpouring of writings about Teresa suggesting that her effectiveness and holiness as a reformer came about precisely because she had managed to overcome her femininity. "When Teresa was proclaimed co-patron saint of Spain, a Carmelite friar declared in a celebratory sermon that she had succeeded in transcending the congenital inferiority of her sex altogether: 'This woman ceased to be a woman, restoring herself to the virile state to her greater glory than if she had been a man from the beginning, for she rectified nature's error with her virtue, transforming herself through virtue into the bone [i.e., Adam's rib] from which she sprang.'"[24]

Teresa wanted her monasteries to reflect the poverty, simplicity, and egalitarianism that would subvert the class structure so entrenched in monasteries of the time. Her own experience of belonging to a recently converted Jewish family meant she had experienced the reality of social and religious class distinctions in sixteenth-century Spain, and their detrimental effect on community life. Therefore, she required that Discalced Carmelites were to adopt religious names as "[a]bandonment of titles, polite forms of address, and family names obliterated ethnic and social distinctions."[25] She insisted on the strict observance of poverty so that any woman, regardless of her socioeconomic status, could become a Discalced Carmelite.

Finally and most difficult of all was the question of gender relations. Though Teresa did not envisage Carmelite nuns and monks meeting together in chapter, she intended her reform to apply to male and female branches of the Discalced Carmelites, as the father general had asked of her in 1578; and so she founded male and female reformed Carmels throughout Spain. She worked closely with Rubeo, the Carmelite superior general, Gracian, the apostolic vicar, and with the Carmelite friar John of the Cross, who despite

---

23. See Marie Anne Mayeskie, *Women Models of Liberation* (New York: Sheed & Ward, 1989), 110-55.

24. Alison Weber, "Little Women: Counter-Reformation Misogyny," in *The Counter-Reformation*, ed. Luebke, citing Fray Franciso de Jesús, in *Relación sencilla y fiel de las fiestas que el rey D. Felipe IIII nuestro Señor hizo . . .* (Facticio volume: Vatican Library, 1627).

25. McNamara, *Sisters in Arms*, 496.

a significant disparity in age became her spiritual director. She wanted her Discalced Carmelite sisters to be free to choose their own confessors; she did not require prioresses to be obedient to priors, and she did not want a male provincial to act as confessor for the nuns. Ten years later, Carmelite monks gained authority over the nuns, and in 1604, discalced monks separated themselves from the nuns and embarked on missionary work.

Teresa is now emerging from the pages of feminist history as a champion of women's right to exercise a public role in the church. She herself resorted to irony to highlight some of the prejudices that worked against women in sixteenth-century Spain. Well aware that women had important pastoral roles in the church's effort to reform itself, she complained about the lack of appreciation for such roles: "Isn't it enough, Lord, that the world keeps us silenced and incapable of doing anything of value for You in public and we don't dare speak of truths we bewail in secret, but you won't hear our rightful petition? I don't believe it of such a good and just lord; you are a just judge, not like the world's judges, who since they are sons of Adam, and are, in short, all men, there is no female virtue they don't view as suspect."[26]

The significance of Teresa's reforming activities in the post-Tridentine church equals that of Ignatius of Loyola (1491-1556), founder of the Jesuits, and the impact of these two Spanish saints on the Catholic Church is unparalleled. Ignatius and the order he founded are identified as missionary, but, given Teresa's contribution to the Catholic Reformation, it is surely appropriate to also designate Teresa as missionary. It is also fitting, given her important literary output, that she was finally honored as a Doctor of the Church in 1970. Pope Paul VI aptly described her as a teacher of "marvelous profundity."[27]

## ANGELA MERICI, 1470-1540

Little is known of the early life of Angela. She was born in Brescia, northern Italy; her father was a peasant farmer, a free man who enjoyed civic rights, and her mother belonged to the lesser nobility. The death of both parents while Angela was still a child meant she was brought up by an uncle and never went to school. It is ironic, given her later importance as an educator, that while she could read, she apparently never learned to write. Though biographical details of her early life are sparse, hagiographical stories speak of Angela having a vision in which she was directed to set up a religious group. Angela first became a Franciscan tertiary and was formed in a spirituality that required the practice of penance, fasting, and poverty, and a min-

---

26. Ahlgren, *Teresa of Avila*, 88, quoting from Teresa de Jesús, *El camino de perfectión*, El Escorial version, 4:1.

27. See *Acta Apostolicae Sedis*, vol. 62, no. 9, 593.

istry to the poor. T. Ledóchowska believes that Angela's involvement with the Franciscans awakened in her a missionary spirit.

> The bond between Angela and the friars also served to widen her spiritual horizons to the limits of Christendom. Her vocation found its directive in their work, in such a way that the strength she had derived from contemplative prayer necessarily flowed into apostolic action; Angela, by her admission into the Third Order, came into contact with the most dynamic forces then working in the Church and found herself in the full current of the pre-Tridentine reform.[28]

The Franciscans were obviously a significant factor in her formation, but other forces were also at work. First, the Christian humanism associated with the Renaissance meant a new emphasis on the human person and, in particular, on the human intellect and the human capacity to strive after love and beauty. It was this that differentiated the human person from the rest of creation. Christian belief in the value of the human person encouraged Christian women from both the upper and middle classes to respond in a public and comprehensive fashion to the social and economic upheaval and therefore distress characteristic of sixteenth-century Lombardy. Second, Mary Malone points out that, following the example of the Beguines and before the Tridentine reform movement got under way, there was a movement among European women that sought to "transcend the invisibility of women's lives and exercise a public role in education, nursing and care of the poor. This was a religious impulse, wholly rooted in a gospel-inspired apostolic life and wholly exercised in the most ingenious and creative ways."[29] Finally, in sixteenth-century Europe, the moral, spiritual, and intellectual laxity characteristic of some monasteries and convents encouraged an impulse toward reform, both within the church and among those who later broke away. Therefore, in such an environment it is not surprising that Luther's ideas, thanks to printing and the use of the vernacular, were widely disseminated and accepted. Peter Waters believes that even as Lutheranism gained influence in North Italy, the "decline in fervor of priests and monks was matched by an increase in religious responsibility designed to protect the interests of the laity and the Church in general by the civil authority and individual laymen."[30] One expression of this lay concern was the founding of the Oratory

---

28. T. Ledóchowska, *Angela Merici and the Company of St. Ursula*, 2 vols. (Rome: Ancora, 1968), 1:29.

29. Mary T. Malone, *Women and Christianity*, vol. 3, *From the Reformation to the 21st Century* (Maryknoll, N.Y.: Orbis Books, 2003), 3:95.

30. Peter Maurice Waters, *The Ursuline Achievement: A Philosophy of Education for Women. St. Angela Merici, the Ursulines and Catholic Education* (North Carlton, Vic.: Colonna, 1994), 23.

of Divine Love in Vicenza, not far from Brescia, in 1495. The Oratory profoundly influenced Angela because it not only drew on the ethos and spirituality of the *devotio moderna* but adapted "comfortably to the Christian humanism of the northern Italian school. It not only cemented the spirituality and consequent charitable enterprise of the pre-Tridentine reform movement, but also became a cradle for post-Tridentine reform initiatives."[31]

By 1530, Lombardy was once again recovering from war, and the subsequent social unrest encouraged Angela to gather like-minded women around her to meet some of the emerging pastoral challenges. Initially she gathered twelve young women who would become the nucleus of a new religious community, the Company of St. Ursula,[32] and in 1536, the community was granted ecclesiastical approbation. Members did not make solemn vows but were required to make promises of poverty, chastity, and obedience. The Company represented a radical departure from the traditional monastic religious orders. The majority of members were from the middle and lower classes, as Angela sought to avoid the social stratification of the older monastic convents. Governance was the responsibility of the mother general, who was assisted by mature and wise women entrusted with responsibility for the welfare of the younger virgins. Four male attorneys provided advice concerning the financial and material aspects of government. Even more radical was the fact that members were uncloistered, able to live alone or in their homes with their families; they undertook apostolic works, such as the education of young women and care of the sick. The influence of Christian humanism is obvious as "Angela's focus was always on practical ways to help women toward a better sense of themselves as women."[33] Angela died in 1540, before Pius V's legislation in 1563, which reintroduced the cloister for all women, impacted her community. The innovative, indeed radical, character of the Company of St. Ursula can be readily gleaned from the three documents Angela had written for members: the *Regola* (Rule), the *Arricordi* (Counsels), and the *Testamento* (Testament).

The growth of the community was extraordinary. By 1540, when Angela died, there were one hundred and fifty members, some of whom lived in community and some of whom chose to remain with their families. The bishop of Brescia had approved of the community, and they were engaged in a variety of apostolic works—care of the poor and the sick, many of whom were syphilitic, burying the dead, and teaching women and girls. However, their very success "raised issues of control, especially in the light of the

---

31. Ibid., 17.
32. According to legend, St. Ursula was a British princess, who with her virgin companions was martyred at Cologne at the close of the third century. During the Middle Ages, Ursula was regarded as a protector of girl students. The universities of Paris, Vienna, and Coimbra named her as their patron. Hildegaard had great devotion to Ursula, as did Elisabeth of Schönau.
33. Malone, *Women and Christianity,* 3:96.

restrictive attitude of the Council of Trent to women's religious organization and its insistence of enclosure of convents."[34] Members of the Company of St. Ursula were to become nuns. This process began with the decision of Lucrezia Lodrone, Angela's successor, that members wear a special dress that emphasized their difference from nonmembers, and live in a common dwelling. In 1566, Charles Borromeo, bishop of Milan and a leading player in the Tridentine reform, insisted that the Ursulines be brought under episcopal authority and that their rule be modified so that their way of life more closely approximated that of monastic nuns. In 1572, Borromeo revised the rule of the Milan Company, which was under his control, and "in effect he remolded Angela's original company into a religious order called the Ursulines, an order quite distinct from the Brescian Company."[35]

Cardinal Borromeo's decision ignored the fact that Angela had sought and received a papal dispensation that freed her sisterhood from diocesan control. However, his own need for dedicated women to work in his diocese as educators (in 1584, there were six hundred Ursulines living in five communities, and running eighteen schools) and caregivers to the poor meant that he did not rigidly impose these laws on members. Though the contemplative dimension of the Ursuline vocation was emphasized, Ursulines were allowed to go out to teach in the various schools established by Borromeo. As Ruth Liebowitz writes, "Without their assistance, he could not have run this catechism program which was his response to the Protestant charges of religious ignorance in Papist lands."[36]

In 1597, the Milanese model was introduced in France, first in the diocese of Avignon, at that time still part of the papal states, so, in effect, the foundation "was a natural extension of the work as it had been established in northern Italy."[37] They spread rapidly so that prior to the French Revolution there were more than 10,000 Ursulines involved in the education, usually free, of girls in 320 institutions. This extraordinary apostolic outreach was achieved at some cost. The Ursulines, responding to a 1612 papal bull, had reverted to a monastic lifestyle: their schools were attached to or inside their convents, and they substituted the *Rule of St. Augustine* for that of Angela.[38]

---

34. Michael A. Mullett, *The Catholic Reformation* (London: Routledge, 1999), 107.

35. Patricia Raft, *Women and the Religious Life in Premodern Europe* (New York: St. Martin's Press, 1996), 106.

36. Liebowitz, "Virgins in the Service of Christ," 143.

37. Waters, *The Ursuline Achievement*, 34.

38. Historically and contemporaneously, Ursulines are divided as to the wisdom of the cloistered lifestyle. Ledóchowska writes, "it was not the austerity of monasticism that repelled them [Ursulines]; on the contrary, the desire for a contemplative life came to them without difficulty. Prayer held the first place in the lives of St. Angela and her daughters. The making of solemn vows was therefore welcomed with joy by Ursulines, in spite of the fear that their work would be hampered by the enclosure which was linked to these vows." See Waters, *The Ursuline Achievement*, 36, citing T. Ledóchowska, *Angela Merici and the Company of St. Ursula*, 165. On the other hand, M. de Chantal Gueudré argues that the French Ursulines believed that

Michael Mullett believes that "the case of France illustrates clearly the complex tensions between pressure towards conventual enclosure and the preservation of an active apostolate."[39] In France, the Ursuline communities attracted intending members from the upper middle classes, "especially its Catholic political class of counselors and *parlementaires*"[40] and its teaching mission "emphasized the systematic production of a future elite of Catholic women, wives and mothers"[41] trained in Catholic doctrine and practice, administration of a household, domestic skills, literacy, and arithmetic.

One important development in France was that Ursulines undertook to teach adults as well as children. This development began in 1616 when Mère de Bermond, a charismatic teacher, preached to the townspeople who gathered in the sisters' chapel on feast days and Sundays. Linda Lierheimer demonstrates that the congregation recognized that de Bermond was preaching a sermon rather than teaching. "The most respected people of the Town were always among the first to arrive; and seats were taken as at a Sermon. This lasted until the year 1623 when the male Superiors (with good reason, for this was an unusual thing) forbade the Sisters to teach any longer in the Church."[42] While Catholic reformers were anxious to involve women religious in apostolic activities such as nursing, teaching children, or works of charity, activities that could rightly be seen as extensions of their domestic work, there was less enthusiasm for women religious moving into the public space and, in effect, becoming preachers. There was certainly scope for Ursulines to minister as teachers and preachers given the magnitude of the task that faced seventeenth-century reformers in France, and many Ursulines "felt justified in taking on public roles that were traditionally the preserve of men. Although the Council of Trent had set the reform of the clergy as one of its central goals, efforts in this area had little effect on parish life in France before the middle of the seventeenth century."[43] Lay people, ecclesial authorities, and indeed the Ursulines themselves recognized the ambiguity of the Ursuline situation. However, the struggle against Protestantism meant that initially the Ursuline activism was welcomed, but as the Protestant threat receded, the position of the French ecclesial authorities toward the Ursulines

---

monasticism was imposed. The Ursulines accepted it "out of obedience to the Church, adding this sacrifice to others; obedience was often a holocaust for them." See Waters, *The Ursuline Achievement*, 36, citing M. de Chantal Gueudré, *Histoire de l'ordre des Ursulines en France*, 3 vols. (Paris: Editions Saint Paul, 1957), 103.

39. Mullett, *The Catholic Reformation*, 108.

40. Ibid.

41. Ibid.

42. Linda Lierheimer, "Preaching or Teaching? Defining the Ursuline Mission in Seventeenth-Century France," in *Women Preachers and Prophets through Two Millennia of Christianity*, ed. B. M. Kienzle and P. J. Walker (Berkeley: University of California Press, 1998), 212, citing Marie-Augustine de Pommereu, *Les Chroniques de l'ordre des Ursulines recueillies pour l'usage des Religieuses du mesme Ordre* (Paris, 1673), vol. 1, part 2, 173.

43. Ibid., 215.

was less ambiguous. Efforts and legislation to ensure a cloistered lifestyle for Ursulines were intended to curtail their public role, but people still flocked to hear them within the convent. Women were to engage in private instruction inside the convent, which necessarily restricted the numbers who could attend, but not in public preaching.

The Ursuline impact on women's involvement in mission was noteworthy. Not only did the various Ursuline congregations enjoy an unprecedented growth, but they provided a model for other women seeking a missionary identity in the church prior to the French Revolution, and, in particular, an identity that focused on the education of girls. In 1628, the Canonesses of St. Augustine of the Congregation of Notre Dame received papal approbation, and on the eve of the Revolution had over four thousand religious involved in the educational apostolate for girls in France and Germany. Irishwoman Nano Nagle founded the Irish Congregation of the Presentation of the Blessed Virgin Mary in 1777, and, like the Canonesses, ensured that her sisters followed a teaching methodology similar to that of the Ursulines.

The French Revolution meant the destruction of much of the education system of the *ancien régime,* and its leaders sought a replacement that ignored the pivotal role of the Catholic Church in education. While the different Ursuline congregations struggled on during the revolutionary era, eventually they were forced to disband; but in 1806 they were once again recognized as a teaching body whose pedagogical philosophies and practices were still important. It is not surprising, therefore, that Madeleine Sophie Barat turned to the Ursuline model when in 1801 she founded her congregation, the Society of the Sacred Heart. The Faithful Companions of Jesus, founded in Amiens in 1820, and the Sisters of St. Brigid, founded in Ireland in 1807, also drew on Ursuline educational philosophy.[44] Angela's innovative approach to the role of the women in mission probably owes more to the lay movements of the late Middle Ages than it does to monasticism. Her charism was one that could adapt to the realities of the changing political and religious realities of sixteenth-, seventeenth-, and eighteenth-century Europe. She inspired countless women to live the evangelical life in new ways and to embrace new ministries within the church, and she deserves to be acknowledged as one of the great missionary and reforming figures of Tridentine Catholicism.

## MARY WARD, 1585-1645

Mary Ward was born into a fervent recusant family in Yorkshire, three years before the defeat of the Spanish Armada, and fourteen years after Pius V's bull *Regnum in Excelsis* demanded that all English Catholics show their allegiance to the pope by attempting to dethrone Queen Elizabeth. The defeat

---

44. See Waters, *The Ursuline Achievement,* 97-109.

of the Spanish Armada meant that the "harsh anti-recusant penal laws reflected the situation of a nation the survival of whose government and indeed, whose very identity were threatened by Catholic Spain under Philip II."[45] Almost all the conspirators in the ill-fated plot masterminded by Guy Fawkes to blow up the House of Parliament in 1605 were Mary's relatives. Mary, then, grew up with the expectation of suffering and possibly of martyrdom, and it was in the context of harsh repression that she conceived of her vocation as working for the conversion of England through the Catholic education of young women. Realizing the difficulties this would entail, she left England for a more Catholic-friendly environment in which to prepare herself.

She journeyed to the Spanish Netherlands in 1606 and joined the contemplative and enclosed Poor Clare community. She soon discerned, however, that she was not called to a contemplative life and returned to England where she made the Spiritual Exercises of St. Ignatius. That, coupled with the example of English Jesuits in England and in Europe, where they ministered to English Catholics who had fled persecution, persuaded her that she was called to found a religious order whose work would be the Catholic education of women. Furthermore, her order would take as its model the Jesuits, whose spirituality and ministry so deeply impressed her. Like Angela Merici, Mary envisaged that her institute would not be cloistered, nor would its members wear a distinctive dress, and it would be governed by women. The apostolic and missionary quality of her vision is apparent. As Lavinia Byrne writes, Mary expected of her companions

> a desire to love and serve God in joy and freedom; the ability to prize truth; an apostolic spirit. As well as opening girls' schools in Europe, they would return to the mission field of England, for there were many families who would shelter active exponents of the Gospel; many homes in which she and her sisters could give the Spiritual Exercises of Ignatius to devout lay people out of the glare of the public eye. They were in less danger than the missionary priests—though the [Anglican] Archbishop of Canterbury said of her that she was "worse than seven Jesuits." Praise indeed.[46]

In 1609, Mary returned to St. Omer in the Spanish Netherlands. She and her companions, calling themselves the Institute of the Blessed Virgin Mary, began a ministry among Catholic émigré adults, and a ministry of education for English children as well as those of local inhabitants. These two groups were soon to be joined by boarders from England, because families who were

---

45. Mullett, *The Catholic Reformation,* 109.

46. Lavinia Byrne, "Spiritual Stars of the Millennium: 25, Mary Ward (1585-1645)," *The Tablet* (June 24, 2000), 878.

already sending their sons to the Jesuit college wanted something similar for their daughters. Margaret Mary Littlehales states that Mary's intention was "to train English girls from Catholic families to be wives and mothers or religious, but all to be apostles for the Faith in England."[47] Mary's students received a comprehensive education in which Latin figured prominently because English recusants regarded Latin as part of their ecclesiastical heritage and all had a great love and respect for the Latin of the Vulgate Bible. "It was part of Catholic belief, and particularly in England, that the vernacular versions, starting with the Tyndale and ending with the King James' version of 1611, were at the root of all the reformers' heresies."[48] Mary, aware of the persecution and deaths of so many English priests, recognized that wives and mothers would have to assume responsibility for religious instruction in the home. By 1611, forty young women had joined her community, despite its noncanonical status. The community suffered financial insecurity, for new members usually arrived without a dowry because parents were wary about giving money to noncanonical groups.

There was growing pressure on Mary from friend and foe alike to adopt one of the four classical rules for religious life: Augustinian, Benedictine, Franciscan, or Teresian (Carmelite). If Mary had followed this advice, then her community would have been transformed into one of enclosed contemplatives, whereas she saw her group as living an apostolic vocation and believed that the Jesuit *Rule,* with its strong missionary focus, lack of cloister, and central governmental structures, was more appropriate for her fledgling community. It was not long before Mary experienced ecclesiastical wrath and, indeed, persecution. In her efforts to ensure an apostolic life for her sisters modeled on that of the Jesuits, she journeyed six times from northern Europe to Rome in order to plead her case before reluctant popes. She was constantly on the receiving end of censure and criticism from clerics in England and in Europe. This opposition did not prevent her institute from establishing houses and schools not only in St. Omer, but also in Liège, Rome, Perugia, Naples, Munich, Pressburg, and Vienna. In 1631 Urban VIII, the pope who condemned Galileo, suppressed the Institute, and this "merely on the basis of English clerical calumnies and calumnies spawned by the hurt pride of ambitious continental clerics."[49] This led to Mary's imprisonment in a Poor Clare convent in Munich, by order of the Roman Inquisition. Mary was described in the papal bull as a "heretic, schismatic, and rebel against

47. Margaret Mary Littlehales, *Mary Ward: Pilgrim and Mystic, 1585-1645* (Tunbridge Wells: Burns & Oates, 1998), 62.
48. M. Emmanuel Orchard, ed., *Till God Will: Mary Ward through Her Writings* (London: Darton, Longman & Todd, 1985), xvii.
49. Lawrence F. Barmann, "Mary Ward: Centuries Her Scroll," *Review for Religious 59* (2000): 612.

holy church." The reason given for the suppression was that "the sisters had 'carried out works by no means suiting the weakness of their sex, womanly modesty, above all virginal purity—works which men, who are most experienced in the knowledge of Sacred Scripture and the conduct of affairs, undertake with difficulty and not without great caution.'"[50] Even though the personal charges against Mary were later dropped, the bull described unenclosed religious communities as "pernicious growths," basically unnecessary, as women are "incapable of the knowledge necessary for teaching scripture."

Her refusal to embrace the enclosure, her vision of apostolic women educating other women, and her desire to follow the Jesuit *Rule* were insurmountable obstacles in the early seventeenth century. Her Institute could survive only "in the approved form of an enclosed religious Order. Ward's mistake had been to create a society which threatened male assumptions about the Church because it was too similar to male structures of authority."[51] By 1703, the prescriptions of the papal bull had been rescinded, and in 1749, Pope Benedict XIV, in *Quamvis Iusto,* approved Mary Ward's Institute of the Blessed Virgin Mary as a bona fide religious congregation. "Though the ruling upheld the right of bishops to local control over all convents in their dioceses, it approved the right of this unenclosed institute to remain organized."[52] Mary had challenged papal and Tridentine constraints on women's orders, in particular the cloister and the need for episcopal rule, asking instead that, like the Jesuits, her community be directly under the authority of the pope. She favored a system of centralized government with an elected superior general. Benedict's decree, *Quamvis Iusto,* still upheld the rights of local bishops to exercise control over convents in their dioceses, but it did approve a new form of religious life, and so did away with an enforced cloistered life as the norm for women. In 1877, the Institute finally received papal approbation, and one hundred years later, after 366 years, the Institute was allowed to adopt the Jesuit Constitutions. Mary died in Yorkshire in 1645, not as a broken woman, but one whose missionary project was "destroyed by little more than unreasoning ecclesiastical anti-feminism and prejudice."[53] In 1983, while in York, Pope John Paul II declared that he wished to beatify her during his pontificate, but unfortunately this had not happened prior to his death in 2005.

---

50. Malone, *Women and Christianity*, 3:109, citing the 1631 papal bull of suppression *Pastoralis Romani Pontificis*.

51. MacCulloch, *Reformation*, 644.

52. Mary Peckham Magray, *The Transforming Power of Nuns: Women, Religion and Cultural Change in Ireland, 1750-1900* (New York: Oxford University Press, 1998), 8.

53. Mullett, *The Catholic Reformation*, 110.

## JEANNE DE CHANTAL, 1567-1641,
## AND LOUISE DE MARILLAC, 1591-1660

In the sixteenth and seventeenth centuries, Catholic reform occurred in two competing ways. First, some Catholics sought reform through a return to the past. After all, the different heresies that appeared so threatening to the church were linked to the use of the vernacular for reading the Bible, theological writings, and discussions, and to the discovery of printing, which proved important for the growth of a more informed and articulate laity. Protestant reformers claimed that they were returning to the scriptures in order to find a scripture-based foundation for their theological thought. Catholic Church authorities believed that virtue could be reclaimed through a return to the "*status quo*—the way Christendom used to be before sin and division came upon it. Catholic reformers looked back to a golden age, an age of faith, and hoped to recreate it by returning the Church to its pristine state, and by rooting out the novelties which they considered akin to heresy."[54] Such a mindset understood reform as restorationist rather than as a forward-looking movement. We have already seen how this posed immense difficulties and trials for Teresa, Angela and the Company of St. Ursula, and Mary Ward.

Second, other Catholic reformers, such as Ignatius and the women founders and refounders, were aware that the times demanded innovation. Catholic reformers were caught "in this clash between reformism and apostolic fervor."[55] Such tension created problems for two French women, Jeanne de Chantal and Louise de Marillac. Both these laywomen were *dévotes*, "pious members of the laity who were identified by their extreme religiosity and practice of social work."[56] As Elizabeth Rapley shows, "*dévot* spirituality was, so to speak, bonded to good works."[57]

Jeanne was born into a wealthy bourgeois family in France, and after the death of her mother, while still an infant, Jeanne was raised and educated by her lawyer father and her aunt. She was given a solid education, which included knowledge of financial and legal matters. Jeanne was widowed after being happily married for eight years to Baron de Chantal. In 1604, she first came into contact with Francis de Sales (1567-1622), bishop of Geneva, a meeting that led to a deeply rewarding spiritual and apostolic partnership. Francis's great gift to the church was to articulate a spirituality for committed lay women and men who wished to serve God in the world. Jeanne was so attracted to this that she asked Francis to be her spiritual director. This

---

54. Elizabeth Rapley, *The Dévotes: Women and Church in Seventeenth-Century France*, McGill-Queen's Studies in the History of Religion 4, ed. G. A. Rawlyk (Montreal: McGill-Queen's University Press, 1993), 23.

55. Ibid., 24.

56. Raft, *Women and the Religious Life*, 118.

57. Rapley, *The Dévotes*, 77.

was fortuitous because Francis, aware of the spiritual and material poverty of many, realized that cloistered monasteries were no longer able to respond to such needs. He saw the need for communities of women, not hindered by solemn vows or the cloister, who could minister to the poor and the sick. At the same time, he recognized the importance of the contemplative dimension of such a life and wanted a community that would "combine Martha's charitable activity with Mary's contemplative virtue."[58] The widowed Jeanne was searching for a life of perfection. Family obligations and her often poor health ruled out the possibility of a strictly observant monastic life, but not a life of prayer and ministry to the poor in the world.

In 1610, six years after Jeanne and Francis first met, the community of the Visitation (Visitandines) was established at Annecy. The new community had a number of goals. First, it sought to provide a place of prayer and quiet, "a simplified monastic routine,"[59] for wives and mothers who would need to return to their families when this was required of them. Second, members were to visit, in a spirit of love, compassion, and concern, the poor and sick. Third, widows were to be welcomed to the community, and, finally, women could stay with the community for times of retreat. This was certainly innovative and suited the needs of women who, like Jeanne, had significant family and administrative responsibilities. Jeanne's obvious administrative and financial skills served her well in the years ahead when she was asked to establish other communities.

In 1615, a community was established in Lyon at the request of Archbishop de Marquemont, but within a year he was forcibly expressing his concern about women moving around freely in public in the exercise of their ministry. Francis responded to such criticism by explaining that the vision that he and Jeanne shared was right for women with family responsibilities who wanted "a life of perfection." Their modified monastic life, their ministry to the poor, their simple vows, their modest dress, and their asceticism allowed for such women to be actively involved in addressing the missionary challenges the church faced in the early seventeenth century. Marquemont also demanded that the title "Visitation" be replaced by his choice, "Présentation de Notre Dame," a nomenclature that clearly indicated that women "were to be confined to the holy place that was their monastery."[60] Francis's response to Marquemont is worth noting: "woman . . . no less than man, enjoys the favor of having been made in the image of God; the honor is done equally to both sexes; their virtues are equal; to each of them is offered an equal reward, and, if they sin, a similar damnation. I would not want a woman to say: I am frail, my condition is weak. The weakness is of the flesh, but virtue, which is strong and powerful is seated in the soul."[61]

---

58. McNamara, *Sisters in Arms*, 465.
59. Malone, *Women and Christianity*, 3:114.
60. Rapley, *The Dévotes*, 36-37.
61. Ibid., 37, citing François de Sales, *Oeuvres Complètes* (Annecy, 1892-1908), 25:291-92.

Francis insisted to Marquemont that his and Jeanne's vision of a non-cloistered lifestyle followed the practice of the early church, as the first Christians' "saintly simplicity did not require such severity."[62] His correspondence with Marquemont illustrated the two different reforming thrusts operative in the Catholic Church and the impact this had on women seeking to develop active, apostolic lives for themselves. Jeanne and Francis sought the involvement of women in society, and believed striving for perfection was an interior task, whereas Marquemont, concerned about innovation that could smack of Protestantism, understood reform as a return to the status quo, and for women a return to a cloistered religious life in which they made solemn vows. Middle- and upper-class parents only too happily acquiesced to Marquemont's thinking. The Tridentine reformers' insistence on women being cloistered and making solemn vows also had important civil implications for nuns (and monks). The absolute renouncement of patrimony and marriage that solemn vows meant was equivalent to civil death, and, in effect, nuns became nonpersons, lacking any power to claim worldly rights or goods. This was reassuring for families "with estates to consider. They [parents] valued the assurance that their children, once entered into the religious state, could not be resurrected to complicate the inheritance."[63] Given the opposition of the church and the wider Catholic Lyonnais population, Francis, acknowledging the archbishop's authority, agreed to his demand.

Like Angela Merici and Mary Ward before them, Jeanne and Francis could not sway powerful church dignitaries with their personal holiness, and they were obliged to accept a cloistered and monastic life for their community. In 1618, the Order of the Visitation was canonically established by Pope Pius V, and in 1624, it had received a papal bull of approbation from Pope Urban VIII. By the end of the seventeenth century, there were one hundred and fifty convents with over six thousand nuns. Jeanne died later in 1641, strenuously resisting ecclesiastical attempts to introduce inspections by appointed clergy in order to supervise the conventual life of the order. Discussions with episcopal authorities concerning the apostolic character of the Visitation community were the responsibility of Francis rather than of Jeanne, although it was the latter who was the inspiration behind the founding and spread of the Order. This indicates that it was easier and more appropriate for Francis to negotiate with Marquemont than it was for Jeanne.

The story of Louise de Marillac and the Daughters of Charity, which she co-founded with Vincent de Paul (1580-1660), is the story of the first apostolic women's congregation to get papal approval for its original rule. This happened in 1633. Louise was born into a middle-class family, though some have suggested that she was illegitimate, and, like Jeanne, she was widowed

---

62. Ibid., citing *Oeuvres*, 25:311.
63. Rapley, *The Dévotes*, 39.

at an early age. Although she had been happily married, she often wondered whether she had a vocation to religious life. In 1623, she met Vincent de Paul, who became her spiritual director and with whom she went on to found a new religious family. Vincent was already involved in wide-ranging apostolic works in which he was supported by laypeople, including a group of aristocratic women, the Ladies of Charity, who worked with the sick and the poor in the slums of Paris. Louise, one of the Ladies, and Vincent recognized that more effective and planned service was required if the needs of the poor were to be adequately met. Just as Francis played an important role to Jeanne, Vincent played an important role to Louise, and he was very clear about what was required: "Your convent will be the house of the sick; your cell, a hired room; your chapel the parish church; your cloister, the streets of the city or the wards of the hospital; your enclosure, obedience; your grating, the fear of God; your veil, holy modesty."[64]

Although the efforts of the Ladies of Charity were commendable, Louise recognized that their aristocratic backgrounds were inadequate preparation for such work, and that younger and stronger women who had some personal experience of poverty would be better suited to the task. In 1633, she accepted into her home four young country women who could be trained in nursing and religion. Vincent supported her in her efforts and, as others were seeking to join her community, she drew up statutes that Vincent, well versed in Canon Law, approved. The growth of the Daughters of Charity was steady; funds were provided by the Ladies of Charity, and Louise was careful to allow entry only to those young women who seemed capable of ministry to the poor and sick. Louise was an extremely capable administrator, and the young community flourished, so that in 1647, Louise and Vincent wrote a Rule for the fledgling congregation, which was to be a prototype secular institute caring for the destitute and sick. In 1658, papal approval was granted.

Louise and Vincent seemed to have realized their aims in a way that eluded other religious founders of the time. A number of reasons account for their success. First, the financial assistance and political support of the aristocratic class; second, the respect that Vincent de Paul enjoyed and his support for Louise legitimated her efforts in a way that was denied to Mary Ward; third, the fact that the Daughters took only annual, private vows without witnesses meant that they could remain uncloistered and hence pursue their ministry to the poor and sick in society—although at the cost of being perceived as less than proper nuns—and finally, given that initially the members came from the lower and poorer classes, concerns about dowries and family reputation were less important. But as Patricia Raft points out, despite

---

64. Vincent de Paul, *Correspondence, Entretiens, Documents*, 14 vols. (Paris: Librarie Lecoffre, 1923), 10:662.

"canon law, inheritance and feudal law, and the social status of women aside, society in general finally realized that these women were providing an irreplaceable service."[65]

The stories of the Ursulines, the Visitandines, and the Daughters of Charity in France do not exhaust the narrative of the role played by women in the sixteenth and seventeenth centuries. These are the stories that have received the most attention, but there were many other new active communities founded, especially in France, in the post-Tridentine era. The papacy and episcopate, aware of the contribution these women were making to church and society, "remained legislatively silent on the issues concerning new active orders until the twentieth century."[66] In 1890, Leo XIII belatedly recognized their contribution in the papal bull *Conditae a Christo*. The lives of women such as Angela Merici, Mary Ward, Jeanne de Chantal, and Louise de Marillac, and the communities they founded, parallel the better-known male foundations or reformed congregations such as the Jesuits and Capuchins. Christian humanism, the Tridentine emphasis on the value of good works, and the Renaissance humanists' praise of the *vita activa* led these women to strive for a more organized and ethical response to social problems. French women, however, did not restrict their efforts to within France, and in the seventeenth century, they journeyed to the New World to participate in the mission there.

## MISSIONARIES TO THE NEW WORLD:
## MARIE GUYART, 1599-1672, AND
## MARGUERITE BOURGEYS, 1620-1700

Marie Guyart, Ursuline, and Marguerite Bourgeys, founder of the Congregation of Notre Dame of Montreal, were two French women who embraced a missionary, apostolic life in Canada. They were not alone; other French women missionaries include Marie Martin and Marie-Madeleine de la Peltrie, who, with the support of the Jesuits and with their own considerable financial resources because of their widowhood, began a Quebec-based mission to the Algonquin and Iroquois peoples. Marie Martin learned their languages and wrote dictionaries and devotional works for these two First Nation peoples. As Malone writes, "the devotional ferment of old France"[67] led to courageous women undertaking to be missionaries in new France.

In 1639, French Ursuline Marie Guyart (Marie de l'Incarnation), departed for Canada, then a French colony, accompanied by three other Ursulines and three nursing sisters. The journey was made possible through the generosity

---

65. Raft, *Women and the Religious Life*, 121.
66. Ibid., 122.
67. Malone, *Women and Christianity*, 3:127.

of Marie-Madeleine de la Peltrie. The group's initial aim was to convert and educate "the dear savages," some of whom would, it was hoped, ask to become part of the Ursuline community. As Marie's correspondence makes clear, she was aware that the numerical and cultural dominance of the settler population posed significant threats to indigenous life and culture. Further, the four Ursulines were obliged to carry out their mission among the young Algonquian, Iroquois, and Huron women and girls during the cold winter season when the harsh climate precluded the young women from being involved in other work. Marie and her companions intended that these young tribal women would interact with, and be integrated into, the settler population. The settlers and the bishops, however, thought otherwise. The Ursulines were forced to segregate the First Nation girls from the settlers' daughters, because the parents of the latter chose to pay for their daughters' education. Settler parents appeared more interested that their daughters become genteel ladies than that they associate with "the savages," hence the need for a segregated, fee-based education.

Although Marie and her companions embraced a noncloistered life, after her death, episcopal decisions obliged the sisters to adopt an enclosed, monastic lifestyle. Further evidence of the patriarchal nature of seventeenth-century church and settler life in Canada can be located in the biography of Marie Guyart that her son, Claude Martin, wrote. He identifies her ministry as ancillary to that of male missionaries. He devotes some energy to distinguishing between preaching and teaching, and although he briefly refers to his mother as a preacher, he is clear that preaching, a public task, did not belong to women because of their "lack of modesty, the sinful propensities of women, the unwillingness of public opinion to accept women in positions of authority, and the association of preaching with priesthood, an office definitely prohibited to women. For this reason, women, he said, could not be called simply apostles, a title reserved for men only, but they could be called apostolic women."[68] He succeeded in making his mother's mission subordinate to that of male missionaries.

Another important example of a woman engaging in mission in Canada is Marguerite de Bourgeoys. Born into an affluent family in Troyes, she left in 1653 for Montreal, where the governor was seeking educators. Initially she taught as *une congréganiste externe*, a type of lay associate with the cloistered nuns of the Congrégation de Notre-Dame of Troyes. In this capacity, she worked in the school associated with the convent and gave religious instruction in the surrounding neighborhood. However, she believed that she had a religious vocation, though not in a contemplative or penitential order. She found in the Lukan story of Mary's visit to her cousin Elizabeth the model for her vision of religious life—ministry exercised for and by laywomen. "It was to be a life without the traditional trappings of religious

---

68. Ibid., 134.

communities, where the poor would be as welcome as the rich, and which, far from just being tolerated for women, was positively enjoined on them by the example of Mary."[69] The severity of Montreal's climate made the establishment of a school for girls difficult, and initially her ministry led her to care for soldiers, whose pastoral needs were significant. In 1658, she was given a building that allowed her to open a school for the education of girls in Montreal. Although the first women who joined her in this ministry undertook to live in obedience and chastity, they were not religious. These were the beginnings of the first noncloistered teaching order in North America, later to be known as the Congregation de Notre Dame. As Rapley points out, the bishop of Montreal approved of them "on condition that they do not in the future aspire to religious life."[70] The young community flourished not only among the children of settlers but also among native girls, who were educated at the mission at Montagne so that they could later integrate themselves into French settler society.

Marguerite had been adamant that her community should practice a quite severe poverty and that it should never charge students for their education. Old age limited Marguerite's ability to be involved actively in decision making. This led younger members, who did not always share her enthusiasm for a life of rigorous poverty, to seek a more moderate lifestyle that reflected their growing importance and status in the colony. Many of the settlers supported them in this. It was argued that Marguerite had not kept up with history; and while the austerity of lifestyle she regarded as appropriate was perhaps suited to a young and struggling colony, many questioned its appropriateness for a rapidly growing and wealthy young nation. Marguerite's vision of religious missionary life had stated,

> We are asked why we prefer to be wanderers rather than cloistered, the cloister being a protection for people of our sex . . . Why do we go on missions which put us in danger of suffering greatly and even of being captured, killed or burned by the Indians? There are signs that the Blessed Virgin has been pleased that there is a company of women to honor the life she led in the world and that this company be formed in Montreal. The Blessed Virgin was never cloistered . . .[71]

But her congregation was now an important educational institution in the colony. The younger Canadian-born members did not share Marguerite's enthusiasm for an educational outreach to the Native American children, partly because fierce intertribal wars were raging, but also because parents

---

69. Ibid., 136.

70. Rapley, *The Dévotes,* 104.

71. Malone, *Women and Christianity,* 3:140, citing Prudence Allen, "Six Canadian Women: Their Call, Their Witness, Their Legacy," *Canadian Catholic Review* 5 (1987): 246-58.

wanted an education for their children that reflected their social and economic ambitions for them.

In summary, the stories of Teresa, Angela, Mary, Jeanne, Louise, Marie, Marguerite, and their companions are stories of women who had the ability to respond in an innovative way to new needs and new demands. This ability was grounded in a spirituality that enabled them to transcend the criticisms, physical danger, and severity of climate that they so often encountered. The energetic and talented women whom we have encountered founded communities that permitted women to extend the scope of their traditional work: care of the sick and the poor, nursing, teaching domestic skills and elementary education to girls and young women. And as the story of the Ursulines in France indicates, they were also able to provide more sophisticated education for middle- and upper-class young women. The origins of the new orders can be traced back to the lay movements of the late Middle Ages such as the Beguines or the laywomen of the Common Life with their emphasis on a contemplative spirituality and ministry to the poor. Ecclesial authorities more often than not were intent on turning such communities into monastic orders. Some women, such as Teresa, used the language of deference and humility in an effort to subvert threats to their reforming and missionary tasks; others, such as Jeanne de Chantal and Louise de Marillac, turned to men who were sympathetic to their aims; and still others, such as Angela Merici, Marie Guyart, and Marguerite Bourgeoys, were at first fortunate that in the extreme situations in which the church found itself in the sixteenth and seventeenth centuries, ecclesial authorities were prepared to ignore the rules in the interests of mission. When the "state of emergency" had passed, they were quick to reimpose the law, usually the requirement of cloister. Diarmaid MacCulloch believes that "the best chance of withstanding being herded into the cloister was to shelter under the authority of a charismatic male sponsor,"[72] a strategy that certainly worked for Louise de Marillac. The success of this tactic in the struggles of the other women we have considered is less obvious.

As we reflect on the struggles and achievements of these women, it could be easy for the contemporary Christian woman to ascribe feminist motivations to them. Certainly religious life offered women freedom from patriarchal family life, educational opportunities, and a certain choice regarding lifestyle and work. These freedoms, however, do not emerge as the key reasons for the momentous decisions they made. Religious reasons—love of God, following Jesus, the wish to serve as missionaries—dominate in all their writings. As Raft states, "They became women religious to become saints, and along the way they became models of human behavior who had tremendous influence on their contemporaries."[73]

---

72. MacCulloch, *Reformation*, 646.
73. Raft, *Women and the Religious Life*, 131.

I began this chapter by asking if the Renaissance, the discovery of the New World, and the Catholic and Protestant Reformations improved the situation of women, and, in particular, enhanced their capacity to be actively involved in the mission of the church. While the protagonists of those events, so momentous for the Western world, did not include the empowerment of women for mission as part of their agenda, the cultural and political shifts of the sixteenth and seventeenth centuries enabled women to forge new missionary identities for themselves in ways that a more stable and settled era would never have tolerated. The fact that they were deeply spiritual, courageous, and prophetic women enabled them to respond with faith and hope to the changing world in which they lived.

# 6

# *Missionary Women in the*
# *Nineteenth Century and until Vatican II*

The nineteenth century witnessed a significant growth in Catholic missionary activity, a growth in which women, lay and religious,[1] played a significant role. There were a number of factors that contributed to this growth: the impact of the French Revolution on European Catholicism, nineteenth-century colonial activity, the emergence of impoverished working classes in the cities of western Europe and the United States, and the cultural revolution in nineteenth-century Ireland. These factors decisively shaped Catholic understanding of mission until Vatican II (1962-1965) initiated equally significant changes in Catholic perceptions of mission. For the most part, this chapter examines the contribution of women to the church's mission prior to 1965; but in the cases of Mother Teresa of Calcutta and Dorothy Day, whose missionary work began in the mid-twentieth century, continuing their stories beyond 1965 helps the reader appreciate better their respective contributions.

It is impossible to underestimate the impact of the French Revolution on nineteenth-century church life. Because the Revolution's leaders created a new and official religion that deified reason, French Catholicism was soon seen as counterrevolutionary. The executions and the enforced and voluntary exile of thousands of priests, religious women, and laity meant that it was difficult "to regard the Revolution as anything but the work of the devil."[2]

---

1. I am using "lay" to describe married or single women who are not professed members of a religious order, while "religious" refers to those women who are professed members of a religious order or congregation. Canonically speaking, women religious are "lay" too, because like "lay" women they are not ordained. According to Canon Law, "order" is used of those women who make solemn vows and normally live a contemplative and enclosed lifestyle. The word "congregation" is used to describe those communities of women who make simple vows and who embrace an apostolic life. Because such canonical nuances may be difficult to appreciate, and both words are used interchangeably, I will use the word "order" when speaking of either orders or congregations.

2. Ralph Gibson, *A Social History of French Catholicism 1789-1914*, Christianity and Society in the Modern World, ed. Hugh McLeod and Bob Scribner (London: Routledge, 1989), 53.

The sufferings of so many help explain "what sometimes seems the mind-lessly reactionary politics of Catholics in nineteenth-century France,"[3] with their rejection of the social and intellectual changes characteristic of the rev-olutionary era.

The French Revolution, however, did not lead to the disappearance of the church, and the nineteenth century was a time of missionary expansion, ini-tially for the French church, but soon for the church in other countries as well. This growth was accompanied by a rejection of Gallican-type[4] rela-tionships between the church and state which had led to the state's inter-vening in and controlling much of church life. It also led to rejection of Enlightenment philosophies and the subsequent critical approaches to theology that they encouraged.[5] These two reactions led to the emergence of Ultramontanism, which literally means, "looking south beyond the moun-tains" to Rome. Ultramontanism, in reaction to Gallicanism, promoted and fostered an emphasis on obedience to, and affirmation of, centralized papal authority. Guiseppe Albergio argues that the "universalist and unidimen-sional concept [of Ultramontanism] increases the centralization of the ecclesial organization, and, in the same time, the horizontal dynamism of communion gives way to an authority descending from the top of the ecclesial pyramid towards the obedience of the rank and the file."[6] As Jeffrey von Arx points out, the "the penchant—one might even say monomania—for unity that we have already noticed as one of the notes of ultramontanism manifests itself most clearly. Because there is only one God there is only one Church and only one truth within that Church, which is enunciated by the Church's single head."[7] Though it originated in France, it gained significant support in the Irish and English Catholic churches and in British colonies such as New Zealand, South Africa, and Australia. It is difficult for many contemporary Catholics to understand the depth of commitment to the Ultramontane cause. However, if Ultramontanism is recognized as a reac-tion against eighteenth-century attempts by Europe's Catholic monarchs to limit the authority of the pope within their countries, it is easier to appreci-ate why many Catholics believed that loyalty to Rome safeguarded impor-

---

3. Ibid., 52.

4. Gallicanism, so called because of its French or Gallic origins, allowed the pope only spir-itual authority, and argued that his teachings required the approval of the entire church. In effect, it severely hindered the authority of the papacy, strengthened the role of the national church, and tolerated the interference of the ruler in the life of a particular church.

5. Pope Pius IX's *Syllabus of Errors*, (1864), which condemned the critical thinking and philosophies associated with nineteenth-century secular liberalism, is perhaps the most notable example of this rejection. See http://www.papalencyclicals.net/Pius09/p9syll.htm.

6. Guiseppe Albergio, "Chrétienté et cultures dans l'histoire de l'église," in *Eglise et his-toire de l'église en Afrique*, ed. Guiseppe Ruggieri (Paris: Beauchesne, 1988), xix-xx.

7. Jeffrey von Arx, ed., *Varieties of Ultramontanism* (Washington, D.C.: Catholic Univer-sity of America Press, 1998), 9.

tant rights and encouraged a more universalist outlook. The Ultramontanists' greatest triumph was the 1870 doctrine of papal infallibility.

There is evidence that Ultramontanism served to advance the church's missionary work. For example, in 1814, the Jesuits were once again able to engage in mission, and the Sacred Congregation for the Propagation of the Faith was reconstituted in Rome in 1817. Nineteenth-century popes—Gregory XVI (1831-46), Pius IX (1846-78), Leo XIII (1878-1903)—personally supported and encouraged Catholic missionary work. Although the nineteenth-century church rightly could be regarded as restorationist and conservative, it was nevertheless a church that took its call to mission seriously, thereby reversing the decline in missionary activity characteristic of the second half of the eighteenth century. Similarly, Ultramontanism also served some women's missionary congregations well as it encouraged many founders to seek exemption from control by the local bishop through asking for and obtaining pontifical status, which allowed them more autonomy.

Another reality that affected the church's understanding of its missionary role in the nineteenth century was colonization, the process of Western expansion into the non-Western world. This colonizing process had begun in the early sixteenth century with the Portuguese and Spanish discoveries of the New World, and accelerated in the succeeding centuries so that by the mid-twentieth century, European rule prevailed over a third of the world's population. In the early nineteenth century, French Catholic missionary activity, numerically the most significant, was driven, first, by religious impulses to restore the church to its rightful place, lost during the revolutionary era, and, second, by a certain romanticism that reacted against the rationalism of the revolutionary era. French author F.-R. Chateaubriand provides an example of such romanticism:

> When regenerated Europe had no more to offer the preachers of the faith than a family of brothers, they turned their eyes to the regions where souls were still languishing in the darkness of idolatry. They were touched with compassion at seeing this human degradation; they were urged on by the desire to shed their blood for the salvation of these strangers. They had to penetrate profound forests, cross impassable swamps, ford dangerous rivers, climb inaccessible rocks; they had to face cruel, superstitious, and jealous nations; they had to surmount the ignorance of barbarism in some and in others the prejudices of civilization. All these obstacles could not stop them.[8]

---

8. F.-R. Chateaubriand, *Gâenie du Christianisme* (Paris: Garnier-Flammarion, 1966), part 4, book 4, chap. 1, quoted by Jean Comby, *How to Understand the History of Christian Mission*, trans. John Bowden (London: SCM Press, 1996), 116.

As the nineteenth century progressed and European powers became more aggressive in their search for colonies, the work of missionaries became more important for the colonizing classes. Thus despite the anticlerical character of French governments in the late nineteenth and early twentieth centuries, French colonial officials "forgot" about anticlericalism when it conflicted with French imperial aims. "Antoine Klobukowski, governor-general in Vietnam from 1908-1919 declared on leaving France that 'clericalism was not for export,' but on arrival in Tonkin, he assured Bishop Gendreau that 'anticlericalism was not for export.' Whatever the sentiments in Paris the reality remained that missionaries were too useful to be flung overboard, and at home the French foreign ministry felt the same."[9]

Closely linked to colonialism was the idea of manifest destiny,[10] the belief that because Western culture was inherently superior to other cultures, Western peoples had a particular obligation to bring Western civilization and values to those being colonized. In addition to their obvious task of evangelization, the role played by missionaries in "civilizing" colonized peoples cannot be underestimated. A popular missionary text in the latter part of the nineteenth century and early twentieth century was John 10:10, "I have come that they may have life and have it abundantly." Commenting on this, Lesslie Newbigin argues that "'abundant life' was interpreted as the abundance of the good things that modern education, healing, and agriculture would provide for the deprived peoples of the earth."[11] On the other hand, even though colonial development was an attempt to socialize non-Western peoples into Western culture and was geared to meet the needs of the colonizing nation, missionary activity associated with such developments

---

9. Adrian Hastings, "The Clash of Nationalism and Universalism within Twentieth-Century Missionary Christianity," in *Missions, Nationalism and the End of the Empire*, ed. Brian Stanley (Grand Rapids, Mich.: Eerdmans, 2003), 17.

10. See David J. Bosch, *Transforming Mission: Paradigm Shifts in Theology of Mission* (Maryknoll, N.Y.: Orbis Books, 1991), 207, 298-303; Stephen B. Bevans and Roger P. Schroeder, *Constants in Context: A Theology of Mission for Today* (Maryknoll, N.Y.: Orbis Books, 2004). Bevans and Schroeder identify "manifest destiny" as a description of Western missionary practice in the second half of the nineteenth century. Two centuries earlier, John Winthrop, governor of the Massachusetts Bay Colony, argued that the Puritan-dominated colony would be a city on a hill living a free and godly life. Nineteenth-century Americans in particular believed that they had a divinely inspired mission to expand and to spread freedom and democracy. This was grounded in a belief in the inherent greatness of the Anglo-Saxon race. Such an ideology and belief in "the white man's burden" were used to justify colonial conquests in Africa and Asia. Bosch argues that in the second half of the nineteenth century, "colonial expansion would once again acquire religious overtones and also be intimately linked with mission!" (*Transforming Mission*, 303). Missionaries, consciously and unconsciously, became agents of the Western imperial task. New Zealand Maori academic Ranginui Walker claimed that "the missionaries were the advance party of cultural invasion." See Ranginui Walker, *Ka Whawhai Tonu Matou: Struggle without End* (Auckland: Auckland University Press, 1990), 85.

11. Lesslie Newbigin, *The Open Secret: Sketches for a Missionary Theology* (Grand Rapids, Mich.: Eerdmans, 1978), 103.

had some positive outcomes. There is little doubt that the educational and health institutions set up by missionaries meant that some missionary activity could be identified as emancipatory. For example, "The role of Christian missions in India's social changes is too well attested to be ignored. Christians, both Indian and missionary, led in the fight against widow-burning, exploitation of laborers on the indigo plantations, and caste barriers."[12]

Western Europe's Industrial Revolution also led to important changes in how mission was understood. Europe's cities began to grow at an unprecedented rate and the appearance of new social classes, the factory working classes (Marx's proletariat), posed enormous challenges for the church. It is almost a cliché to claim that the nineteenth-century French church lost the working classes, but Ralph Gibson's comments about the French church were also true of other parts of industrialized Europe: "The relationship between the Church and the industrial proletariat became increasingly an issue . . . industrial workers, by and large, were less Catholic than the rest of the population, and that many industrial agglomerations were indeed the 'missionary areas' that concerned priests began to beat their breasts about toward the end of the century."[13]

Another important development affecting Catholic missionary activity in the nineteenth century in the English-speaking world was what is called the Irish cultural revolution. In 1829, the British Parliament passed the Roman Catholic Relief Act, commonly referred to as Catholic Emancipation. This granted civil and political rights to Catholics in England and Ireland, and allowed the Catholic Church in both countries to progress in a way previously denied them. Sixteenth-century English efforts to subdue Irish Catholics had meant that Tridentine Catholicism never gained a foothold in Ireland, and England's eighteenth-century penal legislation sought to rid Ireland of Catholicism altogether. Though the Catholic Church struggled against such repressive legislation, its inability to set up any sort of diocesan and parochial structures meant that it was difficult "for the church to combat the thriving popular culture of folk belief and practice so prevalent among the Irish masses."[14] However, thanks to Catholic Emancipation in 1829, important socioeconomic, political, and religious changes led to the emergence of an Irish middle class. In turn, this development, particularly in the south and east, allowed the church to reverse the success of Protestant proselytizing activities and to replace Gaelic Catholic culture with "the construction of new, bourgeois Irish Catholic culture characterized by . . . a

---

12. Samuel Hugh Moffett, *A History of Christianity in Asia, 1500-1900*, ed. Jonathan J. Bonk, Angelyn Dries, and Scott W. Sunquist, 2 vols. (Maryknoll, N.Y.: Orbis Books, 2005), 2:447.

13. Gibson, *A Social History of French Catholicism*, 213.

14. Mary Peckham Magray, *The Transforming Power of Nuns: Women, Religion and Cultural Change in Ireland, 1750-1900* (New York: Oxford University Press, 1998), 4.

greater and even exclusive use of the English language, and greater conformity with post-Tridentine Catholic belief and practice."[15] This contributed significantly to the extraordinary missionary activity associated with the nineteenth- and twentieth-century Irish Catholic Church.

It was in this context of socioeconomic, political, cultural, and ecclesial change that Catholic women, lay and religious, sought to carve out new missionary identities for themselves. Again, it is not possible to do justice to the many and varied stories of these women, and so I propose to examine representative examples of missionary women who sought to respond to new missionary needs.

## MISSION AS CHARITY TOWARD THE POOR

Care of the poor was not a new missionary need as such, but the scale of poverty and the number of poor people increased dramatically in nineteenth-century Europe and the United States because of industrialization, urbanization, and immigration. Governments of the time did not see care of the poor through government initiated social welfare structures as part of their responsibility. Poverty was not confined to Europe. If anything, poverty was more of a problem in Europe's colonies for both the immigrant working classes and the indigenous peoples. In many instances, the latter experienced loss of land, their primary resource. Women missionaries responded to these challenges in different ways.

### Catherine McAuley (1778-1841), Founder of the Sisters of Mercy in Ireland in 1831

In the seventeenth century, Mary Ward had dreamed of a community of apostolic, uncloistered women—a development that was strenuously resisted by ecclesial and secular authorities. Her dream was realized in 1749, when Benedict XIV, in *Quamvis Iusto*, ruled that Mary's institute could remain organized as an uncloistered religious institute. As Mary Peckham Magray states, it was "a precedent-setting ruling, for by conceding the right of religious women to form a new style of religious community, it ended the era of enforced enclosure."[16] Women who chose an apostolic life rather than a cloistered life were given legal existence as members of religious congregations and hence eligible for the title of "sister." *Quamvis Iusto* opened the door to the development of the modern sisterhood.

In the nineteenth century, Catherine McAuley was one of the many

---

15. Ibid., 7.
16. Ibid., 8.

women who benefited from the papal decision, although it is unlikely she set out to found a new order that would evolve into one of the world's largest women's orders. Catherine's life and mission provide an example of the important changes that were occurring in Irish Catholicism with the emergence of a middle class in the late eighteenth and nineteenth centuries. From an early age, Catherine was exposed to Protestant influences, and around 1803, five years after the death of her mother, she went to live with an elderly Protestant childless couple, Catherine and William Callaghan. It was while living with them that she began her apostolate of pastoral visitation and education among the many illiterate and poverty-stricken inhabitants of the neighborhood. At the same time, Catherine immersed herself in Catholic devotional practices and sought advice from trusted priest acquaintances about her developing ministry. Such was her charity and concern for the Callaghans in their old age that when they died they left her their considerable fortune of 25,000 pounds. The money allowed her to undertake her mission of mercy, which focused on educational and social work with the poor, particularly women, and with the sick and the dying.

"Her return to Dublin in 1822 as an attractive heiress from a well-established background and brought up among Protestants threw open the doors of fashionable society to her."[17] However, Catherine turned her attention to Dublin's poor, and believing that "her inherited wealth was a trust to be expended on others,"[18] she served them as both educator and social worker. In particular, she focused on women, believing that "no work of charity can be more productive of good to society or more conducive to the happiness of the poor than the careful instruction of women."[19]

Other newly founded Irish congregations, such as Mary Aikenhead's Sisters of Charity, founded in 1815, were engaged in similar work, but Catherine was not inclined to join them; and only reluctantly did she consider the possibility of founding a religious order. However, as women flocked to join her, the movement toward conventual stability accelerated, and in 1831, she reached the milestone of establishing a new religious order. Catherine's main focus was education—of the poor and of the middle and upper classes—and throughout the 1830s, schools were established in much of south and east Ireland.

By 1839, Sisters of Mercy were also working in England, particularly among Irish immigrants. In 1854, five Sisters of Mercy from Bermondsey, later joined by fifteen Irish Sisters of Mercy, served as nurses with Florence Nightingale during the Crimean War (1854-1856).[20] One of the important

---

17. M. Angela Bolster, *Catherine McAuley in Her Own Words* (Dublin: Dublin Diocesan Office for Causes, 1978), 17.

18. Ibid., 19.

19. Ibid., 21.

20. In 1862 Florence Nightingale wrote to her friend Benjamin Jowett (1817-1893), Oxford scholar and Anglican clergyman: "The most religious mind I ever knew was that of a R.Catholic

effects of this mission was that "much of the [subsequent] increasing pro-
fessionalisation of nursing as a respectable career for women resulted from
the high standards and rigorous discipline set in place by women's religious
communities in the first half of the century."[21]

In 1843, Sisters of Mercy had journeyed to Chicago in the United States,
and when the Civil War (1861-1865) began, the community numbered one
hundred members, had four convents, three parish schools, the city's first
permanent hospital, two orphanages, and two select schools for young
women. Membership in the order offered women the opportunity to address
some of the social problems facing migrant communities, a work that also
effectively counteracted Protestant proselytizing efforts. Kathleen Brosnan
writes, "In achieving these ends, the Sisters of Mercy exercised much greater
autonomy than most American women. Through their institutions they
obtained corporate charters and owned property. Their ministries made of
the nuns the most visible actors of a missionary Catholic Church in an
increasingly anti-Catholic, anti-immigrant Chicago."[22] She later states that
"Protestant women who engaged in charity work rarely replicated nuns'
authority or independence."[23] This public presence, however, did not translate into public advocacy on behalf of the poor. The ability of women religious to speak out was circumscribed by a spirituality that prescribed a
self-imposed silence, and which had its roots in Ireland, where "women did
not publicly question the growing hegemony of the male clergy and middle-
class Catholic men."[24]

By the end of the nineteenth century, the Sisters of Mercy were engaged
in a variety of apostolates—education of working-, middle-, and upper-class
children and young women—in Ireland, England, the Americas, Africa, Australia, and New Zealand, and were well on the way to becoming one of the
largest women's orders. Their success can be attributed to a variety of factors, including the personality and spirituality of Catherine McAuley herself
and her personal wealth, which allowed her a measure of financial autonomy
often denied to other founders. The fact that she did not restrict her aposto-

---

Revd. Mother [Mother Mary Clare Moore] who was so good as to go out with me to the
Crimea. After we came home, I found her one day cleaning out a gutter with her own hands. I
know she did it on no theory. I think she had much better employed a man to do it, but that is
what I mean by a true idea of religious life, and she the only R.Catholic too I have ever known
who never tried to convert me." See John W. Donohue, "Sisters in Mercy" (2001); available at
http://www.americamagazine.org/gettest.cfm?articleTypeID=1&textID=1522&issueI; accessed
July 21, 2005.

21. Barbara Walsh, *Roman Catholic Nuns in England and Wales, 1800-1937: A Social History* (Dublin: Irish Academic Press, 2002), 14.

22. Kathleen A. Brosnan, "Public Presence, Public Silence: Nuns, Bishops, and the Gendered Space of Early Chicago," *Catholic Historical Review* 90 (2004): 473-96.

23. Ibid., 473-96.

24. Ibid.

late to the poor alone, but insisted on the education of middle- and upper-class girls ensured that her order always had a number of young women seeking to join them. Catherine's sisters had an ability to respond to emerging pastoral needs, not only in Ireland but also in those countries where there were significant Irish immigrant communities. Although the importance of their ministry for "the evolution of church and society was well understood by hierarchy and clergy,"[25] their ability to influence church policy in any significant way was limited. Furthermore, in carrying out their various ministries, the sisters were not restricted by the demands of cloister. Though the Sisters of Mercy on occasion could find themselves in conflict with church authorities, such conflicts tended to be based on property rather than on apostolate. In 1852, Archbishop Paul Cullen of Dublin announced that nuns were "the best support to religion."[26] Neither Catherine McAuley nor the first Sisters of Mercy could be described as protofeminists; nevertheless, many women joined the sisters in the hope of effecting social and religious change for women. As the face of the caring local church, the sisters were involved intimately in the lives of those among whom they lived and ministered.

## Mary MacKillop (1842-1909), Founder of the Sisters of St. Joseph of the Sacred Heart in Australia in 1866

One major nineteenth-century Catholic missionary concern was the care of immigrant communities, particularly if these communities were minority Catholic communities within Protestant society. As the rate of immigration increased to countries such as Australia, Canada, New Zealand, or the United States, where climatic conditions favored European settlement, bishops and priests tended to concentrate pastoral resources, personnel, and finances on the Catholic migrant communities rather than on the indigenous peoples, even though such work was often the original focus of the new mission. The pastoral needs of such migrant communities, usually poor and marginalized, meant that a mission of retention directed toward migrant Catholics assumed more significance than a mission of evangelization among indigenous peoples.

Australian bishops, like their counterparts elsewhere, identified the Catholic school system as the cornerstone of their pastoral policy. South Australia was one of Australia's poorer states, with its small Catholic, and predominantly Irish, community, marginalized economically, socially, and politically. Bishops and clergy believed that the financial poverty of church

---

25. Magray, *The Transforming Power of Nuns*, 10.

26. Ibid., quoting from Peadar MacSuibhne, ed., *Paul Cullen and His Contemporaries with Their Letters from 1820-1902*, 5 vols. (Nass: Leinster Leader, 1961-77), 4:50.

and state, and the subsequent inability of both to provide education, contributed to a spiritual poverty and therefore "a gradual attrition resulting from [Catholics'] having too infrequent contact with their pastors and too few opportunities to attend to their spiritual duties."[27] Given the impossibility of obtaining government support for a separate Catholic school system in South Australia, diocesan priest Julian Tenison Woods considered importing religious sisters from overseas. Bishops and priests believed that sisters "could generally be expected to be better educated, to be prepared to live more cheaply [than lay teachers], and to have a more permanent commitment to their work than their lay counterparts."[28] However, the lack of finances prevented such an importation, and Woods turned to Mary MacKillop, a young Australian-born school teacher, whom he had earlier met at Penola, South Australia.

Mary was the daughter of Scottish middle-class migrant parents, but despite the family's status, Mary had experienced firsthand the effects of poverty because her father was a poor provider for the family. This situation forced her to seek work as a teacher in order to support the family, often on "outback stations."[29] This task prevented her from fulfilling her dream of becoming a religious sister. Woods's invitation constituted the first small step taken to found one of Australia's first religious orders. On the feast of St. Joseph, March 19, 1866, Mary adopted a simple black dress and began to live according to a rule drawn up by Woods.[30] Before coming to Australia, the English-born Woods had lived for a short time in France where he came in contact with the Sisters of St. Joseph of Puy, and this experience deeply influenced him. He "recalled that there was no 'fine ladyism' among those French sisters, whose education and standard of living closely resembled that of the people among whom they lived and worked and that they were much loved by all with whom they came in contact."[31] He believed that the Sisters of St. Joseph of Puy provided a model that could work in Australia. In 1874, the young Australian order was approved by Rome, and, to Mary's delight and the consternation of the Australian hierarchy, Mary was able to establish her order with a central government rather than under the direction of individual bishops in the particular dioceses in which the sisters worked. This was important for the sisters, but, as Foale points out, while not dis-

27. Marie Therese Foale, *The Josephite Story* (Sydney: St. Joseph's Generalate, 1989), 4.

28. Ibid., 13.

29. "Outback station" is the name Australians give to huge sheep and cattle farms, often hundreds of square kilometers in size, isolated and distant from towns.

30. See Ann Gilroy, "Mary MacKillop and the Challenge to Her Daughters," *Australasian Catholic Record* 72 (1995): 61-72. Gilroy explains that "Mary chose Joseph as the patron because his characteristics of practicality in his role as parent of Jesus, constancy even in the face of doubt, flexibility so that what needed to be done was done, and attentiveness to the signs of the times, were those she knew her women needed" (65).

31. Foale, *The Josephite Story*, 13.

counting Rome's concern about the sisters' welfare, there were other reasons for Rome's decision: it desired "to maintain close control over the Church in the colonies. From this point of view, the Josephite [sisters] were little more than pawns in an episcopal power game and Rome's move to make them independent of the local bishop was an attempt to check those bishops' power."[32] Mary returned from Rome via Ireland, accompanied by fifteen Irish postulants.

Woods and Mary, however, were drifting apart. Both shared a common dream of education for the poor in Australia, but Mary's more practical approach to life, her awareness of the need for discipline and order, her willingness to accept Rome's decision that they should not depend solely on divine providence for their livelihood ran counter to Woods's more utopian vision. He believed that Mary's approach meant the collapse of his vision, and in 1875, they went their separate ways, because Woods seemingly failed to appreciate that the growth of the order would inevitably entail a greater degree of institutionalization than he could tolerate.

In 1891, when there were over three hundred Sisters of St. Joseph working in Australia and New Zealand, Mary wrote: "Twenty-five years ago we first kept up St. Joseph's day as the special feast of our proposed Institute and little did either of us dream of what was to spring from so small a beginning . . . Our poor Father [Woods] was happy that day, and so was I, but we said little beyond wondering whom God would call to assist us—and how he would make his way clear."[33]

In effect, Woods and Mary founded the first Australian order dedicated to education of the poorer classes in the remote towns of the Australian outback, that enormous hinterland that stretched thousands of miles back from the country's cities, all of which were built around the coastline of the continent. Because the order's work involved them with work among the poor, Woods and Mary decided that all who joined the order had to be prepared to live as the poor lived and among them. "They were to own neither house, land nor money in their own right and were to subsist solely on such school fees as they might receive and the gratuitous offerings of the local people."[34] This, coupled with her more flexible attitude toward community—for example, two sisters could constitute a community—encouraged such a life.

Mary MacKillop emerges as an important figure in the story of the Catholic Church in both Australia and New Zealand. She believed that no one should be excluded from the possibility of a Catholic education because of geographical isolation or socioeconomic status, but more importantly, she was a missionary who recognized the needs of a young, struggling, and mar-

---

32. Ibid., 189.

33. Foale, *The Josephite Story,* quoting from Mary MacKillop, "Circular to the Sisters, 4 March 1891," *Circulars*, 168.

34. Ibid., 18.

ginalized community and who sought to respond to those needs in an innovative and gospel-driven manner.

### Mother Teresa of Calcutta (1910-1997), Founder of the Missionaries of Charity in India in 1950

The missionary work of Mother Teresa of Calcutta, despite the extraordinary growth of her institute, rarely figures in academic articles in missiological journals or in scholarly tomes. That lack of academic study, however, is more than compensated for by hagiographical and devotional publications about Mother Teresa,[35] and, to a lesser extent, by more iconoclastic publications.[36] In order to give an adequate picture of the extraordinary growth of her order, I intend to outline the story of the Missionaries of Charity from their foundation in 1950 through Mother Teresa's beatification in 2003. Today, the Missionaries of Charity number over 4,000 members working out of more than 600 foundations in 125 countries.

In 2003, six years after her death, her best-known admirer, John Paul II, beatified her. As he preached during her beatification homily,

> This Gospel passage, "As you did to one of the least of these my brethren, you did it to me" (Mt 25: 40) so crucial in understanding Mother Teresa's service to the poor, was the basis of her faith-filled conviction that in touching the broken bodies of the poor she was touching the body of Christ. It was to Jesus himself, hidden under the distressing disguise of the poorest of the poor, that her service was directed. Mother Teresa highlights the deepest meaning of service—an act of love done to the hungry, thirsty, strangers, naked, sick, prisoners (cf. Mt 25: 34-36) is done to Jesus himself.[37]

Mother Teresa, who went to India as a member of the Irish Loreto Sisters, began her missionary life as a teacher in Calcutta. While missionaries to nineteenth-century India intuitively and consciously recognized the need to educate women from all strata of Indian society, Mother Teresa believed that a greater need than education was serving the poorest of the poor in Calcutta. After some basic training in medicine and nursing with the American Medical Mission sisters at Patna, she returned to Calcutta to found a new order,

---

35. See Malcolm Muggeridge, *Something Beautiful for God: Mother Teresa of Calcutta* (London: Collins, 1971).

36. See Christopher Hitchens, *The Missionary Position: Mother Teresa in Theory and Practice* (London: Verso, 1995).

37. Pope John Paul II, *Beatification of Mother Theresa of Calcutta* (2002); available from http://www.vatican.va/holy_father/john_paul_ii_homilies/2003/documents/hf_jp-ii_hom_20031019_mother-theresa_en.html; accessed August 31 , 2005.

the Missionaries of Charity, who committed themselves to the poorest of the poor. Before long, she was joined by former pupils from the Loreto school where she had been principal.

By the early 1960s, Missionaries of Charity were also working in other parts of India, and by the mid-1960s houses were being established in Asia, Africa, and in Rome. In the 1980s, Mother Teresa opened houses in many communist countries, including the former Soviet Union, Albania, and Cuba. The Missionaries of Charity Brothers were founded in 1963 and were followed by contemplative branches of the sisters and brothers, the Missionary of Charity Fathers, the Co-Workers of Mother Teresa, the Sick and Suffering Co-Workers, and the Lay Missionaries of Charity. Given such extraordinary numerical growth, it is important to appreciate why Mother Teresa emerges as a controversial figure.

Anne Sebba's 1997 publication[38] offers a wide-ranging critique of Mother Teresa, and concludes that her theology does not take into account the extraordinary developments that resulted from Vatican II, particularly those concerned with the changing nature of religious life, contemporary understandings about human sexuality, or the tension between works of charity and the need for societal change. There is little doubt that Mother Teresa unequivocally favored works of charity rather than works of justice on behalf of the poor. This allowed politicians of extreme right-wing views, such as General Pinochet in Chile or "Doc" Duvalier in Haiti, to readily support Mother Teresa. Mother Teresa seemed to personify the dictum that it was better to give a starving person a fish than to teach him to fish. Such a position ignores the need to work at resolving the causes of poverty. While there is much to commend in an ethics of care, it was an ethic that sits comfortably with powerful economic, political, and church groups, who recognized that social change could adversely affect them. According to Mary Malone, the enthusiasm of church authorities for Mother Teresa occurs because "Mother Teresa could be depended on to side with the ecclesiastical authorities on the controversial issues of the day especially with regard to the sexuality and roles of women . . . Mother Teresa, however, seemed to fit perfectly into the current ecclesiastical vision of the role of women. She lived the ethics of care to perfection and inspired millions. She did not, like the women religious founders of previous ages, tackle the authorities about the causes of the suffering or the economic realities which made the slums of Calcutta inevitable."[39] Her lack of enthusiasm for a feminist agenda and her acceptance of the economic, political, and ecclesiastical status quo in the countries where her sisters work have gained her many admirers who regard her as a role model for contemporary Catholic women missionaries.

---

38. See Anne Sebba, *Mother Teresa: Beyond the Image* (London: Weidenfeld & Nicolson, 1997).

39. Mary T. Malone, *Women and Christianity*, vol. 3, *From the Reformation to the 21st Century* (2003), 3:296.

On the other hand, Edward Chia argues that Mother Teresa offers an important example of orthopraxis. He writes as follows:

> Evangelization must be engaged in one step at a time. The early steps are the most tedious, yet easiest and most important. The Christian witnesses through love, service and deeds in the *dialogue of life*. It is through simple acts of caring, sharing and attending that others see Christ and come to accept the Church and Christianity . . . That accounts for why Mother Teresa has been so well accepted in Asia. Hers is a mission of touch, of love and of service.[40]

While Mother Teresa offers "a contradictory model,"[41] and the implications of her missionary practice can be ambiguous for contemporary missionary women, Chia's insight regarding the importance of "dialogue of life" offers another perspective regarding her approach to mission.

These three examples of founders who were primarily committed to the care of the poor are representative and not exhaustive.[42] They are three examples of women who were convinced that the missionary call was above all an invitation, or better a gospel command, to reach out in practical service to the poor wherever they lived—at home or overseas. Perhaps the Gospel imperative that best captures the essence of that approach is Matthew 25:40, "Truly I tell you, just as you did it to one of these who are members of my family, you did it to me." It was an approach that their followers have continued to embrace, and while the Sisters of Mercy and the Sisters of St. Joseph have revisioned that call in the wake of Vatican II, Mother Teresa's Missionaries of Charity have continued with a mission that prioritizes works of charity.

While all three women were committed to mission as service to the poor, there were important differences among them. Catherine McAuley's vision of ministry to the poor did not prevent her from also seeing the wisdom of teaching middle- and upper-class girls, nor in owning and administering large institutional health, educational, and social facilities that furthered the mission of the Mercy Sisters. On the other hand, Mary MacKillop wanted her sisters to live in small, rural-based communities with a lifestyle that approximated that of the people among whom they lived, and she refused to allow her sisters to teach in middle-class or select schools. In Rangiora, New

---

40. Edward Chia, *Towards a Theology of Dialogue: Schillebeeckx's Method as Bridge between Vatican's 'Dominus Iesus' and Asia's FABC Theology* (Bangkok: privately printed, 2003), 260, cited by Stephen Bevans and Roger Schroeder, "We Were Gentle Among You: Christian Mission as Dialogue," *Australian EJournal* 7 (2006); available from http://dlibrary.acu.edu.au/research/theology/ejournal.

41. Malone, *Women and Christianity*, 3:296.

42. Other important examples include the Sisters of Charity of Seton Hill, founded by Elizabeth Seton in 1809 in the United States, and the Sisters of Compassion, founded in New Zealand in 1892 by Frenchwoman Suzanne Aubert.

Zealand, the French Marist priest Augustine Aubry engineered the removal of the Josephites from the local parish school, ostensibly because "the time of their usefulness in this parish is over and that a change of Order is imperiously demanded by the necessities of the place."[43] It seemed he had ambitions to set up a "select" school in Rangiora, staffed by Euphrasie Barbier's community, the Sisters of Our Lady of the Missions, who taught subjects similar to those offered by the Religious of the Sacred Heart at their school in Timaru, another parish of the diocese. Mother Teresa offered a different model of service to the poor. Whereas both Catherine McAuley and Mary MacKillop recognized that education encouraged a social mobility that allowed the poor to improve their situation, Mother Teresa and the Missionaries of Charity have tended to ignore education as a priority in their ministry to the poor. For them, the immediate physical needs of the destitute have remained their apostolic priority.

## MISSION AS GOING ON THE "FOREIGN MISSIONS"

Another group of women believed that mission meant going to the "foreign missions" to work among those who belonged to the world's great religions or whose religious traditions were indigenous. Such people did not live in Europe, but in the African, Asian, and Oceanic colonies of the different European empires, and in the Americas. For Catholics, mission in the nineteenth century had as one of its primary goals the conversion of pagans, infidels, and heretics through planting the church (*plantatio ecclesiae*) where it had not yet been established. Most Catholics believed that outside of the church there was no salvation, so it was important to baptize as many as possible. Such a perception of mission prioritized the sacramental ministry of priests, and women's work of education, care of the sick, and ministry to the poor was perceived as a preparatory stage. Women's ministry, therefore, was much more holistic than that of the priest. It was about development of the mind, care of the body, and catechesis of the young and the poor.

At the end of the eighteenth century, Catholic missionary work had contracted significantly, but this situation began to change after Napoleon's defeat in 1815. In particular, French missionary activity revived in a remarkable way thanks in part to the development of a groundswell "of popular religious reaction against the radicalism of the revolutionary and Napoleonic regimes."[44] One noteworthy stimulus to missionary revival was the estab-

---

43. Fr. Augustine Aubry, SM, Rangiora, to Rev. Mother, Temuka, December 15, 1897, quoted in Anne Marie Power, RSJ, *Sisters of St. Joseph of the Sacred Heart: The New Zealand Story, 1883–1997* (Auckland: Sisters of St. Joseph of the Sacred Heart, 1997), 80.

44. Patrick J. N. Tuck, *French Catholic Missionaries and the Politics of Imperialism in Vietnam, 1857-1914: A Documentary Survey*, ed. P. E. H. Hair (Liverpool: Liverpool University Press, 1987), 1:22.

lishment at Lyon in 1822 of a powerful new fundraising body, the *Société pour le Propagation de la Foi* (Society for the Propagation of the Faith). It is to the story of its founder that I now turn because it was through the work of the society that the church "resumed its march forward as a Church truly Catholic, that is to say, to be found in every continent, among people of every race and from every culture."[45]

### Pauline Jaricot (1799-1862), Founder of the Society for the Propagation of the Faith in France in 1822

Pauline was born into a wealthy, middle-class, silk-merchant family. Her father, Antoine, was bitterly opposed to the changes that the revolutionary and Napoleonic regimes imposed on the church, and suffered because of that opposition. Pauline, however, lived in a way appropriate to her social standing until 1816, when she came under the influence of Abbé Würtz, a forthright preacher and one who vigorously championed the papacy against Gallican claims. Her meeting with Würtz so changed her life that she began to attend to the sick poor in the Hôtel-Dieu. She was not drawn to religious life but joined three lay organizations devoted to reviving the spirituality and missionary fervor of lay Catholics. Both Pauline and her brother, Philéas, were attracted to the foreign missions; and given the resurgence of enthusiasm and interest in foreign mission that developed in postrevolutionary France, they wondered how their dreams could be fulfilled. They had heard of the success of British Bible societies in raising significant finances for missionary work from tens of thousands of small weekly subscriptions, and set out to achieve something similar among French Catholics. The society's publication, *Annals of the Propagation of the Faith*, asked the faithful if "the sight of these incredible efforts on the part of the heretics (Protestants) to propagate their errors [could] inspire Catholics to a generous emulation? Let us hope that the zeal of the children of light becomes as ardent as that of the children of darkness."[46]

Pauline undertook responsibility for such a collection in Lyon, and her project dragged along for several years, "almost without success; for many people, it was an object of derision. Nevertheless, I never despaired of it."[47] Over the next few years, however, she refined her system for collecting money, despite the opposition of some prominent Lyonnais clergy and laymen; and in 1822, the Society for the Propagation of the Faith was formed.

45. André Latreille, *L'église catholique et la révolution française*, 2 vols. (Paris : Cerf, 1970), 11:9.

46. Comby, *How to Understand the History of Christian Mission*, 118, quoting from *Annals of the Propagation of the Faith* III, 13, 1828.

47. James Waldersee, *A Grain of Mustard Seed: The Society for the Propagation of the Faith and Australia 1837-1977* (Kensington, N.S.W.: Chevalier Press, 2000), 23.

A minority opinion holds that Pauline should not be identified as the society's founder. Rather, this honor belongs to a group of Lyonnais men who gave a definite structure to the vision of Pauline and Philéas Jaricot. However, other scholarly research and papal approbation for her role in establishing the society suggest otherwise.[48]

Pauline emphasized that almsgiving for the missions should be accompanied by prayer of reparation to the Sacred Heart of Jesus. Pauline, like many of her contemporaries, was influenced by French mystic Margaret Alacoque (1647-1690), who had promoted devotion to the Sacred Heart of Jesus, a devotion characterized by an emphasis on human sinfulness and the consequent need for reparation and self-sacrifice. This emphasis resonated with many nineteenth-century French Catholics who had identified the laxity of the eighteenth-century church as one of reasons for the revolutionary attacks on the church. Such laxity and its consequences were best addressed by prayer, penance, and almsgiving for the foreign missions.

The work of the society cannot be underestimated, and Pauline Jaricot, a laywoman, provides an important missionary model for her practical commitment toward the foreign missions, and in recognizing the need for a spirituality in which that commitment was grounded. Dana Robert states that

> the European-based organization that, more than any other, helped to energize the foreign mission vision of American Catholics was the Society for the Propagation of the Faith, an organization approved by the church to support Catholic missions to non-Catholics around the world. As it gradually spread throughout American churches during the early twentieth century, it provided a focus for foreign-mission giving and for recruitment for American personnel to Catholic missions.[49]

Today, the society is one of the four Pontifical Mission Societies, and, under the direction of the Congregation for the Evangelization of Peoples (Rome, Italy), seeks to remain faithful to Pauline's vision through fostering an awareness of universal mission, informing Catholics of the missionary needs of the Catholic Church, and encouraging prayer and financial help for those mission churches. Mission continues to be understood as "foreign missions," that is, as spiritual and financial support for the young churches of Africa, Asia, Latin America, and Oceania.

---

48. Waldersee argues that Pauline Jaricot should not be identified as the founder of the Society for the Propagation of the Faith, a position not held by Hugh Laracy, who writes that in 1822, "Pauline Jaricot, daughter of a Lyon mill owner, founded the *Oeuvre de la Propagation de la Foi.*" See Hugh Laracy, *Marists and Melanesians* (Canberra: Australian National University, 1976), 12. See also T. L. Suttor, *Hierarchy and Democracy in Australia, 1788-1870* (Melbourne: Melbourne University Press, 1965).

49. Dana L Robert, *American Women in Mission: A Social History of Their Thought and Practice* (Macon, Ga.: Mercer University Press, 1996), 343.

*Euphrasie Barbier (1829-1893), Founder of the Religieuses*
*de Notre Dame des Missions in France in 1861*

Euphrasie Barbier came from a lower-middle-class family, and after managing her own laundry, she entered religious life in 1848 in the hope of being sent to the foreign missions. Her order, however, sent her to London, where the needs of English working-class people and Irish Catholics escaping the effects of the Irish famine meant that her wish to be more directly involved in foreign missions was frustrated. This persuaded her to leave the Congregation of Calvary, and under the direction of priests belonging to the Society of Mary (Marists, founded in Lyon in 1816 by Jean-Claude Colin), she undertook to found a new religious order specifically devoted to the foreign missions.

Euphrasie's enthusiasm for foreign missions was reflected in her wish that her sisters make a fourth vow of zeal. She wrote as follows:

> In their ardent desire to love God ever more and more, to offer themselves up with Christ for his glory, to make him known and loved, and in order to imitate and glorify as far as in them lies, the zeal of the Heart of Jesus, the Sisters (those who are allowed to make this fourth vow) undertake always to be ready to go on the foreign missions where Holy Obedience may send them, and to work devotedly there for the greater glory of God and the sanctification of souls.[50]

Her close links with the Marist Fathers meant the first missionary sisters went to New Zealand, where the priests and brothers had been working since 1838 with the Maori, the indigenous people. However, like sisters in other newly founded religious orders, the four French sisters who journeyed to New Zealand in 1864 "in search of a wilderness to tame, and savages to convert, found that they could not get past the vices of baptized Christians."[51] The first apostolic work of the sisters on their arrival in New Zealand was the education of the children of English and Irish Catholic settlers. Even though these first sisters had traveled to the ends of the earth, their work in foreign lands seemed to be more about a mission of retention than a mission of evangelization. Euphrasie's hopes of working among non-Christians came closer to realization in 1867 when the sisters were invited to staff a boarding school for Maori girls, although some of these girls would already have been baptized. Her wish to be more involved in working with non-Christians was realized in 1883 when a groups of sisters arrived in Chit-

---

50. "Draft Constitutions," 11. The Vatican's Sacred Congregation for Religious disallowed the making of this vow. Euphrasie comments, "We were told to keep it simply as a virtue and to apply ourselves to practicing it."

51. Jo Ann Kay McNamara, *Sisters in Arms: Catholic Nuns through Two Millennia* (Cambridge/London: Harvard University Press, 1996), 591.

tagong, then a district capital and important port in the Indian Empire. They soon began teaching catechism lessons, first opening a free school with two classes, and a month later, a more advanced fee-paying school for slightly better-off families. Before long, they had opened houses in Akyab (Burma), Dacca (then Eastern Bengal, now Bangladesh), and Calcutta (India).

Euphrasie's enthusiasm for missionary work, particularly foreign missions, reflected an apocalyptic urgency characteristic of the nineteenth-century French Catholic missionary enterprise. For example, in the "Dedication" she wrote for the *Manual of Prayers*, she exclaims, "In these sad times when our souls are filled with profound sorrow and steeped in bitter grief at the sight of that satanic impiety which, under all possible forms, perverts and ruins our dear France, nay entire Europe, and even its influence to the ends of the earth, blaspheming more than ever Your Holy Name, persecuting and pursuing with infernal hate, Your holy Spouse, the Church our Mother, and multiplies its incomparable and sacrilegious outrages against the Holy Eucharist . . ."[52] It was this sense of urgency that drove her to work in the foreign missions.

Unlike Catherine McAuley, Euphrasie was insistent on the need for a cloister. Her attitude exemplified the anomaly of the nineteenth-century French Catholic Church, which was "at once cloistered by the hostile modern world and expansive in its missionary outreach."[53] Euphrasie was aware of the great struggles of the age between revolutionaries and restorationists, and her sympathies lay more with the restorationists in their opposition to modernism. Her insistence that her sisters be contemplative and her concern about modernism and its attendant dangers of anticlerical and antireligious ideas help explain her insistence on a cloistered lifestyle for her community. Furthermore, Cardinal de Bonald, archbishop of Lyon, had required that the Society of Mary, in the person of Father Favre, superior general of the Marist society, should guide the new community until Rome approved its constitutions. Father Favre insisted that the sisters should observe a rule of semi-enclosure, a decision that coincided with Euphrasie's vision for her congregation.[54]

---

52. Euphrasie Barbier, "Dedication," *Manual of Prayer*, 6. Irish Marist Historian, Donal Kerr argues that Pius IX viewed the world as divided into two camps—good and evil—and that he confidently looked forward to a divine intervention. Kerr cites Pope Pius IX's *Ignis, grando, nix, glacies, spiritus procellarum* (1872). The pope claimed that "nature itself was the instrument of God's punishment of a wicked world and that perhaps the end of was nigh." See Donal Kerr, "Rome, France and the Church 1800-1876: The Background to the Marist Adventure," *Forum Novum* 1 (1990): 297. Euphrasie probably would have resonated with those perceptions that understood the world as a battleground between the cosmic forces of good and evil. Such a sense of apocalyptic urgency about mission highlighted the need to hasten to engage in the battle of winning souls over to the kingdom of God.

53. McNamara, *Sisters in Arms*, 576.

54. See Charles Couturier, *Unswerving Journey: The Life of Mother Mary of the Heart of Jesus, Foundress of the Congregation of Our Lady of the Missions*, trans. Rosemary Sheed (Toulouse: Prière et Vie, 1966), 53-74.

Euphrasie's insistence on the cloister could also suggest that she sought a certain distance from the Marist priests' possible interference in the internal governance of her order. This perhaps explains why some Marist priests who believed the cloister was designed to limit both the missionary work of the sisters and their legitimate contacts with the sisters opposed Euphrasie's wishes concerning a cloistered life. On the other hand, other Marists probably subscribed to the monastic tradition that held that nuns were incapable of governing themselves, and governance should belong to monks of the same religious family or to the legitimate ecclesiastical superior.[55] An interesting footnote to the pre-Vatican II story of the sisters' mission and cloistered lifestyle in New Zealand is found in *Diamond Jubilee Magazine* (1929). There is an account of the visit to the Chatham Islands, eight hundred kilometers southeast of New Zealand, by two sisters in the summer of 1928-1929—Sister Mary St. Blaise and Sister Mary St. Dominica—who had responded to Bishop Brodie's request that religious instruction be given to the Catholic children in the Chatham Islands, part of the Diocese of Christchurch. The sisters spent six weeks instructing the children and visiting both Catholic and Protestant families. They stayed with different families, temporarily forsaking the cloistered lifestyle.[56]

## Holy Spirit Missionary Sisters Founded by Father Arnold Janssen (1837-1909) in Holland in 1889

The German priest Arnold Janssen saw that the German church needed to take the church's call to universal mission more seriously. This led him in 1875 to found the Society of the Divine Word (SVD), a male missionary order. Two women, Helena Stollenwerk and Hendrina Stollenwerk, undertook to serve the community as domestic help. They did this for seven years, and their cheerful and willing service convinced Janssen that if such women were to become Catholic sisters, able and prepared to serve missionary priests in such a way, this would undoubtedly help the priests' work. There seems little doubt that Janssen believed that women were best suited to the domestic care of priests and a ministry of prayer to support the priests in their work. Janssen, apparently unwilling to negotiate with a mother superior, "founded his own order of missionary sisters so that they could be trained specifically to help the Society of the Divine Word, and as long as he was in charge, he forbade them to assist other missions . . . the eagerness of

---

55. "Like many of their contemporaries, the [Marist] Fathers were convinced that no community of women could possibly govern themselves unaided." Roberta Morrissey, RNDM, "The Constitutions of Our Lady of the Missions," 1970. RNDM Archives, Rome,

56. See *Diamond Jubilee Magazine in Commemoration of the Foundation of the Convent of Notre Dame des Missions, Christchurch, New Zealand* (Christchurch: Tablet Publishing Co., 1929), 84-85.

German and Dutch women to participate in mission work was so great that by 1906, there were 400 sisters in the congregation."[57]

The typology of Luke 10:38-42, the story of Martha, who actively served the Lord, and Mary, who sat at the Lord's feet and listened, appealed to Janssen, who envisaged the Holy Spirit Sisters as "Marthas" toiling for the Lord through their ministry of domestic care for priests. In order to provide "Marys" who would pray for the SVD priests and brothers, he founded another order, the Servants of the Holy Spirit of Perpetual Adoration. Janssen's understanding of gender roles has been aptly described as "patriarchally inspired."[58] It is apparent that the life of the SVD religious family—priests, sisters, and brothers—reflected the division of gender and class that operated in the wider ecclesiastical and German and Dutch cultures of which it was part. The difficulties that Janssen's understanding of women's role in mission entailed for women were well captured in the comments of Mother Leonarda Lentrup, provincial of the American foundation of the Holy Spirit Sisters in Illinois. She complained that the "SVDs keep us from rising as a mission house."[59] In the ensuing correspondence, the SVD superior general, Father Blum, stated, "The title 'Mission House' is not appropriate [for women] . . . Besides it is also questionable whether a Sisters' Convent may simply call itself a mission house because it implies first of all an institute for mission priests."[60] In 1910, at the Holy Spirit Sisters' first general chapter, the sisters became independent financially and administratively from the SVDs.

The sisters, however, began to understand mission in categories other than those prescribed by their founder, and were soon engaged in health, social, and educational ministries in the United States, Brazil, Papua New Guinea, China, and Japan. If "patriarchy" best describes the life of SVD communities, then "maternalism" is perhaps the most appropriate description for the sisters. "As their name implies, the dominant image these nuns hold of themselves is one of altruistic service, even servitude. Based on Western and papal notions of patriarchy, 'maternal nurturance' and 'domesticity' are the gendered forms this service was supposed to take toward priests and native people alike."[61]

Sisters could embrace missionary roles that patriarchal culture denied to

---

57. Robert, *American Women in Mission,* 339.

58. Mary Taylor Huber and Nancy C. Lutkehaus, "Introduction: Gendered Missions at Home and Abroad," in *Gendered Missions: Women and Men in Missionary Discourse and Practice,* ed. Mary Taylor Huber and Nancy C. Lutkehaus (Ann Arbor: University of Michigan, 2002), 16.

59. Angelyn Dries, "U.S. Sources for the Catholic Overseas Mission Movement," *U.S. Catholic Historian* 11 (1993): 45.

60. Ibid., quoting from Blum, the SVD superior general to Mother General Theresia, March 1, 1915, cited in Ann Geir, *This Fire Ever Burning: A Biography of M. Leonard Lentrup (Elizabeth)* (Techny, Ill.: Mission Press, 1986), 212.

61. Huber and Lutkehaus, "Gendered Missions at Home and Abroad," 17.

men—mission toward women. Sisters could establish and work in orphanages, dispensaries, and engage in catechetics and instruct women in their homes. The emphasis on mission in homes demonstrated the prevailing idea that the good Catholic home was the seedbed of priestly vocations, or, as Janssen, stated, "Christian families also would be sanctified and the vocations for the priesthood and the missions be increased."[62] However, the cultural, climatic, and geographic conditions in which both SVD and SSpS (Holy Spirit Missionary Sisters) missionaries often found themselves led to a blurring of traditional gendered missionary roles. In Papua New Guinea, for example, it appeared as if the sisters were engaging in tasks that verged on the priestly, such as preparing the dying, or baptizing those in danger of death. This happened so much so that SVD historian Bruno Hagspiel explained that "in such cases, upon their return to the station, [the sisters] report to the missionary, observations which may be useful to the Father on his next visit to the place."[63] This suggests that when missionary women and men worked together in transitional times or places, the prescribed gender boundaries between them would more likely be subverted.

*Mary Josephine Rogers (1882-1995), Founder of the Maryknoll Sisters in the United States in 1912*

Mary Rogers, born into a wealthy Irish American family, emerges as one of the most important missionary women in the story of North American overseas mission. She had been deeply influenced by her contact with the work of the Society for the Propagation of the Faith. After hearing Father James Walsh, the Boston director of the society, at a public lecture, Mary devoted herself first to spreading information about Catholic foreign missions to American Catholics, and then, after Walsh founded the Catholic Foreign Mission Society of America, more commonly known as Maryknollers, she founded the Foreign Mission Sisters of St. Dominic, also known as the Maryknoll Sisters. In 1920, they became the first American order of Catholic sisters to commit themselves to the foreign missions. Like other American missionaries of the time, the Maryknoll Sisters were influenced by the idea that Americans had a particular mission to spread freedom and democracy through addressing social ills. In light of the havoc that World War I had created for European missionary groups, the wider Catholic community, particularly missionary organizations such as the Society for the

---

62. Herman Fischer, *Life of Arnold Janssen: Founder of the Society of the Word and of the Missionary Congregation of the Servants of the Holy Ghost* (Techny, Ill.: Mission Press, 1925), 442.

63. Bruno M. Hagspiel, *Along the Mission Trail: In the Netherlands East Indies*, 5 vols. (Techny, Ill.: Mission Press, 1925), 3:206.

Propagation of the Faith, believed that a young and vibrant, democratic America had much to offer the pagan world.[64]

In the early twentieth century, the American Catholic Church was still an immigrant church with all the attendant pastoral challenges this entailed, but the foundation of the Maryknoll Fathers and Sisters indicated that it was becoming more outwardly focused. The culture of the time, however, also held that the Maryknoll Sisters should see their vocation as an extension of women's traditional tasks—cooking and caring for the men while the latter prepared for mission in China. Mary was opposed to the idea that Maryknoll Sisters should be relegated to domestic chores for the men, and so in 1921, the first sisters began their journey to China, where they "were welcomed into Chinese homes, whereas the men were prevented from such contact by strict Chinese customs."[65] Not only did Maryknoll Sisters visit Chinese homes; they also chose to live in Chinese villages, a noninstitutional approach to mission that ran counter to how women's missionary activity usually occurred.

In 1923, Mary visited China at a time when the country was embroiled in civil wars. This allowed her to further develop her understanding of mission, particularly of the need for adequate professional and spiritual formation for her sisters. On her return to the States, she undertook three important developments: the establishment in 1930 of an institution where the sisters would receive a sound academic formation; the establishment of a cloistered community that was intended to be a prayer powerhouse for the apostolic sisters; and, in 1932, given the extraordinary growth of her community, the building of a large motherhouse. The sisters had first built next to the Maryknoll Fathers, but the new motherhouse was located on a large property on the opposite side of the road, a geographical distancing that hinted at a certain philosophical movement too because by now the sisters were developing a missionary style better suited to their gifts and works. As Robert writes, Mary "had experienced the failure of the Maryknoll Fathers to acknowledge the full calling of the sisters to mission work as 'one of our most perplexing problems.'"[66]

Mary's theology of mission was developing, particularly her Mariology. Initially, she found in Mary, who prepared Jesus for his public ministry, a good role model for her sisters, but as her theology of Mary developed, she came to understand her as the one who gave Christ to others. This shift in emphasis meant that Maryknoll Sisters no longer considered themselves as ancillary staff to Maryknoll priests in their important work of evangelization.

---

64. See Dries, "U.S. Sources," 37-48.
65. Penny Lernoux, Arthur Jones, and Robert Ellsberg, *Hearts on Fire: The Story of the Maryknoll Sisters* (Maryknoll, N.Y.: Orbis Books, 1993), xxix.
66. Robert, *American Women in Mission*, 353.

The sisters too were to be engaged in works of evangelization.[67] "In terms of a model for mission, Mother Mary Joseph had clearly moved from an auxiliary model, symbolized by Mary, to an active model based more directly on the work of Jesus Christ."[68]

It is interesting to compare the founding processes of Euphrasie Barbier's order, the Holy Spirit Sisters, and the Maryknollers. Initially, Euphrasie Barbier certainly relied on the spiritual and financial support of the Marist Fathers, but she was equally clear that she wanted an autonomy for her order that ran counter to the wishes of some of the Marist Fathers who believed that women could not really govern themselves. It was for this reason that she sought pontifical status for her sisters, that is, they were to be obedient to the pope, and responsible to bishops in matters of apostolic activity in a particular diocese. However, neither bishops nor male superior generals could interfere in the internal governance of the order. The Holy Spirit Sisters' situation differed from what Euphrasie envisioned because Janssen was very clear about the gendered nature of missionary activity and governance. Holy Spirit Sisters were there to facilitate the mission of the priests through lives of domesticity and prayer, a situation that changed early in the twentieth century. The situation of the Maryknoll Sisters offered another variant on the governance of women's orders. In 1911, Father James Walsh established the Maryknoll Fathers. Mary Rogers's initial involvement with Father Walsh through her enthusiasm for the Society for the Propagation of the Faith led her to found an order of sisters to work in the foreign missions. Geographically and spiritually there was a significant relationship with the Maryknoll Fathers, even though they had a different perception about the role of missionary women. Mary finally made the decision that those differences meant that a certain separation from the fathers was desirable. This separation did not, however, signal a definitive break between the two communities, who continued to work together in the mission field but in ways that meant the sisters were more than ancillary staff for the priests.

The rationale for the foundation of the three orders also warrants examination. Euphrasie was imbued with a calling to work directly with women and children, but the Holy Spirit Sisters, initially at least, were intended by Janssen to be a back-up to the priest in his important sacramental ministry. Father Walsh too saw the Maryknoll Sisters engaged in similar work, but Mary Rogers realized early on that her sisters were capable of more than domestic work for the priests. The men's gendered perception of women's missionary roles is apparent, and although the modern reader feels a certain discomfort with such male perceptions, it is unlikely that the young congregations would have been founded without clerical support.

---

67. Ibid., 353-57, for a succinct and comprehensive account of Mary Rogers's theology of mission.

68. Ibid., 356.

## MISSION AS WORK WITH INDIGENOUS PEOPLES
## AND MINORITY GROUPS[69]

*Elizabeth Lange (1784-1882), Founder of the Oblate Sisters*
*of Providence in the United States*

Elizabeth Lange was born in the Dominican Republic, and in the late eighteenth century, her family shifted to Cuba before immigrating to the United States about 1812. Soon after her arrival in Baltimore, Elizabeth and two Haitian women began teaching Haitian children in a room at St. Mary's Seminary. In 1829, with French-born Sulpician priest Nicholas Joubert, who had formerly worked in San Domingo, she founded the first black order of women religious in the United States, the Oblate Sisters of Providence.[70] The order received papal approval in 1831. In the 1830s, the Jesuits were still debating whether to sell their slaves, and American Catholic bishops appeared to see nothing unwarranted in the institution of slavery, so to found an order of black women was a radical move. Growth was steady rather than spectacular, and at the time of Elizabeth's death in 1882, there were about fifty members.

The apostolic work of the Oblate Sisters was wide ranging and included the education of freed slaves, some of whom were eventually admitted into the congregation, the education of youth, care of orphans, nursing the terminally ill during the 1832 cholera epidemic in Baltimore, sheltering the elderly, and providing domestic help, when required, for the Sulpician priests in St. Mary's Seminary. The support of Father Joubert in particular and the Sulpician community in general had been significant in ensuring the initial growth of the young order, but after Joubert's death in 1843, that support was no longer available; and three orders, first the Redemptorists, then the Jesuits, and finally the Josephite Fathers and Brothers assumed responsibility for the ecclesiastical direction of the Oblates until this requirement was rescinded in the early twentieth century. Under the influence of the Josephites, the Oblates opened a mission in Cuba in 1900, and later on Old Providence Island in the western Caribbean. Political and economic hardship, however, led to the Oblates' withdrawal from these places, although they continued to work in Costa Rica. The story of Elizabeth Lange and the Oblates offers a striking example of a black women's order undertaking a ministry to other blacks oppressed by racism, ignorance, and illiteracy. Such women had not

---

69. Many indigenous orders were founded in the nineteenth and twentieth centuries, for example, the Daughters of Mary of Bannabikira, Uganda; the Congregation of the Little Sisters of Mary Immaculate, Uganda, founded in 1942; and the Associates of Mary Queen of Apostles, popularly known as the Toomilia Sisters, founded in Bangladesh in 1933.

70. Another black order, the Sisters of the Holy Family, was founded in New Orleans in 1842 by two free women of color, Juliet Gaudin and Henrietta Delille. See Angelyn Dries, *The Missionary Movement in American Catholic History* (Maryknoll, N.Y.: Orbis Books, 1998), 28.

only to confront the reality of sexism in their ministry but the evil of racism in the church and in American society.

### Katharine Drexel (1858-1955), Founder of the Sisters of the Blessed Sacrament for Indians and Colored Peoples in the United States in 1891

Katharine Drexel was the heiress of one of America's wealthiest Catholic families, and she used her inherited wealth to build schools, social agencies for Native Americans and African Americans, a university for African Americans in New Orleans, and to pay teaching staff for schools and nursing staff for hospitals. Her wealth likewise supported the Washington-based Bureau of Catholic Indian Missions, which had been formed to lobby for the church in matters relating to Native Americans, the New York-based Catholic Interracial Council, the NAACP, African American parishes, and the 1930s campaign for antilynching legislation in the southern United States.

In the latter part of the nineteenth century, the American Catholic Church was hard pressed to meet the pastoral and socioeconomic needs of urban immigrants who continued to pour into the United States from Europe, and the needs of isolated small farming communities. Unlike its Protestant counterparts, the American Catholic Church did not prioritize foreign missionary work nor did it pay attention to the pastoral and social needs of the Native American population or of blacks, including the 150,000 or so blacks freed from slavery after the Civil War. The needs of white Catholic immigrant communities outweighed other needs.

Katharine recognized this gap in Catholic pastoral and missionary initiatives, and her wealth made it possible for her to direct monies to Native American converts and to African Americans. Encouraged by Pope Leo XIII, she finally decided to found her own order to work specifically with Native Americans and African Americans, primarily through education. Katharine chose not to rely on her own wealth in establishing her community; instead, she continued to direct it toward the work and activities of other groups. The radical nature of her work is obvious when it is remembered that the American bishops "did not speak out on the constitutional rights of blacks until 1943 and did not make racial discrimination the exclusive subject of a national pastoral letter until *Discrimination and Christian Conscience in 1958*"[71] was published. Her order was initially known as the Sisters of the Blessed Sacrament for Indians and Colored Peoples, and her rule was basically that of the Sisters of Mercy, with some additions from the rule of the Holy Ghost Fathers because they were also working with Native Americans

---

71. Patrick W. Carey, *Catholics in America: A History* (Westport, Conn.: Praeger, 2004), 86.

and African Americans. The growth of her order was extraordinary, and generated both enthusiasm and opposition.[72]

Katharine Drexel emerges from the story of missionary women as "a strong voice for interracial justice and for women and mission in the United States."[73] She perceived a need not being met by existing Catholic groups and sought to respond to it in three different ways. (1) She used her own considerable resources to support Native Americans and African Americans who sought justice for themselves. She did not assume that her support gave her the right to organize the political and social agendas of such people. (2) She provided resources to Native Americans and African Americans so that they had a political voice, and she supported lobbying groups, such as the Bureau of Catholic Indian Missions, in their role as advocates. (3) Without relying on her own wealth, although her social status and economic clout undoubtedly helped her, she undertook to found an order that embraced apostolates that had not previously emerged as significant in the American Catholic immigrant church.

## MISSION AS PROFESSIONAL HEALTH CARE

*Anna Dengel (1892-1980), Founder of the Medical Mission Sisters in the United States in 1925*

Catholic women missionaries have always prioritized care of the sick, dying, and wounded. By the twentieth century, Catholic women faced at least two major problems in such ministries. First, because the task of caring for the sick poor was seen as an extension of women's traditional biological tasks of care and nurturance, initially there was little emphasis placed on the need for professional training. Mary Rogers, for example, was very aware of this lack after she visited the first Maryknoll Sisters working in China in the early 1920s. To say this is not to diminish the efforts of the sisters who worked with Florence Nightingale during the Crimean War or who cared for the sick and wounded during the American Civil War, but by the twentieth century, it was obvious that good will, minimal training, and sincerity were no longer sufficient. Second, the church's Canon Law forbade religious to study medicine, human physiology, or to engage in obstetric work because

---

72. "In Beaumont, Texas, she ran into opposition from the Ku Klux Klan: the Sisters went to Mass one morning to find a sheet of paper nailed to the church door. It read: 'We want an end to services here. We will not stand by while white priests consort with nigger wenches in the face of our families. Suppress it in one week, or flogging and tar and feathers will follow.' On the following day there was a threat to dynamite the church." See Kathleen Jones, *Women Saints: Lives of Faith and Courage* (Maryknoll, N.Y.: Orbis Books; Tunbridge Wells: Burns & Oates, 1999), 273.

73. Bevans and Schroeder, *Constants in Context,* 225.

of "clerical suspicion that the intimacy of medical work was harmful to chastity."[74] Unlike Protestant missionaries in the nineteenth and early twentieth century who set up hospitals and dispensaries, Catholic missionaries, most often members of religious orders, were forbidden to practice such medical work. Given the success of Protestant medical missionary activity, it became obvious that Catholics were missing out on important opportunities for evangelization. As Robert states, "In 1889 for example, there were 61 Protestant missionary hospitals and 44 dispensaries in China, but only 5 Catholic hospitals and 7 dispensaries."[75]

Efforts were made to reverse this situation. In the United States, the Catholic Students Mission Crusade, at its 1922 meeting, decided that Catholic missionaries needed to be trained as medical missionaries in a way similar to that of their Protestant counterparts. In 1925, the Catholic Medical Mission Board recognized the need for a more holistic approach to human welfare. Austrian-born medical doctor Anna Dengel, an influential founding member of the society, had begun working as a missionary doctor in Rawalpindi, Pakistan, in 1920. She directed her medical work toward women because local cultural practices made it virtually impossible for male doctors to attend to them. In 1925, she established the Pious Society, which undertook to provide medical services where most needed, and this evolved into the Society of Catholic Medical Missionaries in 1936, the year when the Vatican ruled that women religious could train as physicians, surgeons, and obstetricians.[76] This was the first Catholic order of women founded to work as professional medical personnel. Dengel defined medical missions as "that branch of missionary work through which skilled medical care is given to the sick and poor of mission countries, as a means of relieving their physical suffering and of bringing them to a knowledge and appreciation of our faith."[77]

There were at least three reasons why approval for Catholic medical missionary women was forthcoming in the twentieth century. First, there was a concern about the promotion of birth control policies other than the "rhythm" method, both overseas and among immigrant communities in the United States. Women medical missionaries would be ideally placed to redress such a promotion. Second, the gendered nature of cultural practices in many places adversely affected the health of women, and it was recognized that suitably trained Catholic medical women could best respond to

---

74. McNamara, *Sisters in Arms*, 626.

75. Robert, *American Women in Mission*, 372.

76. The 1917 Code of Canon Law, canon 139.2, forbade clerics to study medicine or practice surgery without an apostolic indult, while canon 592 required lay religious, women and men, to follow all the obligations of clerics stipulated in canons 124-42. Obedience to such canons effectively precluded religious women from studying medicine.

77. Dries, *The Missionary Movement in American Catholic History*, 104, quoting from Anna Dengel, *Mission for Samaritans: A Survey of Achievements and Opportunities in the Field of Catholic Medical Missions* (Milwaukee: Bruce, 1945), 1.

such situations. Finally, the strenuous nature of the work undertaken by pregnant women meant a high incidence of infant mortality or the death of the mother during childbirth, again a situation that would be improved by the intervention of Catholic medical missionary women. It was not surprising therefore that there was a demand for women missionaries to be trained as health professionals in order to work with women.[78]

Anna Dengel is important for Catholic missionary women because, first, she saw that medical missionary work was rooted in the Gospel stories of Jesus, who healed the sick and wounded. She was adamant that sincerity and what Pius IX referred to as "unenlightened heroism" were insufficient. Second, she believed that such twentieth-century missionary work made progress in redressing the health problems that Europeans had earlier inflicted on non-European peoples across the world. Her understanding of mission pointed to "an incarnational theology of mission based on imitation of Christ combined with professionalization in mission to heal the body of Christ,"[79] and "she viewed professional health care for women among Muslim, Hindu and Buddhist cultures not as a means to conversion *per se* but as a witness to the gratuitous love of God."[80] In embracing her vocation as a healing missionary, Anna was continuing the tradition of the many religious and laywomen who before her had engaged in healing ministries. She was innovative in her insistence that women religious who embraced a healing ministry be professionally qualified as doctors and nurses.

## MISSION AS PRESENCE

*Little Sister Magdeleine of Jesus, Founder of the Little Sisters of Jesus in 1939*

Vatican II is often considered by Catholics to be a watershed in bringing about change in Catholic missionary practice, but even prior to the Vatican Council (1962-1965), there were some who recognized the need for new ways of being missionary. French legionnaire-playboy-turned-hermit Charles de Foucauld (1858-1916)[81] was one person who sought to model a new way of being missionary. Upon his dismissal from the French army in 1881, de

78. See Dries, *The Missionary Movement in American Catholic History*, 102-4.

79. Ibid., 106.

80. Angelyn Dries, "American Catholic 'Woman's Work for Woman' in the Twentieth Century," in *Gospel Bearers, Gender Barriers*, ed. Dana L. Robert (Maryknoll, N.Y.: Orbis Books, 2002), 136.

81. Pope Paul VI, in *Populorum Progressio*, acclaims de Foucauld for his ability to live among the Tuaregs. "We need only mention the efforts of Père Charles de Foucauld: he compiled a valuable dictionary of the Tuareg language, and his charity won him the title, 'everyone's brother.'" See Pope Paul VI, *On the Development of Peoples* (New York: Paulist Press, 1967), no. 12.

Foucauld undertook to explore Morocco for the French Geographical Society, and his exposure to the simple, deep faith of the Muslim Bedouins led to a conversion experience that took him first to the Holy Land and then to Syria, where he spent time as a Trappist monk. During this physical and spiritual pilgrimage he meditated on Jesus of Nazareth, the poor man who worked as a carpenter, and this led him to appreciate better the incarnational dimensions of missionary presence. He acted out his insight in a fairly literal manner as a servant in the Poor Clare convent at Nazareth; and though he apparently failed to impress the nuns with his carpentry skills, he impressed them with his spirit of poverty and contemplation.

After ordination, he returned to Algeria, where he attempted to found a religious community committed to a deeply contemplative life whose members would live and work among the poor. He failed to realize this dream and embraced an eremitic rather than cenobitic way of life in remote and isolated Tamanrasset, where he was killed in 1916 by the Tuaregs. Despite his deeply contemplative and ascetical lifestyle, in other important respects, de Foucauld was a man of his times, particularly in his patriotism. He "believed that the colonial presence could be a positive element in the development of peoples provided that it was based on Christian attitudes of justice. He was just as clear that if the colonial presence was not itself evangelized that it would not only be a shameful exploitation of the Algerian people but counter-productive to French interests."[82]

Despite de Foucauld's failure to found a religious order, his vision did not die with him. In 1936 Frenchman René Voillaume and four companions, calling themselves the Little Brothers of Jesus, left France for the Sahara in an attempt to live a life that allowed them to closely identify with their Muslim neighbors. Women too responded to de Foucauld's vision, and in 1939, Frenchwoman Magdeleine Hutin journeyed with a companion to the Sahara and so began the Little Sisters of Jesus. Cathy Wright explains that the inclusion of "little" in the title "Little Sisters of Jesus" affirms that "littleness" was an essential element of mission, and the idea of "littleness" should not be diminished because it was intended to enliven and sustain faith at the deepest level.[83] Its missionary significance derived from the belief that following the example of Jesus, the village artisan from Nazareth, Little Sisters or Brothers should follow a lifestyle that identified them with those among whom they lived.

Magdeleine had grown up in a small village on the French-German border and was intensely aware of the psychological and physical displacement that the wars of the nineteenth and early twentieth centuries along this bor-

---

82. Cathy Wright, "Nazareth as a Model for Mission in the Life of Charles de Foucauld," *Mission Studies* 19 (2002): 36-52.
83. See Cathy Wright, "Spiritual Childhood and Mission: A Way of Living Hope with Brokenness," *Spirituality* 8 (2002): 373.

der caused people. Her experiences allowed her to empathize better with others whose lives were torn apart by war, and she envisioned a form of religious life that reached out to those who were broken and separated. Charles de Foucauld's life offered a model for her. Her important insight was that although fidelity to de Foucauld's vision demanded living among nomadic Muslims in the Sahara, such a contemplative form of life could be lived elsewhere. Communities of the Little Sisters were to be established in places usually considered unsuitable for missionary activity, such as Islamic countries[84] and areas behind what was then the Iron Curtain. Communities were also founded among migrant farm and fruit workers, gypsies, and traveling circuses. Little Sisters were to support themselves by having some members of the community work in jobs similar to those among whom they were living.

The Little Sisters provide a fascinating alternative model to the more usual expressions of Catholic missionary presence prior to Vatican II. Their way of life was noninstitutional, and this allowed them to anticipate and live out in their communities a more inculturated way of life. For example, when the sisters lived in countries where the people have traditionally embraced the Eastern liturgical rites, they adopted Eastern rites in their communities and became an integral part of the local church. They also anticipated Vatican II's emphasis on interreligious dialogue. In 1955, Magdeleine sent sisters to Aqra, a town in the region of Nineveh, Iraq, where Christians and Kurds lived together. By choosing to live where marginalization, poverty, and violence were the daily lot of many, the Little Sisters anticipated what later was called "an option for the poor." Mission for the Little Sisters was a way "of entering the world of the other as one who comes to learn and of being evangelized by those among whom we live, of being receptive of people and events. At its core ours is a contemplative life. Central to it is the deep desire for a friendship and presence that tries to bridge the gap of exclusion and misunderstanding."[85]

Their ministry has not been without its critics. Muslim men sometimes have argued that it is inappropriate for communities of women to live a nomadic lifestyle in the Sahara. Others ask if a spirituality of presence is enough because it fails to address the problems of poverty and oppression in which so many live. More positively, it is not difficult to locate redeeming features in such an understanding of mission. The notion of presence among the marginalized and poor by living as one with them is not only scripturally based (see John 1:14) but it serves as a powerful countercultural model to the prevailing notion of mission as going to help others with its attendant dangers of appearing culturally superior. The model of evangelizing presence to which the Little Sisters were committed is sometimes referred to as "evan-

---

84. In 1994 they established a community in Afghanistan and were the only Catholic presence in that country until they left in 2002.

85. Wright, "Spiritual Childhood and Mission," 376.

gelization of the milieu by the milieu." It was a concept dear not only to the followers of Charles de Foucauld but to other important Catholic groups such as the Worker Priests and Young Christian Workers. It points to the importance of taking seriously those incarnational theologies that demand being one with the people among whom the missionary lives and works. It is a model that has significant implications for interreligious dialogue as "dialogue of life."

## MISSION AS COMMITMENT TO SOCIAL JUSTICE

*Dorothy Day (1897-1980), Founder of the Catholic Worker Movement*

America's Great Depression started with the collapse of the stock market in October 1929, and before long its resulting massive unemployment and poverty were felt worldwide. In 1930, Pope Pius XI's encyclical *Quadragesimo Anno* asked Catholic laity, through their membership in various Catholic Action groups, to address situations of economic deprivation and depression on the home front. The parameters of mission were changing. Catholic laywoman Dorothy Day, although not part of an officially recognized Catholic Action group, was challenged by such teaching. Eventually this led her to address the problem of economic disenfranchisement experienced by many Americans because of the Depression.

Mother Teresa and Dorothy Day represent the extreme ends of the continuum of Catholic missionary women. As Malone says, "It is unlikely that they ever met, and probably [they] would not have liked or agreed with one another."[86] While Mother Teresa was fasttracked to beatification six years after her death, it will probably take much longer for Dorothy Day to be honored by the institutional church in such a way, given her "stormy bohemian and socialist youth that included a sexual liaison that led to an abortion, a marriage that failed, and common-law relationship that resulted in the birth of a child and subsequent abandonment by the father."[87] Initially attracted to communism because of its critique of capitalist economic structures and the poverty such structures caused for so many, and after the birth of her daughter, Tamar, Dorothy Day was drawn to Catholicism and baptized in 1927.

The radical direction in which her faith would lead her was developed and refined after her meeting with Peter Maurin (1877-1949), the French socialist peasant-philosopher whom she met in 1932, shortly after she participated in the Great Hunger March from New York to Washington. On reaching Washington, Day, aware of the communist role in organizing the protest, was critical of the minimal Catholic involvement in the march. She

---

86. Malone, *Women and Christianity*, 3:295.
87. Carey, *Catholics in America*, 186.

did not hesitate to voice her criticism, and Maurin, having read some of Day's articles, was determined to meet her. He found in Dorothy Day "a woman of destiny, a twentieth century Catherine of Siena, sent by God to renew the church as Catherine had done in her day."[88] There were three important influences on Maurin's thinking that also influenced Day. First, he was deeply influenced by French personalism with its emphasis on the absolute value of each person and its resistance to the dehumanizing ideologies of capitalism, fascism, and communism. He was particularly impressed by the insistence of Léon Bloy (1846-1917) that voluntary poverty was a privileged path to God. Second, he was influenced by the works of Russian anarchist Peter Kropotkin (1842-1921), who argued that people "are naturally cooperative and that society can be organized around these positive tendencies."[89] The third important influence were the English Catholic writers Eric Gill, G. K Chesterton, and Hilaire Belloc, who "favored a broad distribution of land and capital rather than the concentration in the hands of a few."[90] His reading and ideas provided Day with an intellectual framework with which she was able to set out on a missionary journey that had not been embraced before by a woman.

Day and Maurin sought to give to American Catholics and to American society a new expression of Catholic social teaching by word and by action. The "word" dimension would be achieved through *The Catholic Worker,* first published in 1933, while the "action" occurred when she and Maurin established the first Catholic Worker house of hospitality. The Catholic Worker movement expanded rapidly, particularly when it provided houses of hospitality for the unemployed, homeless, and hungry during the Depression years. Day and Maurin also reached out to the black community, arguing that racism had its origins in capitalist structures, because capitalists encouraged racism as a control mechanism in their relations with the working classes. Initially, the Catholic middle and capitalist classes had hoped that the Catholic Worker movement would provide a Catholic answer to the presumed threat of communism. Day's thinking and actions speedily altered that perception. The movement fell into further disrepute when the *Catholic Worker* advocated neutrality at the outbreak of the Spanish Civil War (1936-1939). Day's and Maurin's Catholicism was of the radical rather than mainstream variety, and their standing fell further when they spoke out against the anti-Semitism propagated by Michigan-based Father Charles Coughlin.[91]

---

88. Thomas Bokenkotter, *Church and Revolution: Catholics in the Struggle for Democracy and Social Justice* (New York: Image Books, 1998), 411.

89. Ibid., 413.

90. Ibid., 414.

91. Charles Coughlin (1891-1979), a Catholic priest from Michigan, used the radio to preach to a widespread audience during the Depression. Initially a supporter of Franklin D. Roosevelt's New Deal policies, he became increasingly anti-Semitic, and embraced the fascist ideologies of Mussolini and Hitler as the appropriate response to Communism.

Day's opposition to World War II, the Korean War, the Vietnam War, and the rhetoric and mentality of the Cold War made her highly unpopular in many church circles and in society. Nothing deterred her from her chosen path of pacifism and compassion toward the poor so that she and the Catholic Worker movement became the source of "Catholic radicalism in the United States, a movement that challenged prevailing moral assumptions in the culture."[92] Despite conflict with the church, particularly with Cardinal Spellman of New York, Day remained faithful to the church and above all faithful to the biblical imperative to act justly, walk humbly, and love tenderly. As she asked, "Where shall we go except to the Bride of Christ, one flesh with Christ? Though she is a harlot at times, she is our Mother."[93] Her emphasis on the need for nonviolence, her pacifism, her simple lifestyle, and her compassion for the poor and the marginalized make her a truly countercultural, prophetic figure—something finally recognized in the 1990s when John Cardinal O'Connor of New York began the process that one day could culminate in her beatification. Dorothy Day is truly a missionary for our times, and her willingness to step into the public place and proclaim in word and deed the good news makes her a important role model for contemporary women.

## MISSION TO AND FOR WOMEN

### *The Grail Movement, Founded by Jacques van Ginneken, SJ, in the Netherlands in 1921*

Jacques van Ginneken, a professor at the University of Nijmegen, founded a movement of Catholic laywomen, some of them his students. Van Ginneken "like others, romanticized the past. For van Ginneken, not the Middle Ages but the years of early Christianity provided the inspiration he was looking for. He saw the twentieth century as a mirror of early Christianity. The world needed to be conquered for Christ again."[94] He believed that women possessed gifts and talents that should be used and exploited for Christ's sake. His vision was one that spoke to young women students who did not necessarily feel called to the celibate life associated with religious life nor to marriage and motherhood. The Grail Movement, initially called Women of Nazareth, was established as a prototypical secular institute, although such institutes were not canonically approved until 1947.

---

92. Carey, *Catholics in America*, 186.
93. William Miller, *A Harsh and Dreadful Love* (New York: Liveright, 1973), 337.
94. Marjet Derks, "Lion and Lamb: Jacques van Ginneken and the 'Women of Nazareth' in the 1920s and 1930s." Paper presented at European Social Science History Conference (Amsterdam, 1998), 1-9.

The movement sought to unite married and single women of different races, backgrounds, and professions in an effort to provide Christian witness in an increasingly secular society. The movement was one of the different responses to the papal call for more involvement of laity in the mission of the church.[95] Its founder believed that women had particular gifts that meant the possibility of "a place for women beyond the home,"[96] and that they were called to "give themselves to God in the midst of the world."[97] As Dr. Lydwine van Kersbergen, one of its early leaders, said, the formation of women as missionaries "needed to take into account her intelligence and intuition, her bent toward contemplation and inwardness, and her sense of total dedication and selfless love."[98] By 1940 the Grail Movement had moved to the United Kingdom, Germany, Australia, and the United States, where it established its headquarters in Loveland, Ohio. Influenced by the philosophy of the National Catholic Rural Life Conference, van Kersbergen introduced an agricultural dimension to Grail life and philosophy in the United States by settling on a working farm. This dimension has been reflected to various degrees in the liturgies, communal life, and education programs of Grailville since its founding.[99] The outbreak of World War II meant that the Dutch Grail Movement was driven underground during the Nazi occupation, thus hampering its growth, but in the postwar period, it expanded throughout the Western world and elsewhere.

In the Catholic tradition, missionary activity usually belonged to celibate members of women's and men's religious orders. The Grail Movement, however, pointed to the important missionary part that laywomen, single and married, could play. Grail formation stressed community living, preparation for active involvement in mission, and liturgical prayer, which it believed was foundational for its life. Grail training "focused on the understanding and experience of liturgy as the wellspring of Christian life."[100] It is interesting that the Second Vatican Council approved many of the liturgical innovations that the Grail Movement had earlier initiated. In 1962, "the Grail's vision for

---

95. After World War I, the church acknowledged the need for lay involvement in its mission. See, for example, Pope Pius XI's 1931 encyclical *Quadragesimo Anno* and Pope Pius XII's two mission encyclicals, *Evangelii Praecones* (1951) and *Fidei Donum* (1957).

96. Dries, "American Catholic 'Woman's Work for Woman' in the Twentieth Century," 138.

97. Rachel Donders, *The Grail Movement and American Catholicism 1940-1975* (Cincinnati: Selby Services, 1983), 3, quoting from a 1918 conference by Jacques van Ginneken.

98. Dries, *The Missionary Movement in American Catholic History*, 175, quoting from Lydwine van Kersbergen, *Women: Some Aspect of Her Role in the Modern World* (Loveland, Oh.: Grailville, 1956).

99. See "Christian Engaged Project" *Forum on Religion and Ecology,* Harvard University Center for the Environment. Available at http://environment,harvard,edu/religion/religion/christianity/prjects/grailville.html; accessed April 4, 2004.

100. Janet Kalven, "Living the Liturgy: Keystone of the Grail Vision," *U.S. Catholic Historian* 11 (1993): 29-35.

women radically shifted from building a new Catholic culture for modern times toward emphasizing more active involvement in social, political and economic areas . . . They cultivated ecumenical ties with other women, moving not without pain, from religious certainty to religious search."[101]

Grail members, in common with other communities of Catholic religious and laywomen, were deeply influenced in the 1960s by feminism. Prior to the 1960s, the Grail Movement "reflected a particular understanding of Catholicism rooted in a theology of the cross and testified to an acceptance of the complementary status of women in the Church,"[102] but this was to change. Their Jesuit founder had established a hierarchical structure for the Grail Movement, a model that was no longer considered appropriate as Grail members opted for more participatory and collaborative models of governance and relationships with those among whom they worked, recognizing that such a model better equipped them in their role as agents of social change. Efforts to move beyond a hierarchical structure in their own communities also led them to question whether the term "mission" as a nomenclature for their work was suitable in the world of the 1960s, and they suggested that "international cooperation" "might be a more fitting term to express the reality of how their members were involved in the world."[103] Such shifts were more than verbal and pointed to the desire of Grail members to move toward a theology of mission that anticipated the teaching of *Gaudium et Spes* that the church makes its own "the joys and hopes, the griefs and anxieties of the men of this age, especially those who are poor or in any way afflicted, these too are the joys and hopes, the griefs and anxieties of the followers of Christ" (no. 1).[104] Grail activity was to become less about rechristianizing secular society and more about cooperation with all peoples of good will for the sake of all, and in solidarity with the poor. The Grail Movement is of particular interest because it was a movement of laywomen who realized that the call to mission was not primarily grounded in the charism of a particular religious order. Instead, the movement believed that the call to mission was rooted in one's baptism rather than in religious profession or ordination.

Another important example of a lay missionary organization for women was the group founded by Belgian Vincentian missionary Vincent Lebbe. Lebbe, one of the more significant twentieth-century Catholic missionaries, worked in China from 1901 to 1940, and was committed to bringing about "a Catholic Church rooted in the culture and society of China."[105] To this

---

101. Dries, "American Catholic 'Woman's Work for Woman' in the Twentieth Century," 138.

102. Mary Jo Weaver, "Still Feisty at Fifty: The Grailville Lay Apostolate for Women," *U.S. Catholic Historian* 11 (1993): 3-12.

103. Dries, *The Missionary Movement in American Catholic History*, 237.

104. *Gaudium et Spes,* in Walter M. Abbott, ed., *The Documents of Vatican II* (London: Geoffrey Chapman, 1966), 198-99.

105. Jean-Paul Wiest, "The Legacy of Vincent Lebbe," *International Bulletin of Missionary Research* 23 (1999): 35-37.

end, he founded the Society of the Auxiliaries of the Missions so that secular priests from Europe could work as diocesan priests for native bishops in newly established dioceses. These priests became "living signs of a relationship between sister churches based on equality, sharing and service to one another."[106] In addition, Lebbe founded the Lay Auxiliaries of the Missions, the feminine counterpart of the diocesan priests' organization. This initiative was a radical departure from tradition because religious life was the normal avenue whereby women engaged in mission in foreign countries. As Jean-Paul Wiest comments, "these Lay Auxiliaries opened the way for the development and diversification of lay missionary groups among men and women in the Catholic Church some two decades later."[107]

## SECULAR INSTITUTES

In 1996, Pope John Paul II described members of secular institutes as "a leaven of wisdom and a witness of grace within cultural, economic and political life."[108] Secular institutes are a comparatively new phenomenon in the missionary life of the church and were approved in 1947 by Pope Pius XII in the apostolic constitution *Provida Mater Ecclesia*. Since then the growth of secular institutes has been significant with over two hundred institutes worldwide with as many as sixty thousand members. As we have seen, in the sixteenth century, Angela Merici envisioned a group of women who consecrated themselves to God by the three evangelical counsels, but who carried out their mission as laywomen living in the world without habit or community life. The time had not yet arrived for such a radical understanding of women's missionary endeavors, and her followers were eventually required to live a cloistered life and to wear a religious habit. Since Pius XII's canonical approval of secular institutes in 1947, their members have lived and worked as individuals but recognize and celebrate their particular charism and tradition through annual retreats, meetings, common daily prayer, and friendships that have developed because of their common beliefs.

The impulse that motivated people like Jane de Valois and Magdeleine Hutin to develop new forms of religious life was attractive to women who did not want, or who were not able to embrace, religious life but nevertheless wished to commit themselves to the charism and traditions of orders such as the Visitation Sisters and the Little Sisters of Jesus. Such a desire encouraged the foundation of secular institutes that enabled women to make

---

106. Ibid., 37.

107. Ibid. Pius XII's encyclicals *Evangelii Praecones* (1951) and *Fidei Donum* (1957), and John XXIII's *Princeps pastorum* (1959) asked for and approved the development of a lay mission apostolate.

108. John Paul II, *Vita Consecrata, Apostolic Exhortation* (1996); available at http://www.vatican.va/holy_father/john_paul_ii/apost_exhortations/documents/ hf_jp-ii_exh_2503 1996_vita-consecrata_en.html; accessed May 5, 2006.

vows of poverty, chastity, and obedience according to the spirit of such religious communities. The Secular Institute of Francis de Sales was founded in 1943 in Austria and approved as a secular institute in 1964. Though members' apostolates are personal, they are exercised in union with those of other members. Normally, members work at the diocesan or parish level. The Jesus Caritas Fraternity was founded in France in 1952, and approved as a secular institute in 1996. Faithful to the contemplative tradition of Charles de Foucauld, members seek to bring the good news of God's love to all, particularly to the poor. Members live their own individual lives in their families or alone, but they are required to gather monthly in their local fraternities for prayer, liturgical and personal, sharing the gospel, and participating in a review of life. The review allows individuals to bring to the group their concerns, their joys, and hopes. Members are expected to spend time each day in contemplation and to spend some time in retreat every month in the "desert." With their noninstitutionalized character, secular institutes offer a different model of mission from religious orders as members are involved in a range of apostolic activities that grow out of shared gospel values. As Paul VI rightly said, consecrated seculars are "an experimental laboratory, in which the church tests the ways she relates concretely to the world."[109]

The nineteenth century and the first half of the twentieth century witnessed important developments in women's missionary activity. The potential for women to embrace new missionary tasks that realities such as immigration, colonization, or war offered should not be underestimated. Despite the sheer volume of women's contributions, women's missionary work was still perceived by a patriarchal church and society as an extension of their biological roles as caregivers and nurturers. Because this caring role was supposedly instinctual rather than acquired, the need for professional education of the nun-nurse, nun-teacher, and nun-social worker was downplayed. Even though sisters were often the public face of the Catholic Church, they had little public voice regarding church life or even their own apostolic lives. As New Zealand church historian Christopher van der Krogt notes, "although the vast majority of teachers in Catholic schools were nuns, they seldom spoke in public."[110] They were expected to follow a monastic timetable, and Marie Augusta Neal points out that "the cloister became so sacralized in practice, that through the years, women who banded together . . . not for a contemplative vocation but for common prayer and works of charity were subjected to the same rigid restrictions when they dedicated their lives to works of human service in the local

---

109. Pope Paul VI, cited by Helen St. Denis, *The Growth of Secular Institutes Diocesan and Pontifical "Vocation for the New Millennium"* (2003); available at http://www.secular institutes.org/Vocation.htm; accessed May 7, 2006.

110. Christopher van der Krogt "Good Catholics and Good Citizens," in *Godly Schools? Some Approaches to Christian Education in New Zealand,* ed. Bryan Gilling (Hamilton: University of Waikato and Colcom Press, 1993), 4:18.

community."[111] This was true even if the actual foundation processes differed widely from order to order; a monastic timetable and way of life were appropriate for missionary sisters. Furthermore, a monastic lifestyle reinforced hierarchical structures and ensured a certain distancing from society.

Missionary work, whether in Europe, North America, or the mission fields meant that, at the personal level, women religious often experienced a greater freedom than that available to other Catholic women, and at the institutional level, many of them served their orders as able administrators and managers, thus securing for themselves a measure of financial and managerial autonomy that eluded their Protestant sisters in the mission fields. At the same time, the gendered nature of the works male and female missionaries undertook reflected the reality of their home ecclesial and social cultures, and "this gendered dichotomy also replicated the subordinate role of women within the hierarchy of the Catholic Church."[112] A 1921 publication of the American Society for the Propagation of the Faith insisted that women's missionary work of caring and nurturing children and women, and thereby improving family life, was the indispensable foundation on which a new church could be built. Even though the multifaceted nature of such work required the involvement of many women, numerical superiority did not allow for a significant voice in decision making regarding mission. That role belonged to "the missionary clergy, who required more arduous study and preparation than the sisters."[113]

Missionary women, lay and religious, had a deep love for the institutional church and its eucharistic spirituality, and were conscious of the centrality of daily Mass in their lives. They would have subscribed to the dominant Catholic ecclesiology that upheld the church's claim "to be the one and only true church, and consequently also officially Christian but non-Catholic regions were regarded as mission fields."[114] Therefore, they acquiesced to the belief that the establishment of the church in the foreign missions and in Protestant countries was a priority, and although responsibility and decision making for that activity belonged primarily to popes and bishops, women performed useful ancillary roles.

---

111. Marie Augusta Neal, *From Nuns to Sisters: An Expanding Vocation* (Mystic, Conn.: Twenty-Third Publications, 1990), 21.

112. Nancy C. Lutkehaus, "Missionary Maternalism: Gendered Images of the Holy Spirit Sisters in Colonial New Guinea," in *Gendered Missions: Women and Men in Missionary Discourse and Practice*, ed. Mary Taylor Huber and Nancy C. Lutkehaus (Ann Arbor: University of Michigan), 227.

113. Dries, *The Missionary Movement in American Catholic History*, 130, referring to Paulo Manna, *The Conversion of the Pagan World* (Boston: Society for the Propagation of the Faith, 1921), 168.

114. Yvonne Maria Werner, "Introduction," in *Nuns and Sisters in the Nordic Countries after the Reformation: A Female Counter-Culture in Modern Society*, ed. Yvonne Maria Werner (Uppsala: Swedish Institute of Mission Research, 2004), 10.

Throughout the nineteenth century, the dominance of Ultramontanist theologies and ecclesiologies meant that Vatican influence and control over missionary activity generally minimized the importance of attending to local culture and traditions. This engendered a Eurocentrism among missionaries and a somewhat dismissive attitude toward the cultures in which missionaries worked. Women missionaries enjoyed an advantage over their clerical counterparts because their mission involved them more directly in responding to felt human needs than was true of the sacramental ministry of the priest. However, both women and men generally held that missionary work and the spread of European civilization were complementary tasks. This encouraged a certain ethnocentrism and paternalism or maternalism, and "colonialism was regarded as an act of providence in order to facilitate the easy spread of the Christian faith."[115]

Although the mission of many sisters involved them in improving and fostering family life, their own lifestyles suggested something rather different. The model that sisters unconsciously provided—the possibility of education, travel, freedom from the demands of married life in a patriarchal culture—offered an alternative to the domestic development of Christian families that they consciously promoted in their capacity as missionaries in villages and in parishes. By extension, these alternative models attracted young indigenous women to religious life, thereby assisting in the growth of a newly established church. There is little doubt that religious missionary life provided a partial alternative to patriarchal family demands and allowed Catholic women to transgress contemporary social and religious boundaries. Thus, while religious missionary life at one level reinforced hierarchical and gendered structures in the church, it also helped subvert those same structures as women's missionary potential was realized and it became apparent that they could readily and capably perform roles other than domestic in the mission fields.

The relationship between the institutional church, the regulated life characteristic of nineteenth-century religious orders, and the freedom from familial demands was a complex one. In the exercise of their mission, religiously engaged women "adopted religious and ethical reform ideals that had been formulated by male theologians. By this means, women religious were able to contribute actively to the development of church and society."[116] At the same time, women were restricted by canonical legislation that obliged them to adjust to the church's hierarchical and clerical structures in order to participate actively in the church's missionary activity. Although women religious often found themselves in conflict with local bishops, there was little questioning of either Catholic ecclesiology or theology. This was to occur after Vatican II.

---

115. Isaac Padinjarekuttu, *The Missionary Movement of the 19th and 20th Centuries and Its Encounter with India: A Historico-Theological Investigation with Three Case Studies* (Frankfurt-am-Main: Peter Lang, 1995), 27.

116. Werner, "Introduction," 14.

# Part III

# WOMEN RECLAIMING THEIR RIGHTFUL MISSIONARY ROLE

# 7

# *Missionary Women since Vatican II*

## THE CONTEXT OF MISSION IN THE POSTMODERN ERA

By the middle of the twentieth century, the contours of the postmodern world were taking shape, and this affected the way in which women understood mission. To understand the changes that were to occur in missionary thought and practice, we need to refer first to World War II. The staggering loss of life brought about not only by military conflict but also by the Holocaust, and the bombing of civilian targets such as London, Dresden, and Hiroshima, highlighted the power for good and evil that modern technology offered governments. But the end of the war did not mean the dawn of peace; the dominance of the two super powers, the United States and the Soviet Union, meant an uneasy coexistence that occasionally brought both to the brink of war.

Second, Asian and African nations sought political independence from their former colonial masters. In 1947, the former Indian Empire became two separate nation states—India and Pakistan. In Vietnam political independence was gained only after war first with the French, and then a long civil war between American-supported Vietnamese opposed to communism and the North Vietnamese and their communist backers. In Africa, Ghana gained its independence from British colonial rule in 1957, Nigeria in 1960, and Kenya in 1963. In Africa, too, independence was sometimes preceded by war that pitted Africans against their colonial masters in countries such as Zimbabwe, Kenya, or Algeria. Even when countries gained independence, fierce tribal and ethnic fighting within a country meant great hardship for thousands of civilians, as the examples of Bangladesh, Nigeria, Angola, and the Democratic Republic of Congo made clear.

Political independence meant that mission understood as the movement of One-Third World missionaries to overseas "pagan" peoples became problematic for Two-Thirds World countries, often former colonies of Europe's imperial powers. Similarly, it led to a growing belief that political independence ought to be complemented by ecclesiologies that encouraged the growth of local churches. Wilbert Shenk argued that the "scaffolding" on which nineteenth-century missionary ecclesiologies were erected was no longer suitable for the modern era. He claims that in "many places the scaffolding seemed oppressively heavy or was allowed to stay in place far longer than necessary . . . [but] the scaffolding has been dismantled—at times forcibly, especially in the years since 1945."[1] Raimon Panikkar claimed that the Western missionary endeavor was weakened by the association of missionaries with Western imperialism with its presumed cultural and moral superiority, and its denominational and often divisive character.[2]

However, church growth after independence was significant. Methodist Bishop Hwa Yung of Malaysia points out that

> much of the [church] growth in Africa and Asia has occurred in the post-colonial period. Africa had largely emerged from colonialism by the early 1960s. Between 1964 and 1984, Christian numbers grew from about 60 to 240 million. In Asia, the percentage of Christians relative to the continent's population doubled from 2.3% to 4.7% between 1900 and 1970, and almost doubled again to 8.5% by the year 2000. In particular in Asia, a lot of the growth took place in places where the church was non-existent or weak in the earlier half of the 20th century. These include South Korea which is now 25-30% Christian, and Southeast Asia with some 22%. Places like Nepal that had hardly any Christians before 1960 now has a church of half a million strong![3]

The growth of the Christian community in such countries since political independence suggests that neither the patronage of colonial powers nor the attraction of the West was as significant in the conversion process as was commonly thought. Hwa Yung observes that "if anything, there is clear evidence that western control, either through colonial authorities or missionaries, has contributed significantly to the slow growth of the church in the earlier period."[4] In the case of Africa, there is some evidence that the end of the colonial period inhibited the growth of Islam and spurred the growth of Christianity instead.

China's situation is instructive. Despite the valiant missionary efforts of the nineteenth and early twentieth centuries, in 1949 Catholics numbered

---

1. Wilbert R. Shenk, ed. *Changing Frontiers of Mission* (Maryknoll, N.Y.: Orbis Books, 1999), 165.

2. See Raimon M. Panikkar, *Asia and Western Dominance: A Survey of the Vasco da Gama Epoch of Asian History, 1498-1945* (London: George Allen & Unwin, 1953).

3. Hwa Yung, "The Integrity of Mission in the Light of the Gospel: Bearing the Witness of the Spirit," unpublished manuscript (2004), p. 3.

4. Ibid., 5.

about 3.25 million and Protestants 1.30 million. This slow growth can be attributed to Western and Japanese imperialism in the nineteenth and early twentieth centuries, and to the subsequent xenophobia and Marxism of China's leaders. The slogan "One more Christian, one less Chinese" summed up the feelings of Chinese leaders. Christian leaders, sensitive to this opinion, also recognized that the whole problem was aggravated by missionary control over the budding Chinese church. "It seemed to China watchers in the 1970s that the Communist dictatorship had destroyed Chinese Christianity."[5] But today China watchers "in Hong Kong report that there are between 50 and 70 million Christians and 500,000 house churches."[6] This extraordinary growth of Christian churches in Africa and Asia augurs well for the future of Christian mission in light of the decline of institutional Catholicism in Europe, North America, Australia, and New Zealand. Today missionaries, women and men, Asian and African, are working not only in the Two-Thirds World but in the One-Third World.

Third, the power and growth of global North nations' economic clout in Two-Thirds World countries did little to alleviate the poverty of millions. Even if nations gained political independence, this seldom translated into economic well-being. The growing gap between One-Third World and the Two-Thirds World economies led One-Third World political leaders to promote development as a privileged way to eradicate poverty. In his 1961 inaugural address, President John Kennedy signaled a new sense of purpose in international affairs. He declared, "To those peoples in the huts and villages of half the globe struggling to break the bonds of mass misery, we pledge our best efforts to help them help themselves."[7] In such an atmosphere of hope and optimism, the United Nations launched its first Decade of Development. This sense of optimism was again evident six years later, when the World Council of Churches' Church and Society Conference in Geneva stated that people could "create new possibilities almost at will," and the 1968 Medellín document of the Latin American bishops believed that Latin America was "on the threshold of a new epoch."[8] David Bosch believes that the West was imbued with a false sense of optimism regarding development as the panacea for the poverty of the world's masses, and that development

5. Dana L. Robert, "Shifting Southward: Global Christianity since 1945," *International Bulletin of Missionary Research* 24 (2000): 50-58.

6. Rin Ro Bong, "Asia," in *Evangelical Dictionary of World Missions,* ed. Scott A. Moreau, David Burnett, and Harold Netland (Grand Rapids, Mich.: Baker Books, 2000), 83.

7. John F. Kennedy, Inaugural Address (1961); available at http://www.bartleby.com/124/pres56.html; accessed December 12, 2005.

8. See David J. Bosch, ed., *Transforming Mission: Paradigm Shifts in Theology of Mission* (Maryknoll, N.Y.: Orbis Books, 1991). Bosch is citing from *The Church for Others and the Church in the World* Geneva: World Council of Churches, 1967); see also Gustavo Gutiérrez, *A Theology of Liberation: History, Politics and Salvation,* trans. Caridad Inda and John Eagleson (Maryknoll, N.Y.: Orbis Books, 1988), xvii.

was not "as Paul VI had hoped, a new word for peace, but another word for exploitation. Underdevelopment was not a preliminary stage toward development but its consequence . . . The West's grand schemes, at home and in the Third World, have virtually all failed"[9] to eradicate poverty.

Fourth, unprecedented social and cultural changes were also affecting the way in which women understood mission. Feminism as a movement in secular society accelerated in the 1960s as women sought to redress the injustice of their situation. Though Catholic women were influenced by secular feminist authors such as Marilyn French and Germaine Greer,[10] more important were the works of Catholic feminist theologians such as Mary Daly, Elisabeth Schüssler Fiorenza, and Rosemary Radford Ruether,[11] who introduced women to the androcentric nature of biblical interpretation and theology, and its impact on church life.

Fifth, another significant development was the secularized nature of Western society. This had been noted as early as 1943 when two French authors argued that France was a country without religion.[12] This situation shattered the geographical understanding of mission and Christianity. "How was the traditional 'sender' of mission to become the 'receiver'?"[13] In 1968, a *Time* magazine's cover asked, "Is God Dead?" The question served as a type of shorthand to convey the loss of cultural religion in many Western countries.

When we consider the context of contemporary mission, perhaps the biggest challenge facing the missionary is how to work in such radically different situations and yet remain creatively faithful to New Testament missionary imperatives. Bosch suggests that the apparent opposites that confront today's missionary—"diversity versus unity, divergence versus integration, pluralism versus holism,"[14] demand new ways of theologizing about mission. I hope to demonstrate that Catholic women missionaries have been responsive to that demand; but before embarking on that task, it is important to examine how Catholic teaching on mission provided a springboard for women as they sought to identify new ways of being missionary.

---

9. Bosch, *Transforming Mission*, 357-58, 361.

10. See Marilyn French, *The Women's Room* (New York: Ballantine Books, 1977); Germaine Greer, *The Female Eunuch* (London: McGibbon & Kee, 1970).

11. See Mary Daly, *Beyond God the Father: Towards a Philosophy of Women's Liberation* (Boston: Beacon Press, 1973); Elisabeth Schüssler Fiorenza, *In Memory of Her: A Feminist Reconstruction of Christian Origins* (New York: Crossroad, 1983); Rosemary Radford Ruether, *Sexism and God-Talk: Toward a Feminist Theology* (Boston: Beacon Press, 1983).

12. See Henri Godin and Yvan Daniel, *France, Pays de Mission?* (Paris: Editions du Cerf, 1943).

13. Stephen B. Bevans and Roger P. Schroeder, *Constants in Context: A Theology of Mission for Today* (Maryknoll, N.Y.: Orbis Books, 2004), 248.

14. Bosch, *Transforming Mission*, 367.

## CATHOLIC WOMEN'S CHANGING MISSIONARY IDENTITY AND PRACTICE

Vatican II was one catalyst for significant changes in Catholic missionary practice. Catholic theologian Thomas Stransky writes that "no other world church or international confessional body has undergone such an intensive examination of consciousness and conscience about mission as did the Roman Catholic Church during the four years of the Second Vatican Council."[15] Other factors that encouraged women missionaries to reframe their understanding of mission included liberation theology, feminist theologies, and ecotheologies. In this chapter, I will examine how these different developments have impacted the practice of mission for women religious and laywomen.

### *Vatican II's Importance*

Vatican II shifted Catholic women's perceptions regarding mission in at least three ways: first, the council insisted that through baptism all the faithful are missionary; second, mission no longer pitted the church against the world, or against peoples of other faiths and religious traditions; and third, the council mandated religious orders to review their way of life and their apostolic works so that they could respond more effectively to contemporary missionary needs. Perhaps the most important development was the realization that mission belonged to all believers by virtue of their baptism. Missionary identity flowed from baptism rather than from ordination. This teaching, found in *Lumen Gentium,* the "Dogmatic Constitution on the Church,"[16] represented a significant advance on the earlier position that priests and bishops had "to shoulder the whole mission themselves"[17] in virtue of their ordination. Now, through baptism and confirmation, "all are commissioned to that apostolate by the Lord himself . . . Now the laity are called in a special way to make the Church present and operative in those places and circumstances where only through them can she become the salt of the earth" (*Lumen Gentium* no. 33). Prior to this, the mission of laypeople, including nonordained religious, was considered subordinate to the

---

15. T. F. Stransky, "Evangelization, Missions and Social Action: A Roman Catholic Perspective," *Review and Expositor* 79 (1982): 343-51.

16. Unless otherwise stated, references to documents of Vatican II will be to Austin Flannery, ed., *Vatican Council II: Constitutions, Decrees, Declarations* (New York: Costello Publishing Company, 1996).

17. Richard P. McBrien, *Catholicism,* 2 vols. (East Malvern, Vic.: Dove Communications, 1980), 2:672.

sacramental ministry of the ordained minister. The "Decree on the Apostolate of the Laity," *Apostolicam Actuositatem,* made it clear that laity are full
members of the church, and therefore share in the church's mission, "not
simply by leave of the hierarchy but 'from their union with Christ their Head.
Incorporated into Christ's Mystical Body through baptism and strengthened
by the power of the Holy Spirit through confirmation, they are assigned to
the apostolate by the Lord himself (*Apostolicam Actuositatem* no. 3).'"[18]
These teachings concerning the missionary vocation of all the baptized represented an important development in Catholic tradition. The nineteenth-
century church had emphasized mission as *plantatio ecclesiae.* This had
prioritized the centrality of the ordained minister in mission because of the
foundational nature of the priest's sacramental ministry in establishing a new
church. The work of lay women and men was understood only as an ancillary and preparatory stage.

Second, theologies of mission were influenced by conciliar teachings on
the church's relationship to the world and hence to other religions and traditions. Most significant was the "Pastoral Constitution on the Church in
the Modern World," *Gaudium et Spes.* It was a document concerned with
the church's relationship to the world rather than with the inner life of the
church. The English title of *Gaudium et Spes,* "Pastoral Constitution on the
Church in the Modern World," is important because the preposition *in* in the
title emphasizes that the church is not apart from the world, nor is it set over
against the world, but it is *in* the world. Further, the theology of *Gaudium
et Spes* of "the signs of the times" meant that "the Church has always had
the duty of scrutinizing the signs of the times and interpreting them in the
light of the gospel" (no. 4). This has made it more difficult to hold fast to a
theology that sees the church in opposition to the world. A sense of history
permeated *Gaudium et Spes,* an awareness encouraged by biblical texts such
as Exodus, which demonstrated that it is through historical events that God's
salvific love for humankind is revealed. In this perspective, revelation is not
limited to a particular time, but continues to occur "within the total historical process itself."[19] These teachings had significance for women as they
began to negotiate new mission priorities that flowed from their informed
reading of history and context.

*Gaudium et Spes* affirmed the ongoing importance of the Catholic social
teaching of Pope Leo XIII's *Rerum Novarum* (1891), Pope Pius XI's *Quadragesimo Anno* (1931), and Pope John XXIII's *Mater et Magistra* (1961).[20]
These encyclicals taught that Catholics have a responsibility to respond to

---

18. Ibid., 2:680.
19. McBrien, *Catholicism,* 2 vols. (East Malvern, Vic.: Dove Communications, 1980),
1:231.
20. See McBrien, *Catholicism,* 2:673.

injustice in the world, and along with conciliar teachings they pointed to the need to reframe Catholic ecclesiology so that the church understood itself as the servant of the world, not as separate from it. This responsibility of service in the world required that the church scrutinize "the signs of the times," and discern the missionary implications of these in the light of the gospel (see *Gaudium et Spes* no. 4). The entry point for mission would be the sorrows and sufferings of the world rather than *ad intra* ecclesial concerns. *Gaudium et Spes* signified the essential relationship between religious faith and temporal activity. A more positive attitude toward the world and toward other religions is evident in other documents, such as the "Decree on Ecumenism," *Unitatis Redintegratio*, which teaches that ecumenism is a missionary responsibility of all the baptized. The "Declaration on the Relationship of the Church to Non-Christian Religions," *Nostra Aetate*, states that "humanity forms but one community. This is so because all stem from the one stock which God created to people the entire earth (see Acts 17:26), and because all share a common destiny, namely God" (no. 1). In the same document we also read that "the Catholic Church rejects nothing of what is true and holy in these religions. It has a high regard for the manner of life and conduct, the precepts and doctrines which, although differing in many ways from its own teachings, nevertheless reflect a ray of that truth which enlightens all men and women" (no. 2). Given that many missionaries prior to Vatican II believed that baptism into the church was almost a prerequisite for salvation, such teachings were nothing short of revolutionary, and their effect on mission was immense.

Finally, Vatican II's "Decree on the Appropriate Renewal of the Religious Life," *Perfectae Caritatis*, had implications for mission because the majority of women missionaries were members of religious orders. Religious were mandated to examine their lifestyles and mission in view of the momentous changes that were occurring in church and society in the twentieth century.

## Vatican II and the Mission of Women Religious

Many women's orders recognized the need for renewal prior to Vatican II. For example, the need for tertiary education and professional formation was acknowledged. Orders that embraced a semicloistered lifestyle that owed more to monastic traditions than to apostolic were asking if the cloister still constituted a privileged safeguard of contemplative spirituality. Those that had been founded specifically for work in the "foreign missions" were asking what that meant in a postcolonial age, and what fidelity to the original congregational charism of foreign missionary work required in the second half of the twentieth century. Socio-economic realities, particularly the growing secularization of society and the awareness of the poverty in which millions lived, also alerted religious orders to the need for reassessing mission priorities. These factors helped prepare the way for both attitudinal and structural changes regarding the role of missionaries in church and society.

The council taught that the renewal of religious life "comprises both a constant return to the sources of Christian life in general, and to the primitive inspiration of the institutes and their adaptation to the changed conditions of our time" (*Perfectae Caritatis* no. 2). Three sources for renewal were identified: the scriptures, especially the Gospels; church teaching; and the reclamation of the founder's vision for her community. This meant that Catholic sisters turned to the scriptures, particularly the Gospels, finding in them insights for their exercise of mission. Prior to the council, laypeople had been actively discouraged from reading and studying the scriptures, let alone interpreting them.[21] The return to the scriptures in order to seek a mandate for discerning new missionary tasks proved to be a significant shift of focus. Historical-critical methodologies revealed a God who was on the side of the poor in the Old Testament, and a Jesus who directed his mission of healing toward the poor and marginalized.

Vatican II's theology of "the signs of the times" (see *Gaudium et Spes* nos. 4-10)[22] and the church's social teachings found in the encyclicals of John XXIII, Paul VI, and John Paul II indicated that "the world" was no longer to be avoided through a cloistered lifestyle. Rather, the world was the privileged arena where one met God. The suffering world called women of good will to work at overcoming situations of oppression. God's call to mission was no longer mediated only by church authorities. Women religious were to identify and respond to the new missionary needs that the economic, social, political, and religious imperatives of the day demanded,[23] and which

---

21. See, for example, the *Dogmatic Catechism*. Question. "Would it not be well to make translations of the Bible into the vulgar tongue so that it might be put in the hands of all, even of the laity?" Answer. "The church forbids that the Bible, literally translated into the vulgar tongue should be given to be read by all persons indifferently. She even forbids absolution of sins to be given to those who choose to read it, or retain possession of it without permission. The proof that it cannot be a good thing to put the Bible into the hands of all persons is, that being full of mysteries it would injure rather than profit the ignorant; and this is manifest from the zeal with which Protestants scatter abroad, everywhere and at great expense, an incredible number of vernacular translations of the Bible." *Dogmatic Catechism* (Frassinetti), revised and edited by the Oblate Fathers of St. Charles (London, 1874), quoted by Gerard Rummery in "The Development of the Concept of Religious Education in Catholic Schools 1872-1972," *Journal of Religious History* 9 (1977): 302-17.

22. *Gaudium et Spes* nos. 4-10 describe some of the more significant "signs of the times" as follows: scientific and technological developments and their impact on culture; improved communication structures; the abandonment of religious practices; economic inequalities; lack of hope; and a questioning about the deeper meaning of life.

23. See Sandra M. Schneiders, "Religious Life (*Perfectae Caritatis*)," in *Modern Catholicism: Vatican II and After,* ed. Adrian Hastings (New York: Oxford University Press, 1991), 157-61.

were in harmony with the charism of a particular religious community. This allowed women religious to turn from a "narrow ascetical-juridical understanding of religious life that had constrained religious life,"[24] and to shift the locus of authority from the institutional church to the decision-making processes of their own religious orders in determining mission priorities. Prior to Vatican II, a founder's vision had become obscured by a strict adherence on the part of women religious to episcopal directives in the exercise of mission and by the 1917 Code of Canon Law. The vision was often further dimmed by the excessive institutionalization that had occurred. For example, an original vision of care of the sick poor often had been transformed into an expensive and institutionalized approach to health care for the middle classes which the poor could no longer access. At the same time, orders realized that the founder's vision was not to be replicated unthinkingly. Rather, it was to be creatively interpreted. Vatican II offered an invitation to religious women to step back from thinking of themselves as "indentured servants of the hierarchical church, [whose] life structures were patterned after the patriarchal society and were regulated by Canon Law."[25] Women religious met in chapter to clarify their mission priorities in the light of conciliar teachings and their particular charism. As changes regarding mission were articulated, it became obvious that this would lead to changes in lifestyle, governance, understandings of the vows of poverty, chastity, and obedience, and ecclesiology.

## The Impact of Liberation Theologies

In the early 1970s, women religious were further challenged by Latin American liberation theology.[26] Liberation theology identified and affirmed the place of context and experience, particularly the experience of oppression, in the process of doing theology.[27] In the Latin American context, the

---

24. Ibid., 158.

25. Carmel McEnroy, *Guests in Their Own House: The Women of Vatican II* (New York: Crossroad, 1996), 19.

26. English-speaking Catholics usually were introduced to liberation theology through their reading of Gustavo Gutiérrez, *A Theology of Liberation*.

27. There is disagreement among theologians over the degree to which the context is central or peripheral to the process. "Some would maintain that an emphasis on the contextual dimensions of theology makes theology too self-centered and myopic . . . The contrary argument is that there is now sufficient evidence, particularly from Latin American, feminist, black and indigenous theologies to support the position that all theologies are in fact contextual." See Neil Darragh, "Contextual Method in Theology: Learnings from the Case of Aotearoa New Zealand," *Pacifica* 16 (2003): 45-66.

privileged entry point into the task of theologizing was the constraining economic and political disenfranchisement experienced by millions. Liberation theology insisted that the starting point for theologizing should be peoples' experience of oppression, and that responsibility for doing theology belonged to oppressed communities and not simply to the magisterium and academic communities. When liberation theologians identified experience as the privileged entry point into theologizing, they were thinking of the shared experience of an oppressed community whose reflection on that experience enabled them to recognize and name the causes of their oppression. In turn, that recognition allowed them to identify responses that directed action toward the causes rather than the results of oppression. This contrasted with Catholic missionary practice of the nineteenth and early twentieth centuries, which took as its starting point, with few exceptions, papal and episcopal directives.

One facet of liberation theology that was of particular importance for religious orders was an insistence on "a preferential option for the poor." Liberation theology's methodology of economic analysis argued that the poverty experienced by the urban and rural poor was the result of economic systems that discriminated against the poor, and advantaged the middle and capitalist classes. One way for women religious to help in the liberation of the poor was by making a preferential option for the poor through focusing their energies on assisting the poor in their struggles to overturn unjust economic systems. Within the Latin American context, the preferential option for the poor was an invitation to the church to concentrate its resources on work with the poor in their struggle for liberation from structural poverty. Prior to Vatican II, apostolic religious life was often institutionalized and monastic, with members involved in educational, health, or social institutions. Even in countries such as Australia, Canada, and New Zealand, where women religious often staffed rural or semirural parish primary schools and lived in communities of three to six sisters, they followed a monasticlike routine. However, when women religious made an option for the poor, many of them gave up the security and status associated with an institutional ministry and the lifestyle that accompanied it.

An option for the poor involved women religious in a variety of ministries, as Mary Joseph Maher's description of the work of Immaculate Heart of Mary missionaries in Brazil demonstrates:

> They engaged in a variety of ministries, primarily forming base Christian communities (*communidades ecclesiales de base*) where the people prayed, reflected on their reality in the light of the scriptures, and took action to improve the quality of their life (for example, getting water, cleaning up sewage, obtaining health care, and improving education). In addition, the missionaries coordinated pastoral work, started

women's reflections groups, organized youth groups, and supported workers' rights and the people's rights to land.[28]

An option for the poor was not restricted to the Two-Thirds World. In the Christchurch Diocese in New Zealand, several Sisters of Mercy who had served as high school principals shifted to the poorest suburb in the city and worked in the community as social workers or as teachers in the government-funded school.[29] The Australian Province of the Sisters of Our Lady of the Missions responded to the situation of the Aboriginal peoples by moving to the remote Australian outback to provide primary education for one Aboriginal community's children. This necessitated living in two caravans for some years. The same sisters in a document of their 1990 general chapter stated that they were to work "with oppressed indigenous peoples, work with victims of violence especially women and children, work with others who challenge oppressive government structures, challenge church leadership where there are unjust structures and policies, develop representation and leadership by women, develop inclusive language structures, support land rights and world ecology movements."[30] This and similar statements were representative of the hope and enthusiasm that drove many women's orders and demonstrated the appeal of liberation theology for women religious.

*Impact of Feminist Theologies*

Women religious recognized that liberation theology's methodology—sharing of experiences and stories, analyses of those stories, theological reflection on and engagement with them, and then developing strategies for action—was a useful tool for discerning other mission priorities. First, it encouraged Catholic sisters to reflect on their own experiences as women in a patriarchal and hierarchical church, and to recognize that they too were an oppressed group whose work in the church had been defined as "auxiliary" or "ancillary" to the ministry of the priest. Despite such a designation, over the years "women's attention to the health, education and spiritual needs of people built up the social services and educational institutions wherever they

---

28. Mary Joseph Maher, "Empowering Immaculate Heart of Mary Missionaries," in *Gospel Bearers, Gender Barriers: Missionary Women in the Twentieth Century*, ed. Dana L. Robert (Maryknoll, N.Y.: Orbis Books, 2002), 146.

29. See Pauline O'Regan, *A Changing Order* (Wellington, N.Z.: Allen & Unwin, 1986).

30. "RNDM for Mission: General Chapter 1990 Vision Statement" (Rome, 1990).

served."[31] These services and institutions were often the public face of the church, and women religious made extraordinary sacrifices to provide these services. New Zealand priest-historian Ernest Simmons aptly describes the contribution of women religious to the institutional church in the modern age: "It is difficult to find anything to admire in the blindness that prevented the bishops, the clergy, and the laity from seeing that they were building a church on the bent backs of the nuns."[32]

By the 1970s, women religious were questioning their ancillary role in the church's mission, recognizing that it had its genesis in the male sexism that was part and parcel of patriarchal culture. They found support for their questioning in church teaching. *Gaudium et Spes* no. 29 states that discrimination based on sex is sinful: "Nevertheless, with respect to the fundamental rights of the person, every type of discrimination, whether social or cultural, whether based on *sex,* race, color, social condition, language or religion, is to be overcome and eradicated as *contrary to God's intent*" (italics added). Furthermore, the 1971 synod document *Justice in the World* taught that while "the Church is found to give witness to justice, she recognizes that anyone who ventures to speak to people about justice must first be just in their eyes. Hence we must undertake an examination of the modes of acting and of the possessions and lifestyle found within the Church herself" (no. 40).[33]

In a paper presented to Catholic bishops and congregational leaders of New Zealand, Mercy Sister Elizabeth Julian argues that religious women and men are called to a prophetic ministry within the church.[34] This call is explicit in *Religious and Human Promotion,* which states, "Evangelization, for the Church, means bringing the Good News into all strata of humanity and through it transforming humanity from within: its design for living, opening them up to a total vision of humanity. To accomplish this mission, the Church must search out the *signs of the times* and interpret them in the light of the Gospel, thus responding to persistent human questions. *Religious are called to give singular witness to this prophetic dimension*" (italics

---

31. Angelyn Dries, "U.S. Catholic Women and Mission: Integral or Auxiliary?" *Missiology: An International Review* 33 (2005): 301-11.

32. E. R. Simmons, *A Brief History of the Catholic Church in New Zealand* (Auckland: Catholic Publications Centre, 1978), 107.

33. World Synod of Bishops, *Justice in the World* (1971); available at http://www.osjpm org/cst/jw.htm; accessed March 27, 2006.

34. See Elizabeth Julian, "Creating a Song and Dance—Kiwimaging: The Prophetic Role of Women Religious in the Church in Aotearoa New Zealand Today." Address to the Catholic Bishops and Congregational Leaders of Aotearoa New Zealand (2006); available at http://www .welcom.org.nz/index.php?subaction=showfull&id=1141958457& ucat=1&archive=; accessed March 27, 2006.

added).[35] It was particularly reassuring for women religious to learn that they should

> not fear any obstacle to the generosity and creativity of their projects from the hierarchical nature of the ecclesial communion, because every sacred authority is given for the purpose of harmoniously promoting charisms and ministries. On the contrary, religious are encouraged to be "enterprising in their undertakings and initiatives"; this in keeping with the charismatic and prophetic nature of religious life (*Religious and Human Promotion* no. 27).

*Vita Consecrata* no. 57 affirms that "women's new self-awareness also helps men to reconsider their way of looking at things, the way they understand themselves, where they place themselves in history, and how they interpret it, and the way they organized social, political, economic, religious and ecclesial life."[36] Elizabeth Julian's careful examination of contemporary church teaching on religious life makes it clear that women religious are right to speak and act prophetically about sexual discrimination in the institutional church because this clearly falls within the ambit of their missionary work.

Second, by the 1950s, women religious, aware of their need to be theologically educated—Catholic practice had meant that only seminarians and priests were theologically educated—were seeking theological education for themselves. The United States-initiated Sister Formation program demonstrated the mid-twentieth-century trend of women religious pursuing higher theological education in increasing numbers. After Vatican II, this process accelerated as women religious responded to their own felt need for such theological education. At the same time, a worldwide shortage of priests posed problems for Catholic parish life and hastened the trend whereby women religious and laywomen sought theological education in order to qualify themselves for parish and teaching ministries. Furthermore, it was increasingly obvious that the works traditionally undertaken by women religious as teachers, nurses, and social workers were more than simply

---

35. Plenaria of the Sacred Congregation for Religious and for Secular Institutes, *Religious and Human Promotion* (1978); available at http://www.vatican.va/roman_curia/congregations/ccscrlife/documents/rc_con_ccscrlife_doc_12081980_religious-and-human-promotion_en.html; accessed March 27, 2005.

36. Pope John Paul II, *Vita Consecrata: Post Synodal Apostolic Exhortation* (Libreria Editrice Vaticana, 1996); available at http://www.vatican.va/holy_father/john _paul_ii/apost_exhortations/documents/hf_jp-ii_exh_25031996_vita-consecrata_en.html; accessed March 27, 2006.

extensions of women's biological roles. These ministries required profes- sional competency, and therefore increasing numbers of women religious attended tertiary institutions to prepare themselves professionally for their demanding ministries.

Third, the awareness of women religious of the negative effects of patri- archal culture on women in society and church was a motivation for their reaffirmation of their mission to women and children. While this had tradi- tionally been an apostolic priority for women religious, now the goals of such work included the important dimension of alerting or conscientizing women and girls to the reality of the patriarchal nature of the society or church in which they lived. For example, women religious worked with poor women to set up income-generating projects that gave them independent access to monies to help run their homes and to finance some of the educa- tion of their children. Prior to this, in situations where the father was the only family wage earner, and particularly where he controlled the allocation of monies, most women had no discretionary access to money.

### Care of Creation and Mission

The parameters of women religious' missionary work were further expanded when women recognized that the same patriarchal culture that led to domination of women also encouraged the exploitation of the environ- ment. In *Gaia and God,* Rosemary Radford Ruether writes, "domination of women has provided a key link, both socially and symbolically, to the dom- ination of the earth, hence the tendency in patriarchal cultures to link women with the earth, matter, and nature, while identifying males with sky, intellect, and transcendent spirit." [37] Some orders sought to give an institutional char- acter to this recognition of the oppression of creation through initiatives that would alert others to an awareness of ecological issues. The enthusiasm in many women's orders to embrace the new cosmology associated with Thomas Berry and Brian Swimme has led to "nuns becoming organic farm- ers and gardeners, vegetarian cooks, reiki masters, holistic health practi- tioners, grassroots botanists, astronomy buffs, and teachers/learners of ecology and cosmology—all within the new centers they are founding." [38] Communities of Catholic sisters involved in such new missionary initiatives are now being established in both One-Third and Two-Thirds World countries.

---

37. Rosemary Radford Ruether, *Gaia and God: An Ecofeminist Theology of Earth Heal- ing* (New York: HarperCollins, 1992), 3.

38. Mary Judith Ress, *Ecofeminism in Latin America* (Maryknoll, N.Y.: Orbis Books, 2006), 105-6.

Some of the inspiration for these centers came from Genesis Farm, a learning center for Earth Studies founded in 1980 in New Jersey by the Dominican Sisters of Caldwell. Its members focused on the connections "between the health of our global commons of air, water, land and nature, and the health of our local communities and bioregions. We root ourselves in a spirituality that reverences Earth as a primary revelation of the divine."[39] As one of its founding members, Miriam MacGillis, OP, states, "We're at a moment where there are no guarantees as to the Earth's future. It's a question of our own critical choices. And I think what we're deeply in need of is a transforming vision. . . . A vision that opens the future up to hope."[40] These initiatives are motivating women religious to reassess the role of the three vows of religion in their lives, and suggesting that ecological considerations should inform the manner in which they live their vowed life. Do they express through their vows of poverty, chastity, and obedience awareness that the human person is part of a suffering earth community? In this context, poverty is an invitation to restrain our addiction to consumption; chastity is about bonding to the other in a spirit of mutuality and equality, thereby subverting sexist, militaristic and racist ideologies; and obedience is responding to "creativity at the heart of the universe."[41]

Tabgha Center in New South Wales, Australia, was another such initiative. Established in 1988 by several women's orders, it sought to link care for the earth with works of justice by drawing on traditional and contemporary expressions of Christian spirituality. In its various courses, the center engaged participants in addressing significant questions such as the following: What profound changes are taking place in our world today? In what ways has our understanding of the cosmos changed? People speak of an emergence of spirituality and a dissatisfaction with religion—what do we mean by that? Does a new understanding of the world (cosmos) suggest a new understanding of sacred texts? How can we participate in the promotion of justice that is essential to our time? How can we live today in a way that is both energizing and liberating? Women religious are making the connection between ecological degradation and oppression of the poor, especially poor women. Because ecological degradation "aggravates the social and economic injustice between rich and poor in our global community,"[42] eco-communities are seeking a holistic response to the oppression of people and creation.

---

39. See *Genesis Farm: A Learning Center for Earth Studies;* available at http://www.genesis farm.org/history.htm; accessed March 27, 2006.

40. Ibid.

41. Ress, *Ecofeminism in Latin America,* 107.

42. Denis Edwards, "Celebrating Eucharist in a Time of Global Climate Change," *Pacifica* 19 (2006): 1-15.

*The Impact of Liberation Theology on the Lives and
Mission of Women Religious*

These developments highlight the influence that liberation theology's
methodology has had on women religious as they identified and responded
to the missionary imperatives of the postmodern world. Mary Jo Leddy
believes that it was those orders she identifies as "liberal" that most enthu-
siastically embraced such methodologies.[43] But this approach has not been
without its difficulties. In particular, the willingness of women's orders to
tolerate a diversity of ministries has meant "the absence of a vital and common sense of meaning and direction"[44] that makes it difficult for members
to unite around a common understanding of mission. This is because "statements of mission or charism . . . are vague and general enough to include all
the various interests in a congregation."[45] American Benedictine and com-
mentator on religious life Joan Chittister likewise argues that one of the problems accompanying diversity and flexibility in mission priorities and practice
is "a scattering of efforts and a flippancy of approach. Here today, there
tomorrow, is not service, it is simply social fluttering in the name of religion."[46] She attributes a scattered approach to the failure to acknowledge
that a missionary vision demands fidelity to the daily, long-term grind of
working with people in difficult circumstances. In the final analysis, a utopian
vision that is not grounded can mean that nothing is really achieved, other
than an inefficient use of personnel and resources. Related to this is what
Chittister calls "a pathological individualism. What the group stands for as
a group, what the group is about as a group, gives way to the tyranny of the
person. What was once retreat from the tasks of the time in the name of the
spiritual tradition becomes retreat in the name of self."[47] Although both
Leddy and Chittister are writing out of a North American context, their
insights are also true of communities of women religious in other One-Third
World countries.

Furthermore, international women's orders that can be described as "liberal" find it difficult to attract new members. Even their Two-Thirds World
provinces, although they fare better than their One-Third World counter-

---

43. See Mary Jo Leddy, *Reweaving Religious Life* (Mystic, Conn.: Twenty-Third Publications, 1990), 47-78. In the North American context, and this has significance for other One-
Third World countries, "liberal" means, on the one hand, a ready acceptance of values such as
a high regard for human rights, and, on the other hand, individualism. The material prosperity
of One-Third World countries means their inhabitants can readily fall into the trap of con-
sumerism. She suggests that religious are as prone to this as other sectors in society. This leads
to a loss of the prophetic and countercultural dimensions of religious life.`
44. Ibid., 73.
45. Ibid.
46. Joan Chittister, "Religious Life: Quest and Question," *Priests and People* 10, nos. 8-9
(1996): 312-17.
47. Ibid., 316.

parts, fail to attract as many candidates as the more traditionally structured orders.[48] Anecdotal evidence suggests that when orders have made the decision to opt for the liberal model of renewal—for example, a sister either not wearing a traditional habit, or in the case of Two-Thirds World sisters, wearing one that was more attuned to the local culture and local missionary needs—this has met with limited local approval. Asian, African, and Latin American Catholicism appear to be rejecting the liberalism of important sectors of the One-Thirds World. As Philip Jenkins states, "changes that [liberal] Catholic and other reformers today are trying to inspire in North America and Europe (and that seem essential if Christianity is to be preserved as a modern, relevant force on those continents) run utterly contrary to the dominant cultural movements in the rest of the Christian world."[49] Maryknoller Catherine Harmer, in *Religious Life in the 21st Century*, significantly subtitled *A Contemporary Journey into Canaan*, offers a different interpretation and suggests that the sense of alienation and loss experienced by many women religious in liberal orders is best understood as a time of wandering in the desert, and is hopefully the prelude to new life.[50]

Second, a more holistic approach to mission by women religious meant that "saving souls," or seeking out pagans to prepare them for baptism, has ceased to be an important missionary objective. In her historical analysis of the Maryknoll Sisters' mission in Hong Kong,[51] Cindy Yik-Yi Chu explains how this development occurred. The first Maryknoll Constitutions required that the sisters be sent to pagans in "heathen lands" for their "personal sanctification" and to convert others to Christianity.[52] When the sisters arrived in

---

48. Women religious outnumber deacons, diocesan priests, and male religious, ordained and lay. Nearly half of all women religious are in Europe, while a third are in the Americas. However, the age median in such congregations is at least seventy years plus. "Between 1950 and 2000, the number of women religious declined from 806,233 to 769,142. However, these numbers mask both steep decreases and increases. Significant declines are found in Europe (from 528,893 in 1950 to 366,326 in 2000), North America (from 183,740 to 90,529), and to some degree in Oceania as well (from 12,177 to 11,095). In the rest of the world, the number of women religious increased considerably (from 21,242 to 138,195 in Asia, from 3,280 to 52,583 in Africa and from 56,901 to 110,414 in Latin America)." See Bryan T. Froehle and Mary L. Gautier, *Global Catholicism: Portrait of a World Church*, ed. Bryan T. Froehle and Mary L. Gautier, 3 vols. (Maryknoll, N.Y.: Orbis Books, 2003), 2:42-43.

49. Philip Jenkins, *The Next Christianity* (October 2002); available at http://www.the atlantic.com/cgi/cgi-bin/send.cgi?page=http%3A//www.theatlantic.com/iss; accessed March 3, 2003.

50. See Catherine M. Harmer, *Religious Life in the 21st Century: A Contemporary Journey into Canaan* (Mystic, Conn: Twenty-Third Publications, 1995).

51. See Cindy Yik-Yi Chu, "From the Pursuit of Converts to the Relief of Refugees: The Maryknoll Sisters in Twentieth Century Hong Kong," *The Historian* 65 (2002): 353-76.

52. Penny Lernoux, with Arthur Jones and Robert Ellsberg, *Hearts on Fire: The Story of the Maryknoll Sisters* (Maryknoll, N.Y.: Orbis Books, 1993), 143, citing from "Tentative Constitutions of the Foreign Mission Sisters of St. Dominic (Third Order), Congregation of the Immaculate Conception, at Maryknoll, Ossining, New York, U.S.A.," drafted in 1917; First Constitutions in use after General Chapter of 1925; Constitutions, Maryknoll Mission Archives.

Hong Kong in 1921, they established a training center and language school to prepare themselves for the Chinese mission, which would allow them to fulfill the twin goals of personal sanctification and "saving souls." These objectives changed after Vatican II. The sisters argued that mission was not about bringing God to where God had previously been absent, because "God was already present in the foreign places before the Christian missionaries arrived."[53] By 1990, the Maryknoll Constitutions defined mission as "Wholistic Evangelization meaning Liberation, Inculturation, & Dialogue, Human Development and Reverence for Creation."[54] This expanded understanding of mission was attributable to the renewal initiated by Vatican II and to the influence of post-Vatican II theological developments, both of which prompted the Maryknollers to undertake a variety of works in Hong Kong—relief, welfare, reform, education, civil awareness, advocacy, and work with refugees—none of which had conversion through sacramental baptism as a primary aim. The first *Constitutions* of the Sisters of Our Lady of the Missions included similar statements regarding mission. The sisters were exhorted "to labor more perfectly for their own sanctification" and "to extend the Kingdom of God in souls by devoting themselves to the instruction of children and women above all in infidel and non-Catholic countries."[55] An emphasis on "saving souls" in pagan and infidel countries had been a defining mark of Catholic missionary activity prior to Vatican II. Vatican II and the subsequent renewal that women religious undertook meant a radical shift in perception. As we have seen, conciliar documents, by affirming the Spirit's presence in the world and human history even prior to the Christ event, brought about a change in Catholic understanding of the church's relationship to the other religions.

Third, although the work of women religious was foundational for the church's mission, it was traditionally considered secondary or auxiliary to the main task of missionary work that emphasized the sacramental role of priests in establishing the church in those places where it was not yet established. As the first *Constitutions* of the Sisters of Our Lady of the Missions stated, the work of the sisters was undertaken "under the direction of their Lordships the Bishops or Vicars-Apostolic in order *to assist them in their apostleship*, and to provide, according to the best of their power and ability for the spiritual and corporal needs of the persons entrusted to their care" (italics added).[56] After Vatican II, it was easier for women religious to embrace an

---

53. Chu, "From the Pursuit of Converts to the Relief of Refugees," 358.

54. Ibid., citing Sister Camilla Kennedy, "(Chart of the) Historical Perspective of the Nature and Scope of the Maryknoll Sisters," June 1992, Maryknoll Mission Archives, Maryknoll Sisters, Searching and Sharing: Mission Perspectives (Maryknoll, N.Y., 1970), 10-11.

55. Euphrasie Barbier, *Constitutions of the Daughters of Our Lady of the Missions* (Letchworth: 1936), nos. 1, 2.

56. Barbier, *Constitutions of the Daughters of Our Lady of the Missions*, no. 3.

expanded definition of mission because their educational, health, and social work always had been more broadly based than that of the ordained minister. This allowed women religious to move beyond the narrow ecclesiocentric understandings of mission associated with the pre-Vatican II church because they recognized that their work was no longer ancillary but integral to the church's mission. Angelyn Dries, reporting on a conversation she had with Roseanne Rustmeyer, SSND, executive director of the U.S. Catholic Mission Association, summarizes well the changing reality of women religious' missionary activity:

> Current global conditions which most affect women and children are human trafficking, issues relating to economics such as privatization of water, etc. increased poverty, health issues, violence and ethnic conflicts, little opportunity for women's voices to be heard, the inability of women missioners to keep their institutions, local professional people leaving their countries for more lucrative jobs in other places (nurses trained in India, for example, coming to the United States), and AIDS ministry. A continuous thread of women's traditional socio-economic emphases weaves through the experience of women missionaries in the twenty-first century, even though the theological emphasis in mission has changed from individual conversion to church planting, "*missio Dei*," and the multi-form of expression expressed in *Redemptoris Missio.*[57]

Consciously, and unconsciously, there was a growing belief among women religious that their missionary activity was no longer auxiliary but rather integral and central in hastening the coming of the reign of God.

It has been suggested that the mission of women religious has collapsed into humanitarian work that differs little from that of the major development agencies. This is not so. Obviously the question of personal motivation can help rebut such criticisms, but, more importantly, women religious work out of a mindset that understands the world as the privileged arena of God's activity and see their task as hastening the coming of the reign of God. A reignocentric position can lead to a loosening of ties with the institutional church and to understanding mission as considerably more than assisting bishops in their apostleship. Given that many women religious are sensitive to the historical reality of their place in a patriarchal church and the personal and institutional costs this has entailed, it is not altogether unexpected that they have sought and found a different theological motivation for their exercise of mission.

---

57. Dries, "U.S. Catholic Women and Mission," 303.

Fourth, in those international orders founded in the modern era, mission was often perceived as a movement from One-Third World nations to Two-Thirds World countries, and in the eighteenth, nineteenth, and twentieth centuries, these latter countries were usually colonies. Where colonies such as Australia, Canada, New Zealand, or the United States were settled by Europeans, the indigenous peoples soon became a minority, and vocations to religious life from them were few and far between. The situation was different in those colonies in which the colonizers were a small minority. In countries such as India, Vietnam, and Nigeria, there have been and still are many indigenous vocations to religious life. Thus today, the Sisters of Our Lady of the Missions number 144 in the British Isles, including the Irish Republic, and in India, they number 153. More important though than the numbers is the difference in the median age. In the One-Third World provinces, the median age is in the high seventies, but in the Two-Thirds World provinces it is in the mid-forties,[58] which suggests that responsibility for the future lies with religious life in the Two-Thirds World. This, in turn, means that women religious from the Two-Thirds World are assuming positions of responsibility and undoubtedly will bring new perspectives to bear on the exercise of mission. The emerging and younger African, Asian, and Latin American leadership has not been so decisively shaped by the experiences of Vatican II and the tendency to explain the world and church in pre- and post-Vatican II categories. Given their local contexts, such women will see inculturation and interreligious dialogue as being significant.[59]

Fifth, as women religious move into the third millennium, the optimism with which they greeted Vatican II and the possibility it offered them to renew and radically redirect their mission has somewhat diminished. Karl Rahner's comments in 1991 are worth pondering:

> Although I took part in the elaboration of *Gaudium et Spes* at the Council, I would not deny that its undertone is too euphoric in its evaluation of humanity and the human condition. What it says may be true, but it produces the overall impression that it is enough to observe its norms, and everything will more or less turn out well.[60]

The sense of optimism to which Rahner refers has been shaken since Vatican II as orders seek to discern whether the situation in which they find themselves is a dying process signaling the disappearance of religious life as it has

---

58. See *RNDM Statistics—Year Ending 31 December 2005*. RNDM Archives, Rome.

59. Robert Schreiter, *Toward the Missionary Church of 2025—The Past and the Future* (2002); available at http://www.sedos.org/site/index; accessed April 2, 2006.

60. Karl Rahner, *Theological Investigations* (London: Darton, Longman & Todd, 1991), 22:158.

been known or whether their collective "dark night of the soul" is the prelude to a new and transfigured life. It has been suggested that the decline in religious life in the One-Third World is partially attributable to the adoption of a middle-class lifestyle that has proved inimical to the authentic renewal of religious life. As Michael Crosby writes, "We religious do not want to challenge the status quo because, despite our protestations to the contrary, we benefit from it, and these benefits have numbed us to the injustice being perpetrated by the hierarchical systems that act as though they have been divinely instituted."[61]

## RELIGIOUS ORDERS AND ASSOCIATES

An important development from the 1970s onward was the effort by religious orders to involve laypeople in their mission. These laypeople, often referred to as associates, seek affiliation with a religious institution while maintaining an independent lifestyle. There are at least two reasons as to why this has been happening. First, many orders rightly consider that their founders' charisms are important for the life of the church, not just for their particular order, and so identify ways whereby others can know something of their charism and its implications for mission. Second, the dramatic decline in people seeking a life-long commitment to religious life in the One-Third World, and the equally dramatic increase in the need for committed missionary personnel, persuaded orders that one way of coping with this tension was to invite others to share in their mission. Most orders have moved in this direction, but the process has occurred in a variety of ways.

One of the fastest growing lay associate groups is the Lay Missionaries of Charity (LMC), who whether married or lay, women or men, seek to live according to the spirit and charism of Mother Teresa's Missionaries of Charity. To facilitate this, they make private vows of chastity (conjugal in the case of married couples), poverty, and obedience, and a fourth vow of wholehearted free service to the poorest of the poor beginning with one's own family. Deeply involved in the world, the LMCs live lives of prayer, penance, and works of charity after the example of the holy family of Nazareth.[62] The LMCs were established in 1984 in Rome and today have spread to many parts of the world; they have their own statutes and prayer book. Presently, there are over one thousand consecrated LMCs, and several at different preparatory stages of formation.

The Sisters of Our Lady of the Missions have also recognized the importance of lay associates. Although the Vietnamese Province has a strong lay

---

61. Michael H. Crosby, *Can Religious Life Be Prophetic?* (New York: Crossroad, 2005), 8.
62. Sebastian Vazhakala, *Lay Missionaries of Charity: Who We Are!* available at http://laymc.bizland.com/whoweare.htm; accessed April 5, 2006.

associate group, given the concern about declining numbers of sisters, there has been more enthusiasm for this development in One-Third World provinces. Individual provinces have involved lay associates in activities that best respond to the needs of a particular province and to the situations of those with whom they are associated. One significant development has been the involvement of teachers and senior students from the two Australian secondary schools previously staffed by Mission Sisters in education projects in Vietnam. As yet, there is no detailed plan as to how the congregation or the different provinces could collectively negotiate the role of lay associates.[63]

In New Zealand, the Sisters of St. Joseph of the Sacred Heart invite women and men who are attracted to the spirit of Mary MacKillop to gather for friendship, prayer, and to discern how their enthusiasm for Mary McKillop's spirituality and mission can allow them to make a difference in the world in which they live. Governance in this group is shared among a representative group of lay associates and women religious who regularly meet to plan and share tasks. The Josephite Sisters also have formal lay associate programs in Australia and in Peru.

The Mercy Sisters throughout the world have initiated lay associate programs. Again, the motivation for this has been the wish to continue Catherine McAuley's mission of mercy in contemporary society. For example, in 1978, the Sisters of Mercy in the Americas founded the Mercy Volunteer Corps to serve those in need. Mercy volunteers live in small supportive communities, receive a small monthly stipend, and are involved in a variety of activities that give expression to Catherine McAuley's spirit. These activities may include adult literacy instruction, care of those suffering from AIDS, housing development projects, public relations, social work, and teaching. In addition to the Mercy Volunteer Corps, Mercy Associates enables Catholic women and men to affiliate with a particular regional community and participate in the Mercy mission in their own way while maintaining an independent lifestyle.

The Benedictine Sisters of Erie initiated the Benedicta Riepp Program, named for their Benedictine woman founder in the United States. This is a temporary membership experience in which women choose to live the monastic life for one to three years. During this time temporary members learn more about the Benedictine tradition, literature, spirituality, and prayer life, work in a community ministry, and participate in Benedictine commu-

---

63. The 2002 General Gathering asked that Provincial and Regional Leadership Teams "continue to explore with Associates and other interested people, creative ways of sharing our charism, life and mission" (5). The Congregational Leadership Team was asked to further facilitate research concerning "new forms of membership" ("If You Knew the Gift of God," in *25th General Gathering of the Sisters of Our Lady of the Missions* [Pattaya, Thailand, 2002], 9).

nity life and development. Joan Chittister believes that the membership of women in the Benedictine Riepp Program is in continuity with 1,500 years of Benedictine tradition. She argues that this step is a new way of "dealing with the Middle Ages notion of *claustral* oblates, an old Benedictine term for oblates who live inside the cloister."[64]

Orders see the development of associates as a response to Vatican II's call for laypeople to live a committed spiritual life that can involve them in the ministry of the particular order with which they are affiliated. The type of formation program that introduces associates to the order's charism and mission varies from order to order, as do the requirements regarding the form and duration of commitment. Commenting on the North American scene, Ramon Gonzalez writes,

> The numbers of associates of religious orders is currently estimated at 11,000 in Canada, and 15,000 in the United States. They are represented by the North American Conference of Associates and Religious, a networking organization that connects over 155 religious congregations of women and men who sponsor lay associate groups. Some religious orders in the U.S. have expressed fear that religious orders may lose their identity, and finances, if associates are allowed membership . . . However, many orders have drawn up agreements stating the congregations have no legal or financial responsibilities to the associates.[65]

In a recent publication, Mary Bendyna, RSM, notes that women associates outnumber men by a ratio of approximately seven to one.[66] Furthermore, many male associate groups were not founded until the 1990s. Women and men may associate with religious orders for different reasons: with men there is often more of a desire for community, ministry, and service, whereas women appear to be drawn by a desire for prayer and spirituality.

There are both disadvantages and advantages for lay associates in their relationship with a religious order. On the one hand, there are at least two potential areas of tension: first, associates, like women religious prior to Vatican II, may find that their role is seen as auxiliary to that of the vowed religious with whom they work; second, associates seem to be more involved

---

64. Arthur Jones, "Benedictines Welcome Women to Make Temporary Commitment," *National Catholic Reporter*, December 3, 1999, 11.

65. Ramon Gonzalez, "Sisters Find Lay Associates: As Traditional Vocations Dwindle, Orders Find New Life Working with Laity" (February 7, 2000); available at http://www.wcr.ab.ca/news/2000/0207/layassociates020700.shtml; accessed April 3, 2006.

66. See Mary Bendyna, *Partners in Mission: A Profile of Associates and Religious in the United States: North American Conference of Associates and Religious* (Washington, D.C.: Center for Applied Research in the Apostolate, 2000).

with ministry, prayer, and social activities than with financial management and decision making. On the other hand, the institutional community and financial support that a religious order can offer to laypeople can be a significant factor in enabling them to embrace a mission of solidarity with the poor, either at home or overseas. Religious orders provide more extensive opportunities for formation of prospective missionaries, which increases the probability that they will work effectively in the places to which they are sent. The fact that religious and laypeople, ordained and nonordained can work together gives visible expression to the unity that should be characteristic of the church which teaches that the church is "a kind of sacrament or sign of intimate union with God and of the unity of all mankind" (see *Lumen Gentium* no.1).

A similar development is occurring among those orders who have invited others to join them in their mission though not as associates of a particular community. Perhaps the most significant example of this phenomenon is the Jesuit Refugee Service (JRS). Founded in 1980 and currently operating in more than fifty countries, the JRS serves and defends the rights of refugees and displaced people. Women and men from other orders, laypeople, and diocesan priests join the JRS with the explicit goal of responding to this missionary need. Such people do not become Jesuit Associates nor are they initiated into Jesuit spirituality or tradition; nevertheless it allows them mission possibilities otherwise not so readily available. A positive feature of the JRS is the Jesuits' willingness to appoint women to high-profile public roles that formerly would have been considered the prerogative of men. For example, the JRS is involved in advocacy work on behalf of refugees—work that women have successfully headed. JRS Advocacy and Policy Coordinator Melanie Teff gives some idea of what this work entails. She writes:

In 2004 advocacy work focused on dealing with the following issues in many countries: negative perceptions of refugees, pressure on refugees to return to their countries of origin before it is safe for them to do so; the increasing use of detention for refugees, asylum seekers and migrants, access to fair and efficient asylum procedures, access to quality education for refugees and displaced children, sexual abuse and violence against refugee women and girls, inadequate provision of food rations and non-food items to refugees, access to health services for refugees, recruitment of children to armies, and armed groups and landmines.[67]

---

67. Melanie Teff, "Jesuit Refugee Service and Advocacy," *2004 Annual Report* (Rome, 2004), 6. Available at http://www.with.jrs.net/files/ar2004.pdf (accessed 10 April 2006).

The Christian Brothers through the Edmund Rice Volunteer Scheme,[68] which operates out of Australia and New Zealand, similarly involve women religious and laywomen in their mission to the poor. Women with skills perhaps not normally associated with the brothers, such as nursing, working with mothers and children, and certain domestic skills, have joined this scheme in order to work in places such as East Timor. The *Comunidade Edmund Rice* also makes it possible for selected East Timorese women and men to follow programs in Australia that allow them to work as English teachers when they return home.[69] Moreover, young Australians are invited to share briefly in the life of the East Timorese, a move affirmed by John Paul II in *Redemptoris Missio* no. 82: "Visiting the missions is commendable, especially on the part of the young people who go there to serve and to gain an extensive experience of the Christian life."[70] Likewise, volunteers may work with the Christian Brothers in their Aboriginal Ministry in Australia, and in schools that the brothers operate in Two-Thirds World countries.

## WOMEN LAY MISSIONARIES

In addition to women working with religious orders as associates, there are numerous instances of women, along with men, who work as lay missionaries by being missioned to a particular place by lay missionary organizations that are established under the auspices of a local bishop or a local bishops' conference. Examples of these organizations are many. The Lay Mission-Helpers Association of the Archdiocese of Los Angeles has sent out over six hundred lay women and men who work as teachers, nurses, computer technicians, secretaries, accountants, agriculturalists, and people skilled in a variety of trades. Founded in 1955, its members initially were sent to African and Oceanic nations, and Thailand. The Lay Mission-Helpers Association anticipated Vatican II's teaching on the role and place of laity in the ongoing mission of the church. According to Joan Delaney, "this group, similar to some other lay missionary groups, has witnessed a decline in the number of recruits in recent years owing to the considerable

---

68. The program is named to honor the memory of Irishman Edmund Rice (1762-1844), who founded the Christian Brothers.

69. See the *CER* (*Comunidade Edmund Rice*) *Newsletter* no. 6, which outlines the story of two East Timorese women who attended an intensive ten-week English course at Nudgee International College in Australia. They have returned to their home country to teach English.

70. John Paul II, "*Redemptoris Missio*," in *Redemption and Dialogue: Reading 'Redemptoris Missio' and 'Dialogue and Proclamation,'* ed. William R. Burrows (Maryknoll, N.Y.: Orbis Books, 1993), 48. Unless otherwise stated, all references to *Redemptoris Missio* will be from *Redemption and Dialogue*.

increase in the opportunities for Catholic laity to serve overseas."[71] In its placement of volunteers overseas, Mahitahi:[72] The Project Assistance Agency of the New Zealand Catholic Bishops' Conference requires that volunteers do not undertake tasks that could be carried out by a local person and that their skills be passed on to local people who can continue the work begun by the volunteers. To this end, volunteers' terms do not exceed three years; by the end of that time, a local person should be ready to take over the position. Volunteers receive no remuneration other than their board and keep.

The Hong Kong Catholic Lay Missionary Association was established in 1986 by two lay missionaries, Jessica Ho and Elizabeth Woo, who initially were sent to Tanzania through the Maryknoll Lay Missionary Program. This experience encouraged them to establish the Hong Kong Lay Missionary Association, which sends personnel abroad to work with the poor and marginalized in their struggle for a better life. Members now work in Cambodia, parts of China, and Kenya, often in association with organizations such as the Jesuit Refugee Service. Other important aims include helping those among whom they work to become self-reliant and missionary themselves, encouraging returned missionaries to share their experiences with the local church in Hong Kong, and arranging exposure program that alert participants to missionary needs in countries such as Myanmar.

The role of Catholic laywomen in Papua New Guinea is informative for understanding more about the missionary activity of Catholic laywomen in the Two-Thirds World. Anne Dickson-Waiko, history lecturer at the University of Papua New Guinea, examines the different ways Protestant and Catholic churches have mobilized Papua New Guinean women for ministry.[73] Although the Catholic Church with its "more centralized and its mainly foreign male clergy was slower to encourage indigenous women to combine in groups"[74] for the sake of mission, in 1978 in East New Britain Province, Tolai Catholic women formed a Catholic Women's Association. The economic, religious, and moral goals on the group's agenda aimed at upholding Catholic spiritual, moral, and family values. In 1984, a national

---

71. Joan Delaney, *A Comparative Study of Christian Mission* (Washington, D.C.: U.S. Catholic Mission Association, 1998), 27.

72. *Mahitahi* is a combination of two Maori words and means "work together." It responds to requests for assistance from Pacific Island dioceses who have identified and prioritized development projects. *Mahitahi* seeks to recruit New Zealand expertise to participate in these projects in partnership with local laity, who manage the planning, training, monitoring, and measurement of outcomes.

73. See Anne Dickson-Waiko, "The Missing Rib: Mobilizing Church Women for Change in Papua New Guinea," *Oceania* 74 (2003): 98-119.

74. Ibid., 106.

Catholic Women's Federation was formed. Its constitution indicates that it does not restrict women's role in the church to the domestic realm. It explicitly focuses on economic, social, political, and ecclesial issues in an effort to improve women's place in church and society. It also aims at friendship, unity, and joint action with women of other churches. The Federation, the largest mobilized Catholic lay group, "hopes to assist women in the fulfillment of the national goals and directive principles as outlined in the national constitution."[75] During its first ten years, the Federation set up a network in parishes and dioceses, while "the second decade has seen the raising of issues and activities, especially those identified in the 1995 Beijing Platform of Action."[76] The Federation and its Protestant counterparts are succeeding in mobilizing women in both the rural and urban sectors to "expand their horizons from spiritual and religious to social or to value the experience of fellowship with women from different cultures and backgrounds."[77] In Papua New Guinea, the Federation is playing a vital role in spearheading social change as women unite to prepare the way for a genuine national awareness—an elusive value in a country with over seven hundred different language and cultural groups!

Kenya offers another example of laywomen actively engaging in missionary work. For example, the Kenyan "Catholic Lay Missionaries," established in 1989, brings together Kenyan lay women and men to serve in the most needy rural and urban sectors of Kenya. The CLM has devised a vigorous discernment and selection process for volunteers, culminating in a three-week intensive residential discernment program. Successful candidates serve for a minimum of two years and can renew their contract.[78] Catholic laywoman and senior lecturer at Kenyatta University, Philomena Mwaura, offers some important insights on the missionary role of Kenyan laywomen.[79] For Mwaura, evangelization involves liberation from personal sin, and from all forms of social, economic, cultural, and political oppression. In this perspective, evangelization "implies a regeneration of people in a fundamental way through the power of the gospel."[80] Although the 1994 African Synod insisted on the basic equality that should exist between women and men,

---

75. Ibid., 108.
76. Ibid.
77. Ibid., 109.
78. "Gospel Service: Acknowledgements to New People," *Mission Outlook* (October 2005); available at http://www.missionsocieties.org.uk/MOUT/0510/08_Gospel_Service.htm; accessed April 6, 2006.
79. Philomena Mwaura, "Women and Evangelisation: A Challenge to the Church in the Third Millennium," in *Challenges and Prospects for the Church in Africa: Theological Reflections for the Church in Africa*, ed. Nashashon W. Ndungu and Philomena N. Mwaura (Nairobi: Paulines Publications Africa, 2005).
80. Ibid., 122.

nevertheless "women's rights and dignity are still unattained despite secular and religious efforts to improve the situation . . . [Archbishop] Njue calls for the establishment of appropriate lay ministries in which women can participate. Provisions should also be made for appropriate spiritual formation, and women's involvement in the liturgy and every aspect of the life of the Church."[81] Women's role as primary evangelizers in the family is reaffirmed, and their capacity to nurture and care for others, which allows them to respond to the material and spiritual needs of people in their parishes, is perhaps most suitably acknowledged as an evangelization of touch and healing.

What is just as important, women are increasingly involved in the organization of parish life and outreach to other peoples, Christian and non-Christian. Catholic laywomen have been responsible for the establishment and ongoing life of the Small Christian Communities through their communal prayer, Bible study groups, and their pastoral ministry to Catholics and non-Catholics alike in the area. Women "form 90% of participants in Small Christian Communities."[82] The shortage of priests in many parts of Kenya also means that women are assuming responsibility for paraliturgical assemblies on Sundays and weekdays. Women also engage in evangelization through their membership in groups that endeavor to meet both the spiritual and socioeconomic needs of people. These groups include the Legion of Mary, Catholic Action, Charismatic Renewal, Young Christian Students, and the Grail Movement. Most of these organizations are members of the national Catholic Women's Association (C.W.A.), which has a membership of over 600,000.

The C.W.A. aims at raising awareness of women's dignity, particularly the marginalized, through spiritual formation and socioeconomic activities that serve to empower them. The Association organizes seminars and workshops on issues affecting health and well-being, such as HIV/AIDS, civic education, human rights, gender awareness, leadership training, marriage preparation, parenting, and family skills. Women are enabled to start small income-generating projects in order to finance important family needs, for example, sinking water bore holes, installing electricity in their homes, or helping to meet medical and education costs incurred by family members. These projects are not confined to Kenya, "for example, [in] Tanzania, Uganda, Zambia and Malawi, [national] C.W.A.s contribute to the acceleration of removing obstacles to women's full and equal participation in all spheres of life."[83]

Mwaura identifies as a major concern the fact that in the African church "the only area allowed women in evangelization is that of service,"[84] which

---

81. Ibid., 130-31.
82. Ibid., 134.
83. Ibid., 137.
84. Ibid.

is more likely to occur in the domestic rather than the public sphere. Despite the contribution that C.W.A.s make to the life of the church in many parts of Africa, women are not normally represented in the institutional church's decision-making bodies. In fact, Traditional African Religion allowed women a greater leadership role in the community than do the Christian churches founded by Catholic and Protestant missionaries. In this respect, the mainline churches, including the Catholic, could learn from African Instituted Churches, particularly neo-Pentecostal churches, whose numbers are increasing in a spectacular fashion. One of the main reasons for this increase is that they offer to women leadership possibilities that the mainline churches deny them. While women are expected to play a major role in the task of evangelization, their efforts do not translate into leadership roles and responsibilities at other than the Small Christian Community level. "The Church should come out in 'affirmative action in favor of women' and educate them about their rights in Church and society and also provide them with theological education."[85]

The Maryknoll Lay Missioners grew out of the Maryknoll lay mission program that was begun in 1975, and included the Maryknoll Society (priests and brothers), the Maryknoll Congregation (sisters), the Maryknoll Lay Missioners, and the Maryknoll Affiliates.[86] After discussions with the Vatican in 1994, the Maryknoll lay mission program was directed to become autonomous and self-supporting. Consequently, the Maryknoll Lay Missioners have had to work to build a base of financial support; this means that they are basically dependent on contributions from private individuals to fund their work. According to Randy Young, "Maryknoll lay missioners agree to serve one tour of three and a half years, renewable every three years thereafter. Two thirds of the missioners serve for more than one tour, and about a third for more than ten years." Members may be married or single, and women play an important role as education, health, agricultural, and social workers.

Caritas Internationalis, one of the world's largest humanitarian networks, is a confederation of 162 Catholic relief, development, and social service organizations working to build a better world for the poor and oppressed in over two hundred countries and territories.[87] The various national Caritas

---

85. Ibid., 142.

86. See Randy Young, "Countless Small Victories," *America* 191 (2004); available at http://www.americamagazine.org/gettext.cfm?articletypeID=1&textID=3670&issueID; accessed April 10, 2006.

87. Not all Catholic development agencies go by the name Caritas, even though they are part of the Caritas International Federation. For example, Trócaire is the official overseas development agency of the Catholic Church in Ireland. It was established by the Irish Catholic bishops in 1973 to express the concern of the Irish church for the suffering of the world's poorest and most oppressed people. Similarly, the Catholic Fund for Overseas Development (CAFOD)

organizations can legitimately be identified as part of the missionary out-reach of the church, which involves many laywomen in responding to emer-gency and developmental needs particularly in the Two-Thirds World. In the One-Third World, the major roles for women are fundraising for relief and development overseas, raising the awareness of their local churches to the causes of underdevelopment by introducing people to Catholic social teach-ing. Increasingly, women have a high profile in such organizations as admin-istrators, educators, and fundraisers, though so far not as national directors.[88]

The story of the Grail Movement since Vatican II in some ways is a micro-story of what is happening at the macro level for many women missionaries, both lay and religious. Alden Brown, in *The Grail Movement and American Catholicism*,[89] explains how the movement in the United States evolved from a semimonastic rural movement in the 1940s to a more urban-based and self-confident organization that emphasized international missionary pro-grams in the 1950s, to a self-critical, more feminist-focused, and inclusive movement in the 1960s. The influence of Vatican II, the feminist movement, and liberation theology radically shifted the Grail Movement's self-understanding. Prior to Vatican II, the all-female membership of the Grail Movement tended to be unaware of the limitations that a patriarchal church culture imposed on women, but from the 1960s onward, the feminist move-ment concentrated Grail attention on feminist concerns, for example, on the need for more participatory, democratic structures of government. The Grail Movement's enthusiasm for inclusivity, another value associated with the feminist movement, explains why the American Grail Movement in 1969 voted to admit women of other Christian traditions as full participants, and, in 1975, welcomed Jewish women.

The questioning and self-criticism characteristic of the Grail Movement from the 1960s onward generated new understandings about the movement's missionary goals. In the last two decades of the twentieth century, there has been less emphasis on common, communally organized work. Ministry took on a more individualistic quality as Grail members involved themselves in

---

is the official overseas development and relief agency of the Catholic Church in England and Wales.

88. See Susan Barclay, "Are Mission Agencies Institutionally Sexist?" *Global Connections Occasional Papers* 22 (Spring 2006). Although Barclay is writing about Protestant mission agen-cies, her comments are true also of Catholic development and mission agencies. She writes that mission agencies "each have their own culture, optimized for men who traditionally have been in positions of authority, and embodied in their processes and structures. Gender stereotypes contribute to the overall effect, as does the current generation of leaders. Many of these things are invisible to those within the organization" (4).

89. See Alden V. Brown, *The Grail Movement and American Catholicism, 1940-1975* (Notre Dame, Ind.: University of Notre Dame Press, 1989).

environmental and peace issues particularly as they affected women. Thus the Australian Grail Movement focused on "women's education and personal development, on social and cultural critical analysis, and organized action grounded in conviction."[90] More recently, the Grail Movement has prioritized an ecofeminist agenda. As Rosemary Radford Ruether explains, "an ecofeminist approach that blends feminism, ecology and justice seems to have a particular appeal to Catholic religious women. Ecofeminism brings together spirituality and scientific rationality, prayer and practical management, outreach to society and service to the poor with cultivation of the inner self, critical reason with the poetic, artistic and intuitive."[91]

"Our task" said Edwina Gateley, "is to be faithful idiots in a world that seems to many to be abandoned by God."[92] Thus English-born Edwina Gateley describes the mission undertaken by members of Volunteer Missionary Movement, which she founded in 1969. This independent, Catholic-initiated, lay-run movement spread from England to the United States in 1981. Today the VMM has two branches: VMM-USA and VMM-Europe, and almost two thousand volunteers have served in Central America, North America, Papua New Guinea, and Africa. Membership in the VMM is open to both women and men, but women predominate. From 1964 to 1968, Edwina worked in Uganda as a teacher and lay missionary and established a successful school for Ugandan girls. Experiencing the culture and life of the Ugandan community was formative for Edwina, and on her return to England, prompted her to found a lay missionary movement, or as the VMM Web site states,

> Imagine what it was like to be a layperson in 1969 who wanted to be a missionary. Your choices were pretty much limited to becoming a priest or minister, a religious sister or a brother. While many people felt the call to mission, they didn't always feel called to one of these other ministries. It was exactly this situation that led Edwina Gateley to found the Volunteer Missionary Movement in 1969. Out of her own mission experience in Africa, following the Gospel, she set out to build a community of Christians committed to justice for all peoples.[93]

---

90. See "The Grail (1937–)"; available at http://www.womenaustralia.info/biogs/AWEO 709b.htm; accessed April 10, 2006.

91. Rosemary Radford Ruether, "Sisters of the Earth: Religious Women and Ecological Spirituality," *Witness* (May 2000); available at http://thewitness.org/archive/may2000/may. ruether.html; accessed April 10, 2006.

92. Robert J. McClory, "35 Years on 'the Prophetic Edge': Lay Missionary Movement Takes on World's Inequities," *National Catholic Reporter,* July 16, 2004, 8.

93. See *Volunteer Missionary Movement (VMM-USA): What Is VMM's History?* (2006); available at http://www.vmmusa.org; accessed May 8, 2006.

Volunteers typically serve for two years and often work as part of the volunteer program of an established religious order or Catholic development agency. As a post-Vatican II movement, VMM members readily accept postconciliar missiological developments, acknowledging their implications in their work. Their ability to network with other agencies, to work ecumenically, and to understand that mission priorities are no longer determined geographically suggests that the VMM offers a good model for other young missionary organizations.

Gateley herself has acquired a reputation as a spiritual author and is invited to give retreats and speak on the challenge of urban mission to the poor. Her various books[94] constitute a valuable resource for laypeople, particularly women, in their efforts to identify the shape of a genuine lay missionary spirituality. Her awareness of the sufferings of abused and marginalized women means that she sees retreat work for such women as a personal priority; she is also involved in ministry among women recovering from their experiences as prostitutes. Edwina Gateley models what mission can be for lay women and men: activity directed toward the poor and against violence and poverty, or as she herself says, standing on "the prophetic edge between the world as the 'realm of God' and the 'world as the place of pain and suffering.'"[95] Mission should be inclusive in its outreach; and, mission is a "faith-based operation rooted in the Roman Catholic tradition."[96]

## WOMEN IN MISSION IN THE THIRD MILLENNIUM

In reading and trying to understand the story of women missionaries since Vatican II, we can identify some of the more important developments that have occurred. First, and most notably, the distinctions that previously characterized Catholic missionary work have been blurred. The distinction between the missionary work of women religious and laywomen has almost disappeared with respect to the activities in which they engage. The older division between overseas and local mission, determined by geographical categories, has to some extent been replaced by socioeconomic categories for identifying mission priorities. Mission as a gendered activity is changing—apart from those aspects directly related to the sacramental ministry of the priest. This change is occurring at a different pace in different parts of the Catholic world, as the example of Kenya made clear, but the new works that increasingly engage missionaries, for example, advocacy work, computer

94. See Edwina Gateley, *I Hear a Seed Growing: God of the Forest, God of the Streets* (Trabuco Canyon, Calif.: Source Books, 1990); Edwina Gateley and Louis S. Glanzman, illustrator, *Soul Sisters: Women in Scripture Speak to Women Today* (Maryknoll, N.Y.: Orbis Books, 2002).
95. McClory, "35 Years on 'the Prophetic Edge,'" 8.
96. Ibid.

programming and teaching, research, tertiary and seminary teaching, allow women to work alongside men in ways not possible before. The story of women in mission has indicated that women have often attempted to be missionary as laywomen, or as married women, but a patriarchal church insisted that women who wanted to live out a missionary vocation should do this as women religious subject to Canon Law and clerical directives. Prior to Vatican II, most women missionaries were members of religious orders. This too has changed significantly. Women missionaries may be part of diocesan mission programs, members of secular institutes, associates, or partners with other groups. Intercongregational and interorganization mission, while not the norm, is certainly assuming more importance and will probably continue to do so. Finally, the more individualized ministries of increasing numbers of women religious, and the tendency particularly in some One-Third World countries for women religious to live alone, are diminishing the gap between secular institutes and religious orders.

Second, both women religious and laywomen have reaffirmed that their missionary identity flows from their baptism. Vatican II had insisted on this, and Pope John Paul II reiterated it in *Redemptoris Missio* no. 82. When this teaching is acknowledged in both theory and practice, it ensures that the roles of women religious and laywomen can no longer be identified as auxiliary. The constantly expanding nature of Catholic missionary work and, concomitant to that, the growing contributions that women make to that work mean that women's missionary work now is perceived as integral, and not auxiliary, to mission.

Third, prior to Vatican II, the spirituality of women religious showed the influence of the great masters of the spiritual life, for example, Francis, Dominic, Ignatius, Francis de Sales. Their contribution to the spiritual well-being of both women and men needs to be fully appreciated. From the 1960s onward, however, women religious availed themselves more readily of theological and biblical education, which in turn, introduced them to important women theologians whose nonandrocentric approaches to spirituality have proved enriching. Contemporary women theologians such as Catherine LaCugna,[97] Elizabeth Johnson,[98] and Sandra Schneiders[99] have enabled

97. See Catherine Mowry LaCugna, *God for Us: The Trinity and Christian Life* (San Francisco: HarperCollins, 1991).

98. See Elizabeth A. Johnson, *She Who Is: The Mystery of God in Feminist Theological Discourse* (New York: Crossroad, 1992); idem, *Women, Earth and Creator Spirit* (New York/Mahwah, N.J.: Paulist Press, 1993); idem, *Consider Jesus: Waves of Renewal in Christology* (New York: Crossroad, 1992); idem, *Friends of God and Prophets: A Feminist Theological Reading of the Communion of Saints* (New York: Continuum, 1999); idem, *Truly Our Sister: A Theology of Mary in the Communion of Saints* (New York: Continuum, 2003).

99. See Sandra Schneiders, *With Oil in Their Lamps: Faith, Feminism and the Future* (New York/Mahwah, N.J.: Paulist Press, 2000); idem, *Finding the Treasure: Locating Catholic Religious Life in a New Ecclesial and Cultural Context* (New York: Paulist Press, 2000).

women to identify the parameters of spiritualities that speak and flow into their missionary realities. For example, Johnson's *Women, Earth and Creator Spirit* provides women with a Christian theology in which care of creation can be grounded in ways that honor and draw on the Christian tradition but at the same time use a feminist hermeneutic. While there is much in the emerging spiritualities embraced by women religious that will be important for women lay missionaries, lay missionaries are also identifying the shape of a lay missionary spirituality that can sustain them in their mission. Thanks to the theological and spiritual publications of laywomen such as Edwina Gateley and Mary Judith Ress,[100] laywomen missionaries can now access works written from a lay perspective; and the historical and contemporaneous stories of laywomen such as the Beguines, Angela Merici, Dorothy Day, Jean Donovan, who was martyred in El Salvador, and Sheila Cassidy, the English medical doctor imprisoned and tortured in Chile, offer important models of the contribution of laywomen to mission.

Formation programs for women religious and laywomen tend to have different goals and objectives. Women religious are being prepared for permanent commitment to a particular way of life, of which missionary activity is an integral and essential part, whereas lay missionaries, initially at least, are being prepared for a three-year missionary appointment. Delaney notes that orders of women religious feel "the need to establish some type of precandidacy program. Beyond that, there are a variety of ways in which theological training, ministry experience, cross-cultural training and experience of community life are provided. Since the needs required for living and working long-term in another culture are many, there is an ongoing effort to find the best possible way of preparing personnel for life overseas,"[101] or in another culture even if that is within one's country of origin. Obviously such a lengthy period of formation is not possible for laywomen, but there is now more emphasis on the appropriate formation of laywomen. Those missioned to other cultures participate in programs that include introductions to missionary spirituality and crosscultural living, professional orientation for work to be undertaken, scripture and theology courses, and personal development work. In addition, associate members are introduced to the charism, traditions, spirituality, and mission of the particular order.

Finally, the experience of mission overseas is often a life-changing experience. On returning to their country of origin women realize that they have a genuine missionary role at home in working with the poor, or acting as advocates for the poor because they often know firsthand something of their

---

100. See Ress, *Ecofeminism in Latin America*. Ress is a Maryknoll Lay Missioner, an author, and a founding member of the Con-spirando Collective, a team of women working in ecofeminist theology and spirituality in Chile.

101. Delaney, *A Comparative Study of Christian Mission*, 44.

reality. This is particularly important for women with families with children whose age and needs mean that it is no longer practicable for them to remain in a Two-Thirds World country.

Our story of women in mission since Vatican II is a story that should inspire and encourage contemporary women as they discern the meaning of mission for themselves. The visible changes in women's exercise of mission are obvious enough, but just as important are the less obvious but important theological developments that have led to such changes. It is to these that I now turn.

# 8

# A Feminist Missiology for Contemporary Missionary Women

Throughout the two thousand years of Christian history, Christian women have participated in the mission of the triune God in a variety of different sociocultural contexts—Jewish, Greco-Roman, medieval, modern, African, Asian, Latin American, North American, and, most recently, Oceanic. Despite the variety of situations, one feature common to all these cultures was the strength of patriarchy, which has been defined by Rosemary Radford Ruether as "a developed legal, economic and social system, [which] gives the male head of the family sovereign power over dependents in the household, the wife or wives, children, and slaves. The patriarch is the owner of property passed through the patriarchal lineage: buildings, animals, and land."[1] Almost without exception, male ecclesial leadership in its exercise of authority relied on patriarchal models of governance for the church. Historically, this has meant that in the exercise of their mission, Catholic women have worked in a way that suited the requirements of a patriarchal church.

Thus far we have been considering the story of women in mission, but a story of "the work of women in mission is not the same as a feminist missiology."[2] Today, feminist missiologists, drawing on the insights of contemporary biblical scholars and theologians, are attempting to identify the shape of a feminist missiology.[3] Feminist missiology is a recent undertaking as women identify ways of involving themselves in ministry that observes and respects the insights offered them by feminist biblical hermeneutics and theologies. Traditionally, responsibility for the theological task was entrusted to

---

1. Rosemary Radford Ruether, "Patriarchy," in *An A to Z of Feminist Theology*, ed. Lisa Isherwood and Dorothea McEwan (Sheffield: Sheffield Academic Press, 1996), 174.
2. Letty M. Russell, "Cultural Hermeneutics: A Postcolonial Look at Mission," *Journal of Feminist Studies in Religion* 20 (2004): 23-40.
3. See, for example, *International Review of Mission* 93 (2004), which is devoted to feminist missiology and missionary practice.

ordained ministers whose social location in the institutional church informed their theology. At best, their theologies were paternalistic and kindly disposed toward women, and, at worst, oppressive toward women. Catholic ecclesiology prior to Vatican II "had emphasized that the church was fundamentally an 'unequal society,' composed of 'the pastors and the flock.'"[4] This made it difficult for women to define their missionary role, and, as Indian theologian Samuel Rayan notes, during the period of European expansion, decisions in the church were "made and goods processed at the centre for eventual exportation and consumption by the periphery."[5]

Vatican II began to change this situation. The church was described as a mystery, as "the people made one in the unity of Father, Son and Holy Spirit" (*Lumen Gentium* no. 4). *Ad Gentes* taught that the mission of the church had its origins in the mission of the Son and the mission of the Holy Spirit according to the designs of the Father (see *Ad Gentes* no. 2). These trinitarian developments were of immense importance for the Catholic community as it sought to articulate the shape of missiologies that spoke to the realities of the postmodern world.

Even more important were the emerging articulations of trinitarian theologies that moved beyond those interpretations that subordinated the roles of lay women and men to that of ordained ministers. Traditionally, trinitarian theologies had served a hierarchical church well. Texts such as Matthew 28:19-20 and John 20:21-23 that encouraged hierarchical structures had their foundation in "high" christologies which subordinated the role of the Spirit, who blows where she wills.[6] A number of contemporary theologians—women and men—have begun the task of revisioning trinitarian theologies.

---

4. Stephen B. Bevans and Roger P. Schroeder, *Constants in Context: A Theology of Mission for Today* (Maryknoll, N.Y.: Orbis Books, 2004), 286.

5. Samuel Rayan, "The Ecclesiology at Work in the Indian Church," in *Searchings for an Indian Ecclesiology*, ed. Gerwin Van Leeuwen (Bangalore: ATC, 1984), 196.

6. In the Catholic tradition, Matthew 28:19-20 and John 20:21-23 provide support for the Catholic position that bishops are successors of the apostles in their teaching and pastoral ministries; such an interpretation leads to ecclesiologies that understand the church as hierarchically organized. Commenting on John 20:21-23, Australian theologian David Coffey argues that its "high" christology obscures the mission of the Spirit: "The official doctrine of the Trinity developed from the doctrine of Christ peculiar to the Fourth Gospel . . . I should like to add that John, alone among the Gospels, presented a descending Christology. That is to say, just as the divine Son, Son of Man and Word of God, was sent down from heaven by the Father and in turn sent the Holy Spirit, the 'other Paraclete,' from the Father, so in the Godhead itself the Father generates the Son and the two together breathe forth the Holy Spirit (according to the Western form of the doctrine)." See David M. Coffey, "A Proper Mission of the Holy Spirit," *Theological Studies* 47 (1986): 227-50. Raymond Brown arrives at a similar conclusion: "A later generation of Western theologians called upon [John 20] v. 22 as proof that within the Trinity the Holy Spirit proceeded by spiration and that the Son had a role not only in the mission but also in the procession of the Spirit" (Augustine *De Trinitate* 4.29; PL 42:908). See Raymond E. Brown, *The Gospel According to John XIII-XXI* (New York: Doubleday, 1966), 1023.

They believe that trinitiarian theologies that take as their starting point "high" christologies need to be complemented by theologies that accent the role of the Spirit.

## SCRIPTURE AND THE MISSION OF THE SPIRIT

Old Testament texts point to the universal nature of the Spirit's presence in creation. In Genesis 1:2, God's Spirit is a creative and vivifying presence sweeping across the deep waters ("the earth was a formless void and darkness covered the face of the deep, while the Spirit of God swept over the face of the waters").[7] The Spirit or breath of God that sweeps over the waters is the prelude to God's creative word in Genesis 1:3 ("Then God said, 'Let there be light,' and there was light").

The motif of the Spirit as a creative force is further developed in the Deuterocanonical book of Judith. After her undeniably violent killing of Holofernes, Judith leads the Jewish women in dance and praise. She prays, "Let all your creatures serve you, for you spoke and they were made. You sent forth your spirit, and it formed them" (Jdt 16:14). In the Wisdom of Solomon, there is even greater emphasis on the creative activity of the spirit: "The spirit of the Lord has filled the world, and that which holds all things together knows what is said" (Wis 1:7). Another important spirit text occurs in Wisdom 12:1, a hymn that celebrates the Spirit's indwelling. "You spare all things, for they are yours, O Lord, you who love the living. For your immortal spirit is in all things."

In the book of Wisdom, God's Spirit, often personified as the feminine Sophia, passes into holy souls and makes them friends of God and prophets (Wis 7:27)—an indication that the Spirit-Sophia empowers people for their prophetic mission. The empowering agency of the Spirit-Sophia in God's prophets is attested to elsewhere in the Old Testament. In Genesis 41:38, Pharaoh recognizes that Joseph is one in whom the Spirit of God dwells, and Numbers 11:25 speaks of the Spirit being bestowed on Moses and the seventy elders. But it is in the prophetic books that the empowering agency of the Spirit is most obvious, as Isaiah reveals. The Spirit of the Lord will rest upon the Messiah (Isa 11:2-3) and a spirit of justice will be given to judges (Isa 28:6). In Second Isaiah, God's Spirit overshadows the Servant (Isa 42:1-2), and in Third Isaiah, the prophet is anointed with the Spirit of the Lord God so that his mission to proclaim, heal, liberate, and comfort can be proclaimed (Isa 61:1-2).

---

7. See Herbert G. May and Bruce M. Metzger, eds., *New Oxford Annotated Bible—RSV* (New York/Oxford: Oxford University Press, 1998).

In the New Testament, the Spirit empowered Jesus for his mission. In Matthew's infancy narrative, Jesus is conceived through the power of the Spirit (Matt 1:20). The Spirit rests on Jesus at his baptism (Matt 3:16), and then leads Jesus into the desert as he prepares for his public ministry (Mark 1:12-13; Matt 4:1). A cluster of references to the Spirit occurs in Matthew 12:18-31, the section of the Gospel that details the controversies with the Pharisees that the healing ministry of Jesus has provoked. Matthew understands that Jesus' ministry of healing identifies him as God's chosen servant on whom God's Spirit has come (see Isa 42:1-14). The presence of the Spirit enables Jesus to drive out demons so that entry into the kingdom of God is possible (Matt 12:28).

When Luke writes about the Spirit in the Gospel, he is using the word "spirit" in the sense in which Old Testament tradition understood it: "God's active, creative or prophetic presence to God's world or God's people."[8] In Luke 1:1-12:12, which begins with the infancy narratives and concludes as Jesus begins his journey to Jerusalem, Lukan pneumatology contributes to our understanding of the mission of the Spirit. For Luke, the reign of God had both a present and a future dimension, and the present time before the parousia is the time of the Spirit, the time of mission. Luke's narrative contains references to historical figures whose oppressive rule in Palestine contributed to Israel's sufferings. The very names "King Herod of Judea" (1:5) and "Caesar Augustus" (2:1) evoke a world of political machinations, imperial conquest, economic injustice, and social stratification. The emperor, "the divine savior who has brought peace to the world,"[9] ruled over a brutally pacified world. Palestine was a country that called out for the Spirit's prophetic activity (see 1:51-55; 1:72-79).

Luke 1-4 suggests that Israel's oppression would be overcome through the prophetic mission of Jesus, on whom the Spirit rested. The overshadowing of the Holy Spirit at Jesus' conception means that he was "set apart" for a special mission in God's salvific plan. Joseph Fitzmyer notes that the "highly figurative"[10] language of Luke 1 alerts the reader to "the mysterious intervention of God's Spirit and power, which will bring about Jesus' Davidic role and his divine filiation."[11] Raymond Brown believes that it is appropriate to relate this "action of the Holy Spirit to that of the creative Spirit of God which hovered over the face of the waters in Gen 1:2."[12]

---

8. Joseph A. Fitzmyer, *The Gospel According to Luke I-IX* (New York: Doubleday, 1981), 228.

9. Richard A. Horsley, *The Liberation of Christmas: The Infancy Narratives in Social Context* (New York: Crossroad, 1989), 28.

10. Fitzmyer, *The Gospel According to Luke I-IX*, 337.

11. Ibid., 338.

12. Raymond E. Brown, *The Birth of the Messiah: A Commentary on the Infancy Narratives in Matthew and Luke* (London: Geoffrey Chapman, 1977), 327.

After the descent of the Holy Spirit upon Jesus at his baptism (3:22), Jesus, "full of the Holy Spirit" returns from the Jordan and is led by the same Spirit into the wilderness, where the nature of his future mission is clarified in the temptation narrative (4:1-13). Through the power of the Spirit Jesus would accomplish his mission (4:18), a truth that is confirmed retrospectively in Acts 10:38. The missionary program enunciated by a Spirit-filled Jesus in the synagogue in Nazareth (Luke 4:16-30) suggested that Jesus' mission would transgress, and therefore reverse, Israel's socially determined boundaries, which excluded people on the bases of religion (4:27; cf. 6:1-16), ethnicity (4:27; cf. 1 Kgs 17:1-16), and economic status (4:18; cf. 6:20; 19:2). Luke's Gospel convincingly demonstrates that Jesus understood himself as one whose mission was dependent on the power of the Spirit (11:20), as a prophet (13:33), and as one whose prophetic mission would hasten the eschatological reign of God (11:20).

## THEOLOGIANS, CHURCH TEACHING, AND THE MISSION OF THE SPIRIT

Theologians have been turning to tradition and church teaching for new insights regarding the role of the Spirit in the mission of the Trinity. Belgian theologian Jacques Dupuis, who lived and worked for many years in India, believes that the different non-Christian religions are revelatory and salvific. Dupuis moves beyond exclusivist, pluralist, and inclusivist positions and argues that the Spirit and the *Logos* were active in human history before the incarnation, and therefore active in other religious traditions. He locates patristic evidence, particularly in the writings of Irenaeus, to support his position. He approvingly notes that prior to the incarnation, "the Word and the Breath [Spirit] of God, whom St. Irenaeus saw as the 'two hands of God' (Saint Irenaeus, *Contra Haereses*, IV, 7, 4: SC 100:462-65) [are] conjointly doing his [God's] work"[13] in creation.

Catholic feminist theologian Catherine LaCugna[14] is another whose careful critique of patristic teaching offers fresh insights into the Trinity. LaCugna demonstrates that God's relationship to humankind as revealed in the biblical stories of creation and redemption was gradually undermined by an emphasis, particularly in Western theology, on the inner life of the Trinity.

---

13. Jacques Dupuis, *Toward a Christian Theology of Religious Pluralism* (Maryknoll, N.Y.: Orbis Books, 1997), 195; J. Mambino, "Les deux mains de Dieu dans l'oeuvre de Saint Irénée," *Nouveau revue théologique* 69 (1957).

14. See Catherine Mowry LaCugna, "The Relational God: Aquinas and Beyond," *Theological Studies* 46, no. 4 (December 1985), 647-63; idem, ed., *Freeing Theology: The Essentials of Theology in Feminist Perspective* (New York: HarperCollins, 1993); idem, *God for Us: The Trinity and Christian Life* (San Francisco: HarperCollins, 1991).

According to Patricia Fox, LaCugna recognized that Augustine's theology meant "an ontology of substance eventually came to replace the centrality of a trinitarian theology of relation."[15] LaCugna believes that "the consequences of Augustine's digression from the Cappadocian ontology of the Trinity [which emphasized the relations of the three persons] were more than merely doctrinal. The changed metaphysical options for the theology of God changed politics, anthropology, and society as well."[16] LaCugna explores the nature of *perichoresis*, the reciprocal presence of the three divine persons in one another in mutual giving and receiving without subordination or domination. She believes that this model of reciprocal presence should be lived out in the church, the sacrament of the triune God. If the missionary appreciates the relational nature of the Trinity, she will want to embrace an ethos that models the importance of mutual and reciprocal relations in her own mission. When the missionary accepts "the essentially relational character of God, the relational character of human existence, and the interdependent quality of the entire universe,"[17] then mission can be understood as working for life-giving relationships in church, society, and creation.

Vatican II offers important teaching regarding the mission of the Spirit. For example, *Gaudium et Spes* no. 26 directs attention to the Spirit's activity in the "secular" dimension of life and affirms that "the Spirit of God who with wondrous providence, directs the course of time and renews the face of the earth, assists at this development." The "development" referred to is the improvement of social conditions required to enhance human dignity. This development "must be founded on truth, built on justice and, animated by love; in freedom it should grow every day toward a more humane balance" (*Gaudium et Spes* no. 26). Because the Spirit "directs the course of time and renews the face of the earth," it follows that the mission of God embraces all of human and cosmic history.

The role of the Spirit in the mission of the triune God is well described by John Paul II in *Redemptoris Missio* no. 21: "the Holy Spirit remains the transcendent and principal agent for the accomplishment of this work in the human spirit and in the history of the world (*Dominum et Vivificantem* 42[18]) . . . The Holy Spirit is indeed the principal agent of the whole of the Church's mission" (*Redemptoris Missio* no. 28). An affirmation of the Spirit as the principal agent of mission may wrongly suggest a dichotomy between the work of the Spirit and the work of Jesus. Frederick Crowe's insight regarding the roles of the Spirit and Jesus in the mission of the Trinity is helpful.

---

15. Patricia Fox, "The Trinity as Transforming Symbol: Exploring the Trinitarian Theology of Two Roman Catholic Feminist Theologians," *Pacifica* 7 (1994): 273-94.

16. LaCugna, *God for Us*, 101.

17. Ibid., 289.

18. *Dominum et Vivificantem* ("The Lord and Giver of Life: On Holy Spirit in the Life of the Church and the World"), encyclical letter of Pope John Paul II (May 1986).

Commonly we think of God first sending the Son, and of the Spirit being sent in that context, to bring to completion the work of the Son. On the contrary, God first sent the Spirit, and then sent the Son in the context of the Spirit's mission, to bring to completion—perhaps not precisely the work of the Spirit, but the work of God conceived as one work to be executed in two steps of the twofold mission of first the Spirit and then the Son.[19]

To emphasize God's first sending the Spirit does not mean subverting the trinitarian foundations of Christianity. If we think of the mission of the Spirit as invisible, while the mission of the Son is revealed to humankind at a privileged moment in human history, in the fullness of time, in the visible mission of Jesus of Nazareth, the relationship of the Spirit to the Son is easier to grasp. What is visible is recognized first "in the cognitional order of discovery."[20] At the beginning of time, God gifted creation with the Spirit, and in the fullness of time, God gifted creation with the gift of the Son, sent "not in opposition, but in unity, not in subordination, but in complementarity."[21] In this perspective, both Spirit and Son continue the work of God, as do those in whom the Spirit of God dwells. The mystery of the Spirit's universal presence in the world and the gift of the Spirit from the risen Jesus to his disciples oblige us to hold two seemingly contradictory positions: on the one hand, "Christ sent the holy Spirit from the Father" (*Ad Gentes* no. 4), and, on the other, "the holy Spirit was at work in the world before Christ was glorified" (*Ad Gentes* no. 4). There is one divine economy, in which the functions of the Spirit and Son are complementary. The incarnation is at the center of salvation history, but it is actualized in history through the action of the Holy Spirit (cf. Luke 1:35; Matt 1:18).

John Paul II continues:

The Spirit offers the human race "the light and strength to respond to its highest calling" (*Gaudium et Spes* no. 10); through the Spirit "man comes by faith, attains in faith to the contemplation and appreciation of the divine plan" (*Gaudium et Spes* no. 15) . . . The Spirit's presence and activity affect not only individuals but also society and history, peoples, cultures, and religions. Indeed the Spirit is at the origin of the noble ideals and undertakings which benefit humanity on its journey through history . . . Thus the Spirit who "blows where he wills (cf. Jn

---

19. Frederick E. Crowe, "Son of God, Holy Spirit and World Religions: The Contribution of Bernard Lonergan to the Wider Ecumenism," Chancellor's Address II (Toronto: Regis College, 1985), 8.

20. Ibid., 11.

21. Ibid.

3:8), who was "already at work in the world before Christ was glorified" (*Ad Gentes* no. 4), and who "has filled the world, . . . holds all things together [and] knows what is said" (Wis 1:7), leads us to broaden our vision in order to ponder his activity in every time and place. (*Redemptoris Missio* no. 28)

Papal teaching on the universality of the Spirit's presence has implications for missiology and for ecclesiology. Missiologically, it suggests that other religions can mediate God's salvation, and this has consequences for our understanding of both entry into, and outcomes of, interreligious dialogue. It invests all of human and cosmic history with religious significance, thereby subverting the sacred/secular dichotomy. Ecclesiologically, within the church, the dominant christological emphasis has argued that authority be understood "as permeating from the top downward."[22] However, a pneumatology of the Spirit's universal presence asserts that the Spirit "has been sent to everyone in the church, enabling all to rediscover Christ,"[23] an assertion that means traditional understandings of authority need reassessing. According to liberation theologian José Comblin, the hierarchy has responsibility for maintaining "visible unity, but they have no more initiative than any other Christians,"[24] who together can discern what mission requires of them.

## EXPERIENCE AND UNDERSTANDING
## THE MISSION OF THE SPIRIT

American Catholic feminist theologian Elizabeth Johnson, in developing a trinitarian theology, takes as her starting point our experiences of the Spirit, whose presence we intuit in creation, in our relationships, personal and interpersonal, which can mediate either the absence or presence of the Spirit, and in society's institutions, which function as liberating or oppressive. Johnson understands the Spirit as a Spirit of mutuality and connectedness, and, by extension, these values should be characteristic of the relationships that the missionary builds with those among whom she ministers.

Johnson is aware that an exclusive and excluding use of Father-Son language in trinitarian theologies may serve to maintain patriarchal culture in church and society. In articulating a feminist christology, Johnson seeks to resolve the damage that such language causes by speaking of Jesus as Sophia-incarnate. She does this through reference to the figure of Sophia in the Old

---

22. José Comblin, *The Holy Spirit and Liberation*, ed. Leonardo Boff et al.; trans. Paul Burns (Maryknoll, N.Y.: Orbis Books, 1989), 118.
23. Ibid.
24. Ibid., 119.

Testament wisdom literature, where Sophia is described as giver of life (Prov 4:13; 8:35; Sir 24:5) and as a savior who rescues Israel from Egypt (Wis 10:18). Johnson argues that "Sophia is in reality God herself in her activity in the world, God imaged as female acting subject."[25] But this insight has been obscured in the New Testament texts, because the *Logos* (word) became flesh as the man Jesus of Nazareth, and this meant a movement away from the rich female imagery associated with Sophia. "Jesus is *Sophia* incarnate; Jesus is *Logos* incarnate. Inclusive christological reflection that makes room for female imagery has the potential to contribute in theory and practice to the appreciation of the dignity of women."[26] Failure to do this and to insist on understanding Father-Son language in trinitarian discourse as literal rather than as metaphorical mean that women are defined as "mentally, morally and physically inferior to men, created only partially in the image of God, even a degrading symbol of evil."[27]

In *Women, Earth and Creator Spirit,*[28] Johnson directs attention to the presence of the Spirit in creation, a presence that is an invitation to "extend moral consideration to species beyond our own, and moral standing to ecological systems as a whole."[29] It alerts us to the creative agency of the Spirit (see Gen 1:1; Wis 7:22; 8:1). In order to extend "moral consideration" to ecological systems, Johnson relies on a liberationist analysis to critique patterns of domination and exploitation, and uncovers the causal nature of the depletion of nature's resources by humankind. This depletion constitutes a critical environmental problem, particularly for those who are already economically diminished, and an ethical problem for those responsible for such depletion. Her analysis of patriarchal culture means that nature, like women, becomes the "other," to be exploited, tamed, and controlled by man. As Johnson observes, "Women, whose bodies mediate physical existence to humanity thus become symbolically the oldest archetype of the connection between social domination and the dominion of nature,"[30] for both nature and women are vulnerable to patterns of domination.

Women can be significant protagonists on behalf of exploited nature. By itself, however, a critique of patriarchal culture, and the oppression of women and nature that it encourages, may not be sufficient to resolve envi-

---

25. Elizabeth A. Johnson, *She Who Is: The Mystery of God in Feminist Theological Discourse* (New York: Crossroad, 1992), 274-75.

26. Elizabeth A. Johnson, "Jesus, the Wisdom of God: A Biblical Basis for Non-Androcentric Christology," *Ephemerides Theologicae Lovanienses* 61 (1985): 289.

27. Johnson, *She Who Is,* 22.

28. Elizabeth A. Johnson, *Women, Earth and Creator Spirit* (New York/Mahwah, N.J.: Paulist Press, 1993).

29. Ibid., 66-67.

30. Ibid., 13.

ronmental degradation. Such an ethical response needs to be grounded in a new theology. A theology that focuses attention on the immanence of the Spirit in creation offers humankind the possibility of moving beyond an anthropocentric view of the world to an ecocentric one that enables us to reframe our relationship to nature, conscious of our common origins and our common goal of reconciliation in the *eschaton* (see Eph 1:13-14). This response is predicated on not accepting different ontological levels in the order of creation. Destruction of any particular species by humankind has profound influences on the rest of creation because of the connectedness of all. This is a radical option which involves significant theological and cultural shifts.

Letty Russell believes that women missionaries need "a feminist missiology that is life-giving for all as we participate in God's action of mending creation."[31] Russell's experiences of ministry have convinced her that the conversion required by mission today is to move beyond maternalistic relationships to relationships of mutuality. In her important work on ecclesiology, *Church in the Round*,[32] she uses the image of hospitality, of a *shalom* meal around the table, to carry her theology of mutuality—an image which she has continued to develop. "Hospitality is about the joy of sharing love for others and the unexpected gifts that come in that encounter with those who are different from us. It is also about the hospitality of a God who continually lives in relationship, sharing love between all three members of the Trinity: Source of Life, Word of Truth, Spirit of Love, reaching out to us in love and inviting us to share that welcome with others."[33] Like Johnson, her point of entry into trinitarian theology is the human experience of "the presence of God through the work of the Holy Spirit in our lives and in the world around us."[34] The presence of God's Spirit invites the church to enter into the mission of the Trinity, which she describes as an embrace of the world, "an embrace made flesh in Jesus but accomplished already in the past, present, and continuing presence of the Holy Spirit."[35]

## THE SHAPE OF A FEMINIST MISSIOLOGY

Reclaiming a trinitarian theology of mission that accents the prior role of the Spirit in God's work of creating and redeeming the world is significant

---

31. Russell, "Cultural Hermeneutics," 34.
32. See Letty M. Russell, *Church in the Round: Feminist Interpretation of the Church* (Louisville, Ky.: Westminster John Knox Press, 1993).
33. Letty M. Russell, *The Practice of God's Hospitality* (1999); available at http://www .worldywca-org.ac.psiweb.com/common_concern/june1999/thecredalbasisoftheworldywca .html; accessed June 2, 2006.
34. Russell, "Cultural Hermeneutics," 31.
35. Ibid.

for women in several ways. While it endorses the ecclesial dimension of mission, it liberates women from understanding mission in ecclesiocentric categories. When the major focus of Catholic missionary activity was establishing the church in those places where it had not yet been established, the centrality of the priest's sacramental role meant that women's work often was designated as a preparatory task. Women's ministry of caring and nurturing, while of immense significance for the peoples among whom they worked, was sometimes thought of as "a softening-up" process that would encourage "pagans" to embrace the Catholic faith. Rather than understanding that the church had a particular role to play in furthering the reign of God, this perspective viewed mission as something done for the sake of the institutional church. Stephen Bevans's reflections concerning the Spirit and the ecclesial reality of mission are helpful.

Bevans[36] argues that the Spirit calls the church to mission, and it is through the Spirit's action that the church comes into being—a story that unfolds in the Acts of the Apostles. It is through the actions of the Spirit that the church embraces her role in the mission of God in a way analogous to that of Jesus who similarly began his mission through the empowering agency of the Spirit. The creation of the church is an ongoing process as it repents of its previous faults in the exercise of mission, responds to new situations, and faces up to new challenges. The Spirit equips the church to be missionary through the charisms bestowed on its different members, lay and ordained. All too often in the Catholic tradition, gifts were thought of as restricted to ministers, particularly to bishops and popes, in their exercise of teaching ministries. Through the Spirit, charisms are given to everyone in the church for the sake of mission. "The Spirit's creative activity of bestowing charisms on baptized men and women, therefore makes of the church—simply by the way it lives—a missionary church."[37] Such a pneumatological understanding of the ecclesial dimension of mission demolishes any suggestion that women's missionary role is subordinate to that of the ordained minister. It allows women to see how hieratic christologies have often diminished women's contribution to the church's mission.

Feminist theologies of the Trinity have shown how damaging an exclusive use of masculine God-language has been for women historically and contemporaneously. Its dominance in speaking of the mystery of the Trinity reflects the dominance of patriarchal culture in the church. As Elizabeth Johnson points out, how to speak about God is "a crucial theological question. What is at stake is the truth about God, inseparable from the situation

---

36. See Stephen Bevans, "The Church as Creation of the Spirit: Unpacking a Missionary Image," *Missiology* 35, no. 1 (January 2004): 5-21.
37. Ibid., 7.

of human beings, and the identity and mission of the faith community itself."[38] If God is "imagined and imaged as a male monarch who is absolutely self-sufficient and all powerful [this] will be reflected almost certainly in a male-dominated, rigid faith community that understands mission as a way to extend itself and so extend God's glory."[39] Patriarchal culture believed that women most fittingly fulfilled their God-given (and biologically determined) role in the domestic sphere, and so their missionary tasks were simply extensions of their biological roles of nurturing and caring. When we use a nongendered language or a feminine language of the triune God, as Johnson does in *She Who Is,* it can transform how women and men think of their place in the Christian community. Johnson believes that "no language about God will ever be fully adequate to the burning mystery which it signifies. But a more inclusive way of speaking can come about that bears the ancient wisdom with a new justice."[40]

Women missionaries have recognized that relationships among themselves, and with those among whom they work, need to be grounded in mutuality and inclusivity. This recognition represents a departure from the view of relationships of an earlier age when missionary activity often enough was seen as the cultural arm of European expansion into the rest of the world. Then the relationships that often developed were maternal and colored by notions of cultural superiority. A trinitarian theology that accents the universal presence of the Spirit actively present in other cultures and religious traditions makes maternalistic and culturally superior attitudes toward others less credible. It also subverts the idea of mission understood as "saving souls," an expression that suggests a serious moral or religious deficiency in the other.

Where the universal presence of the Spirit in other cultures and religious traditions is honored, then interreligious dialogue is precisely that. It is not a backdoor to proselytization. The modern age long understood mission as proclamation and by extension as conversion, but when dialogue complements or overtakes monologue as an important way of being missionary, then mission as conversion loses much of its importance. This does not rule out people embracing the Christian faith, but church growth becomes organic rather than organized. In this way the presence of the Spirit outside of the church is respected, and the reign of God flourishes.

Vatican II's reclaiming of the trinitarian nature of all mission has been and is important for Catholic missionaries and those among whom they live and work. It has a particular significance for women missionaries. First, it allows

---

38. Johnson, *She Who Is*, 6.
39. See Stephen Bevans, "Reimagining God and Mission," in *Reimagining God and Mission: Perspectives from Australia,* ed. Ross Langmead (Adelaide: ATF Press, 2007), 3-23.
40. Johnson, *She Who Is*, 273.

them to redefine their role in mission in a way that acknowledges their dignity as made in the image and likeness of God. Second, when they draw on the insights regarding the relations of the Spirit and the *Logos* in scripture, in the fathers, and in church teaching, they are able to expand the parameters of mission. When missionary practice is grounded in such theologies, it cannot be anything other than life-giving for all.

# Conclusion

The two-thousand-year story of women's efforts to fully participate in mission is not only a struggle to survive in harsh natural environments, as would surely have happened when people like Leoba and Walburga made their way from well-established monasteries in England to the forests of Germany, or seventeenth-century French women undertook to minister to Amerindians in North America, or nineteenth-century women journeyed to Asia, Africa, and Latin America, or twentieth-century women labored even to death in oppressive political environments such as El Salvador, Brazil, or Liberia. These sorts of struggle are to be expected, and it is hard to imagine any woman missionary who would have considered them to be anything other than part and parcel of missionary life.

It was also a struggle to survive in a church whose leaders often had fixed ideas about women's role in mission. When women sought to reshape their ecclesial role in a church in which decision making was the prerogative of men, normally the ordained minister, their efforts were rebuffed. Clerical culture required that women's missionary roles be identified by, controlled by, and when it suited them, ended by men. It did not take too long for Paul's understanding of women as "co-workers," as "apostles," "deacons," or "leaders" of household churches to be replaced by understanding women as "obedient" and "submissive" wives, or as "widows" committed to inculcating in younger wives an awareness of their need to be obedient and submissive. Women struggled sometimes successfully against such patriarchal perceptions but, more commonly, women's efforts to live out the implications of their baptismal call to mission were thwarted. Pope Boniface VIII's decree *Periculoso*, making the cloister mandatory for nuns, gave institutional expression to the need to keep aspiring women missionaries fenced in literally and figuratively.

Women persisted, however, in their efforts to be missionary, as the example of the late Middle Ages demonstrates; and while there is evidence of this in the lives of nuns such as Hildegaard, even more noteworthy was the development of groups of middle-class laywomen, often of independent financial means, who sought to live out the gospel life through prayer and mission to the poor. Eventually their efforts were frustrated by clerical opposition, or else women were forced to embrace a cloistered lifestyle in order to exercise their mission, as happened in the case of the followers of Angela Merici when the modern era dawned. In fact, the cloister became the instrument par excellence for keeping women in their place, as the stories of Mary Ward and Jeanne de Chantal exemplify. Though neither of these founders wanted a cloistered and monastic lifestyle, the Tridentine church could envisage no other alternative for women. It took canon lawyer Vincent de Paul and Louise de Marillac to work out a new structure so that women could exercise their missionary vocation without the restriction of a cloister.

Despite such persistent setbacks, women never lost their enthusiasm for mission, and after the French Revolution, there was an extraordinary outburst of missionary enthusiasm among women. However, for women to be missionary, they had first to be religious, bound by Canon Law, and either as pontifical or episcopal groups, bound by the directives of the pope or bishops. Despite their numerical strength women's missionary works were judged as ancillary or auxiliary, and therefore subordinate to the work of the missionary priest. With few exceptions this situation prevailed until the mid-twentieth century when significant shifts began to appear. First, women religious began to challenge their auxiliary status and, second, laywomen recognized that women could be missionary without becoming a professed religious in a religious order.

Vatican II proved a watershed for Catholic mission, particularly for women religious and laypeople as it laid to rest the idea that their work was of secondary importance in the grand scheme of things—a necessary first step in the all-important work of conversion and establishment of the institutional church in those places where it had not yet been planted. Laywomen found it easier to engage in mission without first having to be a member of a religious order. The growth of religious life in the Two-Thirds World ensured that the previous efforts of One-Third World women religious would be continued, albeit in different ways and with different emphases.

As the twenty-first century unfolds, mission is undoubtedly going to be very different from what it has been precisely because future missionaries are going to come from Asia, Africa, Latin America, and Oceania rather than from Europe, North America, and those Oceanic countries where the dominant culture is Western. Mission in the twenty-first century has to face the extra-ecclesial missionary challenges of responding to environmental degradation, including diminishing energy resources, ethnic conflict, the ongoing oppression of women and girls, and the negative impact of globalization on so many peoples. Women, lay and religious, have already begun courageous responses to these new needs, particularly to those areas that they have identified as resulting from patriarchal culture's domination of women and the environment.

Intra-ecclesial missionary imperatives are significant and basically flow from different perceptions as to how power should be exercised within the church. Many women missionaries no longer believe that the Roman model, with its emphasis on centralized clerical decision making, is appropriate for tomorrow's world. In fact, power and control and how they are exercised seem to be foundational to many issues that face the Catholic Church today. This is certainly the case when it comes to identifying the roles of women and laypeople in the church, and to ensuring that the local church is an inculturated church. In such instances, those at the center, that is, the pope in the universal church, Vatican curial offices, bishops in their dioceses, and parish priests in their parishes, tend to think they know what is best for those who live and work on the margins.

This explains why the trinitarian theologies articulated by theologians such as Elizabeth Johnson, Catherine LaCugna, Stephen Bevans, and some of the teachings of John Paul II are of significance for women missionaries. These theologies, with their developed pneumatologies, allow the missionary to recognize and affirm the universal presence of the Spirit in other cultures and traditions. Prior to Vatican II, however, the emphasis was more on the particular presence of the Spirit in pope and bishops and the guidance of the Spirit as they pursued their teaching and missionary tasks. This emphasis on the particularity rather than the universality of the Spirit's presence had as its corollary the development of hierarchical structures in the church. It was assumed that the higher up the hierarchy one was positioned, the more of the Spirit one had, and therefore the greater one's capacity to know what was best for those further down. Slowly but surely this perception is changing within Catholic tradition, and women missionaries, increasingly aware of the Spirit-Sophia present in them and empowering them for mission, and present also in those among whom they minister, are expanding the parameters of Catholic missionary endeavors in the world today.

# Selected Bibliography

*Acta Apostolicae Sedis*, Vol. 62, no. 9 (1970). Vatican City: Commentarium Officiale Sanctae Sedis. 1.

Ahlgren, Gillian T. W. *Teresa of Avila and the Politics of Sanctity*. Ithaca and London: Cornell University Press, 1966.

Allen, Prudence. "Six Canadian Women: Their Call, Their Witness, Their Legacy." *Canadian Catholic Review* 5, no. 7 (1987): 246-58.

Allison, Robert W. "Let Women Be Silent in the Churches (1 Cor 14:33b-36): What Did Paul Really Say and What Did It Mean?" *Journal for the Study of the New Testament* 32 (1988): 27-60.

Anderson, Bonnie S., and Judith P. Zinsser. *A History of Their Own: Women in Europe from Prehistory to the Present*. 2 vols. New York: Harper & Row, 1989.

Anderson, Janice Capel. "Matthew: Gender and Reading." *Semeia* 28 (1983): 3-27.

Balch, David L. "Household Ethical Codes in Peripatetic Neopythagorean and Early Christian Moralists." In *SBL Seminar Papers* 11. Atlanta: Scholars Press, 1977.

Barbier, Euphrasie. *Constitutions of the Daughters of Our Lady of the Missions*. Letchworth, 1936.

Barclay, Susan. "Are Mission Agencies Institutionally Sexist?" *Global Connections Occasional Papers* 22 (Spring 2006): 1-4.

Barmann, Lawrence F. "Mary Ward: Centuries Her Scroll." *Review for Religious* 59 (2000): 608-13.

Bassler, Jouette M. "The Widow's Tale." *Journal of Biblical Literature* 103 (1984): 23-41.

Bauckham, Richard A. *Gospel Women: Studies of the Named Women in the Gospels*. Grand Rapids: Eerdmans, 2002.

Baumert, Norbert. *Woman and Man in Paul: Overcoming a Misunderstanding*. Translated by Patrick Madigan and Linda M. Maloney. Collegeville, Minn.: Liturgical Press, 1996.

Beard, Anne. "The Visionary Life of Elisabeth of Schönau: A Different Way of Knowing." In *Medieval Women Monastics: Wisdom's Wellsprings*, ed. Miriam Schmitt and Linda Kulzer, 167-82. Collegeville, Minn.: Liturgical Press, 1996.

Beirne, Margaret M. *Women and Men in the Fourth Gospel: A Genuine Discipleship of Equals*. Journal for Study of New Testament Supplement 242. Sheffield: Sheffield Academic Press, 2003.

Bendyna, Mary. *Partners in Mission: A Profile of Associates and Religious in the United States: North American Conference of Associates and Religious*. Washington, D.C.: Center for Applied Research in the Apostolate, 2000.

Bevans, Stephen. "Reimagining God and Mission." In *Reimagining God and Mission: Perspectives from Australia*, ed. Ross Langmead, 3-23. Adelaide: ATF Press, 2007.

————. "The Church as Creation of the Spirit: Unpacking a Missionary Image." *Missiology* 35, no. 1 (January 2004): 5-21.

Bevans, Stephen B., and Roger P. Schroeder. *Constants in Context: A Theology of Mission for Today.* Maryknoll, N.Y.: Orbis Books, 2004.

————. "We Were Gentle among You: Christian Mission as Dialogue." *Australian EJournal,* no. 7 (2006). Available at http://dlibrary.acu.edu.au/research/theology/ejournal/.

Bockmuehl, Marcus. *The Epistle to the Philippians.* Black's New Testament Commentary. London: A & C Black, 1998.

Bokenkotter, Thomas. *Church and Revolution: Catholics in the Struggle for Democracy and Social Justice.* New York: Image Books, 1998.

Bolster, M. Angela. *Catherine McAuley in Her Own Words.* Dublin: Dublin Diocesan Office for Causes, 1978.

Bong, Rin Ro. "Asia." In *Evangelical Dictionary of World Missions,* ed. Scott A. Moreau, David Burnett and Harold Netland, 80-84. Grand Rapids: Baker Books, 2000.

Bosch, David J. *Transforming Mission: Paradigm Shifts in Theology of Mission.* Maryknoll, N.Y.: Orbis Books, 1991.

Bovon, François. *Luke 1: A Commentary on the Gospel of Luke 1:1–9:50.* Translated by Christine M. Thomas. Hermeneia. Minneapolis: Fortress, 2002.

Boyarin, Daniel. *A Radical Jew: Paul and the Politics of Identity.* Berkeley: University of California Press, 1994.

Briggs, Sheila. "Galatians." In *Searching the Scriptures.* Volume 2, *A Feminist Commentary,* ed. Elisabeth Schüssler Fiorenza, 218-35. New York: Crossroad, 1994.

Brooten, Bernadette J. "Feminist Perspectives on New Testament Exegesis." *Concilium* (1980): 55-61.

————. *Women Leaders in the Ancient Synagogue: Inscriptional Evidence and Background Issues.* Brown Judaic Studies 36. Chico, Calif.: Scholars Press, 1982.

————. "Early Christian Women and Their Cultural Context: Issues of Method in Historical Reconstruction." In *Feminist Perspectives on Biblical Scholarship,* ed. Adela Yarbro Collins, 65-91. Chico, Calif.: Scholars Press, 1985.

Brosnan, Kathleen A. "Public Presence, Public Silence: Nuns, Bishops, and the Gendered Space of Early Chicago." *Catholic Historical Review* 90 (2004): 473-96.

Brown, Alden V. *The Grail Movement and American Catholicism, 1940–1975.* Notre Dame Studies in American Catholicism. Notre Dame, Ind.: University of Notre Dame Press, 1989.

Brown, Peter. *The Rise of Western Christendom: Triumph and Diversity A.D. 200–1000.* 2nd ed. Oxford: Blackwell, 2003.

Brown, Raymond E. *The Gospel according to John: Introduction, Translation, and Notes.* 2 volumes. Anchor Bible 29, 29A. Garden City, N.Y.: Doubleday, 1966, 1970.

————. "The Resurrection in Matthew 27:62–28:20." *Worship* 20 (March 1990): 157-68.

————. *An Introduction to the New Testament.* New York/London: Doubleday, 1997.

Burrows, William R., ed. *Redemption and Dialogue: Reading 'Redemptoris Missio' and 'Dialogue and Proclamation.'* Maryknoll, N.Y.: Orbis Books, 1993.

Bynum, Caroline Walker. *Holy Feast and Holy Fast: The Religious Significance of Food to Medieval Women.* The New Historicism: Studies in Cultural Poetics 1. Berkeley and Los Angeles: University of California Press, 1987.

Byrne, Brendan. *Romans.* Sacra Pagina 6. Collegeville, Minn.: Liturgical Press, 1996.

Byrne, Lavinia. "Spiritual Stars of the Millennium: 25, Mary Ward (1585–1645)." *The Tablet* (June 24, 2000): 878.

Cardman, Francine. "Women, Ministry and Church Order in Early Christianity." In *Women and Christian Origins,* ed. Ross Shepard Kraemer and Mary Rose D'Angelo, 300-329. New York/Oxford: Oxford University Press, 1999.

Carey, Patrick W. *Catholics in America: A History.* Westport, Conn.: Praeger, 2004.

Carter, Nancy A. "The Acts of Thecla: A Pauline Tradition Linked to Women. Conflict and Community in the Corinthian Church." Available from http://gbgm-umc.org/umw/corinthians/theclabackground.stm. Accessed June 17, 2006.

Carter, Warren. "'To See the Tomb': Matthew's Women at the Tomb." *Expository Times* 107 (1996): 201-4.

Castelli, Elizabeth A. "Romans." In *Searching the Scriptures.* Volume 2, *A Feminist Commentary,* ed. Elisabeth Schüssler Fiorenza, 272-300. New York: Crossroad, 1994.

———. "Paul on Women and Gender." In *Women and Christian Origins,* ed. Ross Shepard Kraemer and Mary Rose D'Angelo, 221-35. New York/Oxford: Oxford University Press, 1999.

Chadwick, Owen. *The Early Reformation on the Continent.* 1st paperback ed. Oxford History of the Christian Church. Oxford: Oxford University Press, 2003.

Chu, Cindy Yik-Yi. "From the Pursuit of Converts to the Relief of Refugees: The Maryknoll Sisters in Twentieth Century Hong Kong." *The Historian* 65, no. 2 (2002): 353-76.

Colgrave, B., and R. A. B. Mynors, eds. *Bede: Ecclesiastical History of the English People.* Oxford Medieval Series. Oxford: Oxford University Press, 1969.

Collins, Raymond F. *First Corinthians.* Sacra Pagina 7. Collegeville, Minn.: Liturgical Press, 1999.

Comblin, José. *The Holy Spirit and Liberation.* Translated by Paul Burns. Theology and Liberation Series. Maryknoll, N.Y.: Orbis Books, 1989.

Connolly, R. Hugh, ed. *Didascalia Apostolorum.* Oxford: Clarendon Press, 1929.

Corley, Kathleen E. "Salome and Jesus at Table in the *Gospel of Thomas.*" *Semeia* 86 (1999): 85-97.

———. "1 Peter." In *Searching the Scriptures.* Volume 2, *A Feminist Commentary,* ed. Elisabeth Schüssler Fiorenza, 349-60. New York: Crossroad, 1994.

Cotter, Wendy. "Women's Authority Roles in Paul's Churches: Countercultural or Conventional?" *Novum Testamentum* 36 (1994): 350-72.

Couturier, Charles. *Unswerving Journey: The Life of Mother Mary of the Heart of Jesus, Foundress of the Congregation of Our Lady of the Missions.* Translated by Rosemary Sheed. Toulouse: Prière et Vie, 1966.

Crosby, Michael H. *Can Religious Life Be Prophetic?* New York: Crossroad, 2005.

Crusé, C. F., ed. *The Ecclesiastical History of Eusebius Pamphilus.* London: G. Bell & Sons, 1897.

Daly, Mary. *Beyond God the Father: Towards a Philosophy of Women's Liberation.* Boston: Beacon Press, 1973.

D'Angelo, Mary Rose. "Colossians." In *Searching the Scriptures.* Volume 2, *A*

*Feminist Commentary*, ed. Elisabeth Schüssler Fiorenza, 312-24. New York: Crossroad, 1994.

———. "Women Partners in the New Testament (Rom 16:12; Phil 4:2; Luke 10:38-42; John 11:2, 12)." *Journal of Feminist Studies in Religion* 6 (1990): 66-86.

Darragh, Neil. "Contextual Method in Theology: Learnings from the Case of Aotearoa New Zealand." *Pacifica* 16 (2003): 45-66.

Davies, Stevan. *The Gospel of Thomas Annotated and Explained.* Skylight Illuminations. Woodstock, Vt.: Skylights Paths, 2002.

Delaney, Joan. *A Comparative Study of Christian Mission.* Washington, D.C.: U.S. Catholic Mission Association, 1998.

Dengel, Anna. *Mission for Samaritans: A Survey of Achievements and Opportunities in the Field of Catholic Medical Missions.* Milwaukee: Bruce, 1945.

Derks, Marjet. "Lion and Lamb: Jacques van Ginneken and the 'Women of Nazareth' in the 1920s and 1930s." Paper presented at European Social Science History Conference, Amsterdam, 1998.

Dickson-Waiko, Anne. "The Missing Rib: Mobilizing Church Women for Change in Papua New Guinea." *Oceania* 74 (2003): 98-119.

Dix, Gregory, and Henry Chadwick, eds. *The Treatise on the Apostolic Tradition of St. Hippolytus of Rome.* London: Alban, 1992.

Dodd, C. H. *Historical Tradition in the Fourth Gospel.* Cambridge: Cambridge University Press, 1963.

———. *The Interpretation of the Fourth Gospel.* Cambridge: Cambridge University Press, 1968.

Donders, Rachel. *The Grail Movement and American Catholicism 1940-1975.* Cincinnati: Selby Services, 1983.

Donohue, John W. *Sisters in Mercy.* 2001. Available from http://www.americamag azine.org/gettest.cfm?articleTypeID=1&textID=1522 &issueI. Accessed July 21, 2005.

Dries, Angelyn. "U.S. Sources for the Catholic Overseas Mission Movement." *U.S. Catholic Historian* 11 (1993): 37-48.

———. *The Missionary Movement in American Catholic History.* Maryknoll, N.Y.: Orbis Books, 1998.

———. "American Catholic 'Woman's Work for Woman' in the Twentieth Century." In *Gospel Bearers, Gender Barriers*, ed. Dana L. Robert, 127-42. Maryknoll, N.Y.: Orbis Books, 2002.

———. "U.S. Catholic Women and Mission: Integral or Auxiliary?" *Missiology: An International Review* 33 (2005): 301-11.

Drury, Clare. "The Pastoral Epistles." In *The Oxford Bible Commentary*, ed. John Barton and John Muddiman, 1220-33. Oxford: Oxford University Press, 2001.

Dube, Musa W. "Toward a Post-Colonial Feminist Interpretation of the Bible." *Semeia* 78 (1997): 11-26.

Dupuis, Jacques. *Toward a Christian Theology of Religious Pluralism.* Maryknoll, N.Y.: Orbis Books, 1997.

Edwards, Denis. "Celebrating Eucharist in a Time of Global Climate Change." *Pacifica* 19 (February 2006): 1-15.

Fander, Monika. "Historical-Critical Methods." In *Searching the Scriptures*. Volume 1, *A Feminist Introduction*, ed. Elisabeth Schüssler Fiorenza, 205-24. New York: Crossroad, 1993.

Fatum, Lone. "1 Thessalonians." In *Searching the Scriptures*. Volume 2, *A Feminist*

*Commentary*, ed. Elisabeth Schüssler Fiorenza, 250-62. New York: Crossroad, 1994.

Filoramo, Giovanni. *A History of Gnosticism.* Translated by Anthony Alcock. Oxford: Basil Blackwell, 1990.

Fischer, Herman. *Life of Arnold Janssen: Founder of the Society of the Word and of the Missionary Congregation of the Servants of the Holy Ghost.* Techny, Ill.: Mission Press, 1925.

Flannery, Austin, ed. *Vatican Council II Constitutions, Decrees, Declarations.* New York/Dublin: Costello/Dominican Publications, 1996.

Flemming, Leslie A., ed. *Women's Work for Mission: Missionaries and Social Change in Asia.* Boulder, Colo./San Francisco: Westview Press, 1989.

Foale, Marie Therese. *The Josephite Story.* Sydney: St. Joseph's Generalate, 1989.

Forcucci, James F., ed. *Relics of Repentance: The Letters of Pontius Pilate and Claudia Procula.* Lincoln, Neb.: Issana Press, 1990.

France, R. T. *The Gospel of Mark.* New International Greek Testament Commentary, ed. I. Howard Marshall and Donald A. Hagner. Grand Rapids: Eerdmans, 2002.

French, Marilyn. *The Women's Room.* New York: Ballantine Books, 1977.

Frend, W. H. C. *The Rise of Christianity.* Philadelphia: Fortress Press, 1984.

Froehle, Bryan T., and Mary L. Gautier. *Global Catholicism: Portrait of a World Church.* Maryknoll, N.Y.: Orbis Books, 2003.

Fox, Patricia. "The Trinity as Transforming Symbol: Exploring the Trinitarian Theology of Two Roman Catholic Feminist Theologians." *Pacifica* 7 (1994): 273-94.

Furey, Constance. "'Intellects Inflamed in Christ': Women and Spiritualized Scholarship in Renaissance Christianity." *Journal of Religion* 84 (2004): 1-22.

Gateley, Edwina. *I Hear a Seed Growing: God of the Forest, God of the Streets.* Trabuco Canyon, Calif.: Source Books, 1990.

Gateley, Edwina, and Louis S. Glanzman (Illustrator). *Soul Sisters: Women in Scripture Speak to Women Today.* Maryknoll, N.Y.: Orbis Books, 2002.

*Genesis Farm: A Learning Center for Earth Studies.* Available from http://www.gen esisfarm.org/history.htm. Accessed March 27, 2006.

Getty-Sullivan, Mary Ann. *Women in the New Testament.* Collegeville, Minn.: Liturgical Press, 2001.

Gibson, Ralph. *A Social History of French Catholicism 1789-1914.* Christianity and Society in the Modern World, ed. Hugh McLeod and Bob Scribner. London: Routledge, 1989.

Gillman, F. M. *Women Who Knew Paul.* Collegeville, Minn.: Liturgical Press, 1992.

Gilroy, Ann. "Mary MacKillop and the Challenge to Her Daughters." *Australasian Catholic Record* 82 (1995): 61-72.

Godin, Henri, and Yvan Daniel. *France, Pays de Mission?* Paris: Editions du Cerf, 1943.

Gonzalez, Ramon. "Sisters Find Lay Associates: As Traditional Vocations Dwindle, Orders Find New Life Working with Laity." February 7, 2000. Available from http://www.wcr.ab.ca/news/2000/0207/layassociates020700.shtml. Accessed April 3, 2006.

"Gospel Service: Acknowledgements to New People." *Mission Outlook* (October 2005).

Graham, Susan Lochrie. "Silent Voices: Women in the Gospel of Mark." *Semeia* 54 (1991): 147-58.

Green, Joel B. *The Gospel of Luke.* New International Commentary on the New Testament. Grand Rapids: Eerdmans, 1997.

Greer, Germaine. *The Female Eunuch.* London: McGibbon & Kee, 1970.

Gueudré, M. de Chantal. *Histoire de l'ordre des Ursulines en France.* 3 volumes. Paris: Editions Saint Paul, 1957.

Gutiérrez, Gustavo. *A Theology of Liberation: History, Politics, and Salvation.* Translated by Caridad Inda and John Eagleson. Maryknoll, N.Y.: Orbis Books, 1988.

Hagspiel, Bruno M. *Along the Mission Trail: In the Netherlands East Indies,* volume 3. 5 volumes. Techny, Ill.: Mission Press, 1925.

Hanson, K. C., and Douglas E. Oakman. *Palestine in the Time of Jesus: Social Structures and Social Conflicts.* Minneapolis: Fortress Press, 1998.

Hare, Douglas. *Matthew.* Interpretation: A Bible Commentary for Teaching and Preaching. Louisville, Ky.: Westminster John Knox Press, 1993.

Harline, Craig. "Actives and Contemplatives: The Female Religious of the Low Countries before and after Trent." *Catholic Historical Review* 81 (1995): 541-67.

Harmer, Catherine M. *Religious Life in the 21st Century: A Contemporary Journey into Canaan.* Mystic, Conn.: Twenty-Third Publications, 1995.

Harrington, Daniel J. *The Gospel of Matthew.* Collegeville, Minn.: Liturgical Press, 1991.

Harris, Stephen L. *Understanding the Bible.* 6th ed. Boston: McGraw-Hill, 2003.

Hastings, Adrian. "The Clash of Nationalism and Universalism within Twentieth-Century Missionary Christianity." In *Missions, Nationalism and the End of the Empire,* ed. Brian Stanley, 15-33. Grand Rapids: Eerdmans, 2003.

Heil, John Paul. *The Death and Resurrection of Jesus: A Narrative-Critical Reading of Matthew 26-28.* Minneapolis: Fortress Press, 1991.

Hilkert, Mary Catherine. "Women Preaching the Gospel." *Theology Digest* 33 (1986): 423-40.

Hillberg, I., ed. *Epistulae.* Vienna, 1912.

Hitchens, Christopher. *The Missionary Position: Mother Teresa in Theory and Practice.* London: Verso, 1995.

Horgan, Maurya P. "The Letter to the Colossians." In *The New Jerome Biblical Commentary,* ed. R. E. Brown et al., 876-82. Englewood Cliffs, N.J.: Prentice-Hall, 1990.

Horrell, David. "Leadership Patterns and the Development of Ideology in Early Christianity." *Sociology of Religion* 58 (1997): 323-41.

Huber, Mary Taylor, and Nancy C. Lutkehaus. "Introduction: Gendered Missions at Home and Abroad." In *Gendered Missions: Women and Men in Missionary Discourse and Practice,* ed. Mary Taylor Huber and Nancy C. Lutkehaus, 1-39. Ann Arbor: University of Michigan, 2002.

Huber, Mary Taylor, and Nancy C. Lutkehaus, eds. *Gendered Missions: Women and Men in Missionary Discourse and Practice.* Ann Arbor: University of Michigan Press, 1999.

"If You Knew the Gift of God." Paper presented at 25th General Gathering of the Sisters of Our Lady of the Missions. Pattaya, Thailand, 2002.

Irvin, Dale T., and Scott W. Sunquist. *History of the World Christian Movement: Earliest Christianity to 1453.* Maryknoll, N.Y.: Orbis Books, 2001.

Jenkins, Philip. *The Next Christianity.* October 2002. Available from http://www.the atlantic.com/cgi/cgi-bin/send.cgi?page=http%3A//www.theatlantic.com/iss. Accessed March 3, 2003.

Jensen, Anne. *God's Self-Confident Daughters: Early Christianity and the Liberation of Women.* Translated by O. C. Dean. Louisville: Westminster John Knox Press, 1996.

John Paul II. *Vita Consecrata.* Post Synodal Apostolic Exhortation. Vatican City: Libreria Editrice Vaticana, 1996.

Johnson, Elizabeth A. "Jesus, the Wisdom of God: A Biblical Basis for Non-Androcentric Christology." *Ephemerides Theologicae Lovanienses* 61 (1985): 261-94.

———. *Consider Jesus: Waves of Renewal in Christology.* New York: Crossroad, 1992.

———. *She Who Is: The Mystery of God in Feminist Theological Discourse.* New York: Crossroad, 1992.

———. *Women, Earth and Creator Spirit.* Madeleva Lecture in Spirituality. New York/Mahwah, N.J.: Paulist Press, 1993.

———. *Friends of God and Prophets: A Feminist Theological Reading of the Communion of Saints.* New York: Continuum, 1999.

———. *Truly Our Sister: A Theology of Mary in the Communion of Saints.* New York: Continuum, 2003.

Johnson, Luke Timothy. *Letters to Paul's Delegates: 1 Timothy, 2 Timothy, Titus.* Valley Forge, Pa.: Trinity Press International, 1996.

Johnson, Paul. *A History of Christianity.* New York: Touchstone, 1976.

Jones, Arthur. "Benedictines Welcome Women to Make Temporary Commitment." *National Catholic Reporter,* December 3, 1999: 11.

Jones, Kathleen. *Women Saints: Lives of Faith and Courage.* Maryknoll, N.Y.: Orbis Books; Tunbridge Wells: Burns & Oates, 1999.

Julian, Elizabeth. "Creating a Song and Dance—Kiwimaging: The Prophetic Role of Women Religious in the Church in Aotearoa New Zealand Today." Address to the Catholic Bishops and Congregational Leaders of Aotearoa New Zealand, 2006. Available from http://www.welcom.org.nz/ index.php?subaction=show full&id=1141958457&ucat=1&archive=. Accessed March 27, 2006.

Kahl, Brigitte. "Toward a Materialist-Feminist Reading." In *Searching the Scriptures.* Volume 1, *A Feminist Introduction,* ed. Elisabeth Schüssler Fiorenza, 225-40. New York: Crossroad, 1993.

Kalven, Janet. "Living the Liturgy: Keystone of the Grail Vision." *U.S. Catholic Historian* 11, no. 4 (1993): 29-35.

Käsemann, Ernst. *Commentary on Romans.* Translated and edited by G. W. Bromiley. Grand Rapids: Eerdmans, 1980.

Keener, C. S. "Family and Household." In *Dictionary of New Testament Background,* ed. Craig A. Evans and Stanley E. Porter, 353-68. Downers Grove, Ill.: InterVarsity Press, 2000.

Kelly, Joan. "The Social Relation of the Sexes: Methodological Implications of Women's History." In *Women, History and Theory: The Essays of Joan Kelly,* ed. Joan Kelly, 1-14. Chicago: University of Chicago Press, 1984.

Kelly-Gadol, Joan. "Did Women Have a Renaissance?" In *Becoming Visible—Women in European History,* ed. Renate Bridethal, Claudia Koonz, and Susan Stuard, 174-201. Boston: Houghton Mifflin, 1987.

Kennedy, John F. Inaugural Address, 1961. Available from http://www.bartleby.com/ 124/pres56.html. Accessed December 12, 2005.

Kienzle, Beverly Mayne, and Pamela J. Walker, eds. *Women Preachers and Prophets through Two Millennia of Christianity*. Berkeley: University of California Press, 1998.

King, Karen L. "Prophetic Power and Women's Authority. The Case of the *Gospel of Mary* (Magdalene)." In *Women Preachers and Prophets through Two Millennia of Christianity*, ed. Beverly Mayne Kienzle and Pamela J. Walker, 21-41. Berkeley: University of California Press, 1998.

———. *The Gospel of Mary of Magdala: Jesus and the First Woman Apostle*. Santa Rosa, Calif.: Polebridge Press, 2003.

LaCugna, Catherine Mowry, ed. "The Relational God: Aquinas and Beyond." *Theological Studies* 46, no. 4 (1985): 647-63.

———. *God for Us: The Trinity and Christian Life*. San Francisco: HarperCollins, 1991.

———. *Freeing Theology: The Essentials of Theology in Feminist Perspective*. New York: HarperCollins, 1993.

Laracy, Hugh. *Marists and Melanesians*. Canberra: Australian National University, 1976.

Layton, Bentley, ed. *The Gnostic Scriptures: A New Translation with Annotations and Introductions*. New York/London: Doubleday, 1987.

Leddy, Mary Jo. *Reweaving Religious Life*. Mystic, Conn.: Twenty-Third Publications, 1990.

Ledóchowska, T. *Angela Merici and the Company of St. Ursula*. 2 vols. Rome: Ancora, 1968.

Lernoux, Penny, Arthur Jones, and Robert Ellsberg. *Hearts on Fire: The Story of the Maryknoll Sisters*. Maryknoll, N.Y.: Orbis Books, 1993.

Liebowitz, Ruth P. "Virgins in the Service of Christ: The Dispute over an Active Apostolate for Women during the Counter-Reformation." In *Women of Spirit: Female Leadership in the Jewish and Christian Traditions*, ed. Rosemary Ruether and Eleanor McLaughlin, 131-52. New York: Simon & Schuster, 1979.

Lierheimer, Linda. "Preaching or Teaching? Defining the Ursuline Mission in Seventeenth-Century France." In *Women Preachers and Prophets through Two Millennia of Christianity*, ed. B. M. Kienzle and P. J. Walker, 212-26. Berkeley: University of California Press, 1998.

Lieu, Judith. *Neither Jew nor Greek? Constructing Early Christianity*. Edinburgh: T & T Clark, 2003.

Lipsius, R. A., and M. Bonnet, eds. "Acts of Paul and Thekla." In *Acta Apostolorum Apocrypha*, vol. 1. Hildesheim: G. Olms, 1959.

Littlehales, Margaret Mary. *Mary Ward: Pilgrim and Mystic, 1585-1645*. Tunbridge Wells: Burns & Oates, 1998.

Louth, Andrew, ed. *Early Christian Writings: The Apostolic Fathers*. Penguin Classics. London: Penguin Books, 1987.

Lutkehaus, Nancy C. "Missionary Maternalism: Gendered Images of the Holy Spirit Sisters in Colonial New Guinea." In *Gendered Mission: Women and Men in Missionary Discourse and Practice*, ed. Mary Taylor Huber and Nancy C. Lutkehaus, 207-35. Ann Arbor: University of Michigan Press.

MacCulloch, Diarmaid. *Reformation: Europe's House Divided 1490-1700*. London: Allen Lane, 2003.

MacDonald, Margaret Y. "Reading Real Women through the Undisputed Letters of Paul." In *Women and Christian Origins*, ed. Ross Shepard Kraemer and Mary Rose D'Angelo, 199-220. New York/Oxford: Oxford University Press, 1999.

————. *Colossians and Ephesians*. Sacra Pagina 17. Collegeville, Minn.: Liturgical Press, 2000.

MacHaffie, Barbara J. *Her Story: Women in Christian Tradition*. Minneapolis: Fortress Press, 1986.

MacSuibhne, Peadar, ed. *Paul Cullen and His Contemporaries with Their Letters from 1820-1902*. Nass, Ireland: Leinster Leader, 1961-77.

Macy, Gary. "The Ordination of Women in the Early Middle Ages." *Theological Studies* 61 (2000): 481-507.

Magli, Ida. *Women and Self-Sacrifice in the Christian Church: A Cultural History from the First to the Nineteenth Century*. Translated by Janet Sethre. Jefferson, N.C.: McFarland, 2003.

Magray, Mary Peckham. *The Transforming Power of Nuns: Women, Religion and Cultural Change in Ireland, 1750-1900*. New York: Oxford University Press, 1998.

Maher, Mary Joseph. "Empowering Immaculate Heart of Mary Missionaries." In *Gospel Bearers, Gender Barriers: Missionary Women in the Twentieth Century*, ed. Dana L. Robert, 143-56. Maryknoll, N.Y.: Orbis Books, 2002.

Malone, Mary T. *Who Is My Mother? Rediscovering the Mother of Jesus*. Dubuque, Ia.: Wm. C. Brown, 1984.

————. *Women and Christianity*. Volume 1, *The First Thousand Years*; Volume 2, *From 1000 to the Reformation*; Volume 3, *From the Reformation to the 21st Century*. Maryknoll, N.Y.: Orbis Books, 2001, 2001, 2003.

Maloney, Linda M. "The Pastoral Epistles." In *Searching the Scriptures*. Volume 2, *A Feminist Commentary*, ed. Elisabeth Schüssler Fiorenza, 361-80. New York: Crossroad, 1994.

Manna, Paulo. *The Conversion of the Pagan World*. Boston: Society for the Propagation of the Faith, 1921.

Manson, T. W. "St. Paul's Letter to the Romans—and Others." In *The Romans Debate: Revised and Expanded Edition*, ed. K. P. Donfried, 3-15. Peabody, Mass.: Hendrikson, 1991.

Marjanem, Antti. "The Mother of Jesus or the Magdalene? The Identity of Mary in the So-Called Gnostic Christian Texts." In *Which Mary? The Marys of Early Christian Tradition*, ed. F. Stanley Jones, 31-42. Atlanta: Society of Biblical Literature, 2002.

Martin, Clarice J. "The Acts of the Apostles." In *Searching the Scriptures*. Volume 2, *A Feminist Commentary*, ed. Elisabeth Schüssler Fiorenza, 763-99. New York: Crossroad, 1994.

May, Herbert G., and Bruce M. Metzger, eds. *New Oxford Annotated Bible—RSV*. NewYork: Oxford University Press, 1998.

Mayeskie, Marie Anne. *Women Models of Liberation*. New York: Sheed & Ward, 1989.

McBrien, Richard P. *Catholicism*. 2 volumes. East Malvern, Vic.: Dove Communications, 1980.

McClory, Robert J. "35 Years on 'the Prophetic Edge': Lay Missionary Movement Takes on World's Inequities." *National Catholic Reporter*, July 16, 2004, 8.

McGinn, Sheila E. "The Acts of Thecla." In *Searching the Scriptures*. Volume 2, *A Feminist Commentary*, ed. Elisabeth Schüssler Fiorenza, 800-828. New York: Crossroad, 1994.

————. "The Household Codes of the Later Pauline Traditions." *The Catechist* 37 (2004): 50-54.

McNamara, Jo Ann Kay. *Sisters in Arms: Catholic Nuns through Two Millennia.* Cambridge, Mass./London: Harvard University Press, 1996.

Meeks, Wayne. "The Image of the Androgyne: Some Uses of a Symbol in Earliest Christianity." *History of Religions* 13 (1974): 165-208.

Metzger, Bruce M., and Roland E. Murphy, eds. *The New Oxford Annotated Bible with the Apocryphal/Deuterocanonical Books.* New York: Oxford University Press, 1993.

Miller, William. *A Harsh and Dreadful Love.* New York: Liveright, 1973.

Moffett, Samuel Hugh. *A History of Christianity in Asia, 1500-1900.* 2 volumes. Maryknoll, N.Y.: Orbis Books, 2005.

Moloney, Francis J. *The Gospel of John.* Sacra Pagina 4, ed. Daniel J. Harrington. Collegeville, Minn.: Liturgical Press, 1998.

Monter, William. "Protestant Wives, Catholic Saints, and the Devil's Handmaid: Women in the Age of the Reformation." In *Becoming Visible—Women in European History,* ed. Renate Bridethal, Claudia Koonz and Susan Stuard, 202-19. Boston: Houghton Mifflin, 1987.

Morris, Joan. *The Lady Was a Bishop: The Hidden History of Women with Clerical Ordination and the Jurisdiction of Bishops.* New York: Macmillan, 1973.

Morrissey, M. Roberta. "The Constitutions of the Congregation of Our Lady of the Mission." 1970. RNDM Archives, Rome.

Muggeridge, Malcolm. *Something Beautiful for God: Mother Teresa of Calcutta.* London: Collins, 1971.

Mullett, Michael A. *The Catholic Reformation.* London/New York: Routledge, 1999.

Munro, Winsome. "Women, Text and the Canon: The Strange Case of 1 Corinthians 14:33-35." *Biblical Theology Bulletin* 18 (1988): 26-31.

Murk-Jansen, Saskia. *Brides in the Desert: The Spirituality of the Beguines.* Maryknoll, N.Y.: Orbis Books, 1998.

Musurillo, H., ed. *The Acts of the Christian Martyrs.* Oxford Early Christian Texts. Oxford: Oxford University Press, 1972.

Mwaura, Philomena. "Women and Evangelisation: A Challenge to the Church in the Third Millennium." In *Challenges and Prospects for the Church in Africa: Theological Reflections for the Church in Africa,* ed. Nashashon W. Ndungu and Philomena N. Mwaura. Nairobi: Paulines Publications Africa, 2005.

Newbigin, Lesslie. *The Open Secret: Sketches for a Missionary Theology.* Grand Rapids: Eerdmans, 1978.

Niccum, Curt. "The Voice of the Manuscripts on the Silence of the Women: The External Evidence for 1 Cor 14:334-5." *New Testament Studies* 43 (1997): 242-55.

O'Brien, P. T. *Colossians, Philemon.* Word Biblical Commentary 44. Waco, Tex.: Word Books, 1982.

O'Collins, Gerald. "The Fearful Silence of Three Women." *Gregorianum* 69, no. 3 (1988): 489-503.

Okin, S. Moller. *Women in Western Political Thought.* Princeton, N.J.: Princeton University Press, 1979.

O'Malley, John. "Was Ignatius Loyola a Church Reformer? How to Look at Early Modern Catholicism?" In *The Counter-Reformation,* ed. David M. Luebke, 66-82. Malden, Mass./Oxford: Blackwell, 1999.

Orchard, M. Emmanuel, ed. *Till God Will: Mary Ward through Her Writings.* London: Darton, Longman & Todd, 1985.

O'Regan, Pauline. *A Changing Order.* Wellington, NZ: Allen & Unwin/Port Nicholson Press, 1986.

Osiek, Carolyn. "Philippians." In *Searching the Scriptures*. Volume 2, *A Feminist Commentary*, ed. Elisabeth Schüssler Fiorenza, 237-49. New York: Crossroad, 1994.

Padinjarekuttu, Isaac. *The Missionary Movement of the 19th and 20th Centuries and Its Encounter with India: A Historico-Theological Investigation with Three Case Studies*. Frankfurt am Main: Peter Lang, 1995.

Panikkar, R. M. *Asia and Western Dominance: A Survey of the Vasco Da Gama Epoch of Asian History, 1498-1945*. London: George Allen & Unwin, 1953.

Paul, Vincent de. *Correspondence, Entretiens, Documents*. 14 vols. Paris: Librairie Lecoffre, 1923.

Perkins, Pheme. *Gnosticism and the New Testament*. Minneapolis: Fortress Press, 1993.

Petersen, Joan M., ed. *Handmaids of the Lord: Contemporary Descriptions of Feminine Asceticism in the First Six Christian Centuries*. Kalamazoo: Cistercian Publications, 1996.

Rader, Rosemary. *Breaking Boundaries: Male/Female Friendship in Early Christian Communities*. New York/Ramsey, N.J.: Paulist Press, 1983.

Raft, Patricia. *Women and the Religious Life in Premodern Europe*. New York: St. Martin's Press, 1996.

Rahner, Karl. *Theological Investigations*. Volume 22. London: Darton, Longman & Todd, 1991.

Rapley, Elizabeth. *The Dévotes: Women and Church in Seventeenth-Century France*. 1st paperback ed. McGill-Queen's Studies in the History of Religion 4, ed. G. A. Rawlyk. Montreal: McGill-Queen's University Press, 1993.

Rayan, Samuel. "The Ecclesiology at Work in the Indian Church." In *Searchings for an Indian Ecclesiology*, ed. Gerwin Van Leeuwen, 191-212. Bangalore: ATC, 1984.

Reid, Barbara E. *Choosing the Better Part? Women in the Gospel of Luke*. Collegeville, Minn.: Liturgical Press, 1996.

*Religious and Human Promotion*. 1978. Available from http://www.vatican.va/roman_curia/congregations/ccscrlife/documents/rc_con_ ccscrlife_doc_1208 1980_religious-and-human-promotion_en.html. Accessed March 27, 2005.

Ress, Mary Judith. *Ecofeminism in Latin America*. Women from the Margins. Maryknoll, N.Y.: Orbis Books, 2006.

Robert, Dana L. *American Women in Mission: A Social History of Their Thought and Practice*. Macon, Ga.: Mercer University Press, 1996.

———. "Shifting Southward: Global Christianity since 1945." *International Bulletin of Missionary Research* 24 (2000): 50-58.

Robinson, J. M., ed. *The Nag Hammadi Library in English*. New York: Harper Collins, 1988.

Rosenblatt, Marie-Eloise. "Jude." In *Searching the Scriptures*. Volume 2, *A Feminist Commentary*, ed. Elisabeth Schüssler Fiorenza, 392-98. New York: Crossroad, 1994.

Ruether, Rosemary Radford. *Sexism and God-Talk: Toward a Feminist Theology*. Boston: Beacon Press, 1983.

———. *Gaia and God: An Ecofeminist Theology of Earth Healing*. New York: Harper Collins, 1992.

———. "Patriarchy." In *An A to Z of Feminist Theology*, ed. Lisa Isherwood and Dorothea McEwan, 173-74. Sheffield: Sheffield Academic Press, 1996.

———. "Sisters of the Earth: Religious Women and Ecological Spirituality." *Witness* (May 2000): 1-4.

Russell, Letty M. "Cultural Hermeneutics: A Postcolonial Look at Mission." *Journal of Feminist Studies in Religion* 20 (2004): 23-40.

———. *The Practice of God's Hospitality*. 1999. Available from http://www.world ywca-org.ac.psiweb.com/common_concern/june1999/thecredalbasisoftheworld ywca.html. Accessed June 2, 2006.

———. *Church in the Round: Feminist Interpretation of the Church*. Louisville: Westminster John Knox Press, 1993.

Ryan, Hildegaard. "St. Hildegaard of Bingen (1098-1179) and Bl. Jutta of Spanheim (1084-1136): Foremothers in Wisdom." In *Medieval Women Monastics: Wisdom's Wellsprings*, ed. Miriam Schmit and Linda Kulzer, 149-64. Collegeville, Minn.: Liturgical Press, 1996.

Sales, François de. *Oeuvres Complètes*. Volume 25. Annecy, 1892-1908.

Schaberg, Jane. "Luke." In *The Women's Bible Commentary*, ed. Carol A. Newsom and Sharon H. Ringe, 275-92. London: SPCK; Louisville: Westminster John Knox Press, 1992.

Schneemelcher, W. "The Gospel of Mary." In *Gospels and Related Writings*, 1:340-43. London: Lutterworth Press, 1963.

Schneiders, Sandra. *Finding the Treasure: Locating Catholic Religious Life in a New Ecclesial and Cultural Context*. Mahwah, N.J.: Paulist Press, 2000.

———. *With Oil in Their Lamps: Faith, Feminism and the Future*. Mahwah, N.J.: Paulist Press, 2000.

Schottroff, Luise. *Let the Oppressed Go Free: Feminist Perspectives on the New Testament*. Translated by Annemarie S. Kidder. Louisville: Westminster John Knox Press, 1993.

———. *Lydia's Impatient Sisters: A Feminist Social History of Early Christianity*. Translated by Barbara Rumscheidt and Martin Rumscheidt. London: SCM Press, 1995.

Schottroff, Luise, Silvia Schroer, and Marie-Theres Wacker. *Feminist Interpretation: The Bible in Women's Perspective*. Minneapolis: Fortress Press, 1998.

Schottroff, Luise, and Wolfgang Stegemann. *Jesus and the Hope of the Poor*. Translated by Matthew J. O'Connell. Maryknoll, N.Y.: Orbis Books, 1986.

Schreiter, Robert. *Toward the Missionary Church of 2025—the Past and the Future*. 2002. Available from http://www.sedos.org/site/index. Accessed April 2, 2006.

Schüssler Fiorenza, Elisabeth. "The Apostleship of Women in Early Christianity." In *Women Priests: A Catholic Commentary on the Vatican Declaration*, ed. Leonard Swidler and Arlene Swidler, 135-40. New York: Paulist Press, 1977.

———. *In Memory of Her: A Feminist Theological Reconstruction of Christian Origins*. New York: Crossroad, 1983.

———. *Bread Not Stone: The Challenge of Feminist Biblical Interpretation*. New York: Crossroad, 1986.

———. "Missionaries, Apostles, Co-Workers: Romans 16 and the Reconstruction of Women's Early Christian History." *Word and World* 6 (1986): 420-33.

———. *Discipleship of Equals: A Critical Feminist Ekklesia-logy of Liberation*. New York: Crossroad, 1993.

Schüssler Fiorenza, Elisabeth, ed. *Searching the Scriptures*. Volume 1, *A Feminist Introduction*. New York: Crossroad, 1993.

———. *Searching the Scriptures*. Volume 2, *A Feminist Commentary*. New York: Crossroad, 1994.

Sebba, Anne. *Mother Teresa: Beyond the Image*. London: Weidenfeld & Nicolson, 1997.

Seim, Turid Karlsen. "The Gospel of Luke." In *Searching the Scriptures*. Volume 2, *A Feminist Commentary*, ed. Elisabeth Schüssler Fiorenza, 728-62. New York: Crossroad, 1994.

Senior, Donald, ed. *The Catholic Study Bible: New American Bible*. New York: Oxford University Press, 1990.

Shenk, Wilbert R. *Changing Frontiers of Mission*. Maryknoll, N.Y.: Orbis Books, 1999.

Simmons, E. R. *A Brief History of the Catholic Church in New Zealand*. Auckland: Catholic Publications Centre, 1978.

Simons, Walter. *Cities of Ladies: Beguine Communities in the Medieval Low Countries, 1200-1565*. Philadelphia: University of Pennsylvania Press, 2001.

Spencer, F. Scott. "Out of Mind, Out of Voice: Slave Girls and Prophetic Daughters in Luke-Acts." *Biblical Interpretation* 7 (1999): 133-55.

St. Denis, Helen. *The Growth of Secular Institutes Diocesan and Pontifical "Vocation for the New Millennium."* 2003. Available from http://www.secularinstitutes.org/Vocation.htm. Accessed May 7, 2006.

Stransky, T. F. "Evangelization, Missions and Social Action: A Roman Catholic Perspective." *Review and Expositor* 79 (1982): 343-51.

Suttor, T. L. *Hierarchy and Democracy in Australia, 1788-1870*. Melbourne: Melbourne University Press, 1965.

Tanzer, Sarah J. "Ephesians." In *Searching the Scriptures*. Volume 2, *A Feminist Commentary*, ed. Elisabeth Schüssler Fiorenza, 325-48. New York: Crossroad, 1994.

Teff, Melanie. "Jesuit Refugee Service and Advocacy." *2004 Annual Report*. Rome: Jesuit Refugee Service, 2004. Available at http://www.with.jrs.net/files/ar2004.pdf. Accessed 10 April 2006.

Thurston, Bonnie. *The Widows: A Woman's Ministry in the Early Church*. Philadelphia: Fortress Press, 1989.

Tilley, Maureen A. "The Passion of Felicity and Perpetua." In *Searching the Scriptures*. Volume 2, *A Feminist Commentary*, ed. Elisabeth Schüssler Fiorenza, 829-58. New York: Crossroad, 1994.

Torjesen, Karen Jo. "Reconstruction of Women's Early Christian History." In *Searching the Scriptures*. Volume 1, *A Feminist Introduction*, ed. Elisabeth Schüssler Fiorenza, 290-310. New York: Crossroad, 1993.

Tuck, Patrick J. N. *French Catholic Missionaries and the Politics of Imperialism in Vietnam, 1857-1914: A Documentary Survey*. Liverpool Historical Studies 1. Liverpool: Liverpool University Press, 1987.

Tugwell, Simon, ed. *Early Dominicans: Selected Writings*. Classics of Western Spirituality. Ramsey, N.J.: Paulist Press, 1982.

Valerio, A. "Women in the 'Societas Christiana': 10th–12th Centuries." *Theology Digest* 33 (1986): 155-58.

van Kersbergen, Lydwine. *Woman: Some Aspect of Her Role in the Modern World*. Loveland, Oh.: Grailville, 1956.

Vazhakala, Sebastian. *Lay Missionaries of Charity: Who We Are!* Available from http://laymc.bizland.com/whoweare.htm. Accessed April 5, 2006.

von Arx, Jeffrey, ed. *Varieties of Ultramontanism*. Washington, D.C.: Catholic University of America Press, 1998.

Wainwright, Elaine. "The Gospel of Matthew." In *Searching the Scriptures*. Volume 2, *A Feminist Commentary*, ed. Elisabeth Schüssler Fiorenza, 635-77. New York: Crossroad, 1994.

————. *Towards a Feminist Critical Reading of the Gospel According to Matthew.* Behefte zur Zeitschrift für die neutestamentliche Wissenschaft 60. Berlin: de Gruyter, 1991.

Waldersee, James. *A Grain of Mustard Seed: The Society for the Propagation of the Faith and Australia 1837-1977.* Kensington, N.S.W.: Chevalier Press, 2000.

Walker, Ranginui. *Ka Whawhai Tonu Matou: Struggle without End.* Auckland: Auckland University Press, 1990.

Walsh, Barbara. *Roman Catholic Nuns in England and Wales, 1800-1937: A Social History.* Dublin: Irish Academic Press, 2002.

Waters, Peter Maurice. *The Ursuline Achievement: A Philosophy of Education for Women. St. Angela Merici, the Ursulines and Catholic Education.* North Carlton, Vic.: Colonna, 1994.

Weaver, Mary Jo. "Still Feisty at Fifty: The Grailville Lay Apostolate for Women." *U.S. Catholic Historian* 11 (1993): 3-12.

Weber, Alison. "Little Women: Counter-Reformation Misogyny." In *The Counter-Reformation: The Essential Readings,* ed. David M. Luebke, 143-62. Malden, Mass./Oxford: Blackwell, 1999.

Wemple, Suzanne Fonay. "Women from the Fifth to the Tenth Century." In *Silences of the Middle Ages.* Vol. 2, *A History of Women in the West,* ed. Georges Duby and Michelle Perrot, 167-201. Cambridge, Mass.: Belknap Press, 1992.

Werner, Yvonne Maria. "Introduction." In *Nuns and Sisters in the Nordic Countries after the Reformation: A Female Counter-Culture in Modern Society,* ed. Yvonne Maria Werner, 5-20. Uppsala: Swedish Institute of Mission Research, 2004.

Wiest, Jean-Paul. "The Legacy of Vincent Lebbe." *International Bulletin of Missionary Research* 23 (1999): 35-37.

Williams, Rowan. *Teresa of Avila.* Outstanding Christian Thinkers. London: Geoffrey Chapman, 1991.

Williamson, G. A., ed. *Eusebius: The History of the Church from Christ to Constantine.* New York: Penguin Classics, 1990.

Wire, Antoinette. *The Corinthian Women Prophets.* Philadelphia: Fortress Press, 1990.

————. "1 Corinthians." In *Searching the Scriptures.* Volume 2, *A Feminist Commentary,* ed. Elisabeth Schüssler Fiorenza, 154-95. New York: Crossroad, 1994.

Wright, Cathy. "Nazareth as a Model for Mission in the Life of Charles de Foucauld." *Mission Studies* 19 (2002): 36-52.

————. "Spiritual Childhood and Mission: A Way of Living Hope with Brokenness." *Spirituality* 8 (2002): 373-378.

Wright, C. J. H. "Family." In *The Anchor Bible Dictionary,* ed. David Noel Freedman, 2:761-69. New York: Doubleday, 1992.

Wybourne, Catherine. "Leoba: A Study in Humanity and Holiness." In *Medieval Women Monastics: Wisdom's Wellsprings,* ed. Miriam Schmitt and Linda Kulzer, 81-96. Collegeville, Minn.: Liturgical Press, 1996.

Young, Randy. "Countless Small Victories." *America* 191 (2004). Available at www.americamagazine.org/gettext.cfm?articletypeID=1&textID=3670&issueID.

# Index

Wire, Antoinette, 8, 10
Women of Nazareth. *See* Grail Movement
women
  in *Acts of Thecla*, 39-44
  as *adelphē* (sister), 15, 18
  affirmation of: in noncanonical texts, 39
  in ancillary roles to ordained clergy, 117, 144, 159
  in apocryphal and gnostic texts, 63-68
  as apostles, 17, 43, 57, 58
  and asceticism, 41, 42
  in authentic Pauline letters, 4-22
  authority over men in gnostic texts, 64
  black: and ministry to blacks, 145, 146
  in canonical resurrection narratives, 53-60
  clerical and ecclesiastical control over, 80, 81, 92, 93, 97, 98, 119, 130, 139, 159
  in Constantinian church, 78-81
  as co-workers of Paul, 11, 13, 14, 17, 19, 20, 21, 35
  as deacons (*diakonoi*), 14, 17, 18, 32
  as disciples of Jesus, 50, 58
  as donors and patrons, 7, 13, 18
  and eremitic life, 79, 80
  and evangelical life, 79, 80
  and evangelization of the family, 190
  in first-century Judaism, 7
  as homemakers in post-Pauline letters, 23-44
  as householders, 12
  in late Middle Ages, 87-94
  lay and religious, 121n1
  as males, 65, 66, 74
  martyrdom of, 74
  as medical missionaries, 147-49
  and mission in early church, 63-68
  missionary role: in Gospels, 51, 58, 59
  as models of faith, 57
  in passion narratives, 48-53

professional education for mission, 158, 159, 160, 175, 176
prophetic actions of, 10, 11, 49, 50, 60-63
promotion of education by, 82, 108, 109, 110, 119, 129, 130, 131
role of: in Corinthian church, 9-10
status in Roman world, 12
subordination of, 10, 11
suppression of public role, 85, 86
as synagogue leaders, 7
and trinitarian theology of mission, 207-10
as witnesses to the resurrection, 55, 56, 57
*See also* women religious
women religious
  and care for environment, 176-77, 196
  and clerical control, 106, 111, 113, 114, 119
  and domestic care of priests, 140, 141
  and feminist theology, 173-76
  and growth of local churches, 160
  and liberation theology, 171-73, 178-83
  missionaries to the New World, 116-20
  and new understanding of mission, 179-81
  and patriarchal culture, 176
  preaching and teaching, 107-8
  prophetic ministry, 175
  theological education of, 175, 176
Woo, Elizabeth, 188
Woods, Julian Tenison: and Mary MacKillop, 130, 131
Worker Priests, 152
worship: at home, 16, 17
Wright, Cathy, 150
Würz, Abbé, 136
Wybourne, Catherine, 83

Young, Randy, 191
Young Christian Students, 190
Young Christian Workers, 152
Yung, Hwa, 164

The American Society of Missiology Series, published in collaboration with Orbis Books, seeks to publish scholarly work of high merit and wide interest on numerous aspects of missiology—the study of Christian mission in its historical, social, and theological dimensions. Able proposals on new and creative approaches to the practice and understanding of mission will receive close attention from the ASM Series Committee.

## Previously Published in
## The American Society of Missiology Series